The World of
the Mexican Worker in Texas

Number Forty-four:
The Centennial Series of the Association
of Former Students,
TEXAS A&M UNIVERSITY

Emilio Zamora

The World of the Mexican Worker in Texas

Texas A&M
University Press
College Station

Library of Congress Cataloging-in-Publication Data

Zamora, Emilio.
    The world of the Mexican worker in Texas /
Emilio Zamora.
        p. cm. — (Centennial series of the Association of Former
Students, Texas A&M University ; no. 44)
    Includes bibliographical references and index.
    ISBN 0-89096-514-5 (alk. paper); 0-89096-678-8 (pbk.)
    1. Trade-unions—Texas—History—20th century. 2. Trade-unions—
Mexico—History—20th century. 3. Mexicans—Employment—Texas—
History—20th century.   I. Title.   II. Series.
HD6517.T4Z363   1993
331.6'2720764'09041—dc20   92-24813
                                                                 CIP

Para Clarita

Tambien dedico este trabajo a Ángela Valenzuela, a María Olga
Zamora, a mis padres y abuelos,
  Emilio Hinojosa Zamora,
  Eudelia Solís Zamora,
  Bruno Treviño Solís,
  Higinia González Solís,
  Estéfana Hinojosa Zamora,
  José Árgel Cantú Zamora,
y a la memoria de El Rancho Solís, Texas, y El Horcón,
Tamaulipas, antiguas tierras de nuestra juventud que a
través de la frontera han ligado fuentes de mi identidad.

Contents

Illustrations

Preface

This study began within a fortuitous intellectual environment at the University of Texas at Austin during the early 1970s. I had as colleagues a group of doctoral students that included Victor Nelson-Cisneros, Roberto Villarreal, and José Limón, then Acting Director of the Center for Mexican American Studies. Professor Juan Gómez-Quiñones joined our circle in 1972 as a visiting scholar in Mexican history and contributed to our development with his guidance and example. Together, we formed a bond of friendship and scholarship devoted to making scholarly contributions to knowledge on the Mexican worker from the United States, in particular from South Texas. At the time, Professor Américo Paredes was the senior Mexican scholar in residence at the Department of Anthropology. He won our respect and admiration for his formidable ability and seriousness of purpose.

With the advice and guidance of Professor Gómez-Quiñones, we agreed on a research strategy which focused on Mexican labor history in Texas during the twentieth century according to three twenty-year periods beginning in 1900 and ending in 1960. I selected the first two decades, a period that witnessed dramatic economic growth and expansion and impressive labor organizing among Mexicans. Our goal was to identify the available documentary information that would allow us to explain changes and continuities over time in the position and condition of Mexicans in the Texas labor market. We were also interested in determining the extent to which Mexican workers waged organizing and strike activity. Our work became an early successful challenge to the prevalent view that Mexicans failed to take an active part in determining their own history. Although we continued collaborating and expanding the scope of our work, my years at Austin were the most formative in my career as a Mexican labor historian.

I have chosen the term Mexican to designate persons of Mexican extraction for several reasons. It is the English equivalent of the most popular self-referent used at the time by Mexicans in Texas. Also, the use of this term acknowledges the fact that Anglos generally disregarded the question of nativity and categorized all persons of Mexican extraction under the popularized heading of Mexican. Moreover, the term reflects an attachment with Mexico that was current. Lastly, it is simply impossible in most cases to determine the workers' nativity due to the mixed composition of many of their organizations. Of course, when it is necessary and possible to make the distinction, I use such terms as U.S.-born and Mexico-born. My focus is on South Texas, or the area below an imaginary line that begins at Galveston on the Gulf Coast, extends through Houston, Austin, and San Antonio and ends at Del Rio, on the international border. I have chosen this admittedly broad geographical definition because it is a convenient way to distinguish the general area of greatest Mexican concentration from the rest of the state.

The people who have consistently helped and supported me during the preparation of this manuscript include my parents, Emilio Hinojosa Zamora and Eudelia Solís Zamora, and the rest of my family, María Olga, Noelia, Rolando, Elia, Cecilia, Leticia, Norma Alicia, Ricardo, and Aida. I am grateful for the guidance, support, and encouragement given me by my friends and colleagues, especially Juan Gómez-Quiñones, José Limón, Victor Nelson-Cisneros, Roberto Villarreal, Mario Montaño, David Montejano, Estevan Flores, Devón Peña, Ines Hernández, Teresa McKenna, Joseph Glatthaar, John Hart, Devra Weber, and Dennis Valdez. I also wish to acknowledge Carlos Arce and the staff of the National Chicano Research Network at the University of Michigan, Ann Arbor, and the National Chicano Council on Higher Education for their support. A research grant from the University of Houston, and postdoctoral fellowships from the Rockefeller Foundation and the University of California President's Minority Fellowship Program also provided me with the necessary assistance to complete the research for this study. Finally, I wish to thank my closest friend and dear companion, Ángela Valenzuela. Your love and patience give me strength.

Emilio Zamora—

The World of
the Mexican Worker in Texas

Introduction

When I began this study I was faced with two seemingly irreconcilable propositions. On the one hand, the Mexican civil rights movement, in particular the Mexican farmworkers' struggle in California, the Midwest, and Texas, indicated that Mexicans were prone to protest and challenge their condition. On the other hand, some labor leaders and journalists claimed that Mexican workers and voters were not inclined to organize or to wage effective and sustained action. The proliferation of numerous Mexican workers' organizations and the impressive voter registration drives that occurred during the 1970s and 1980s have long since discredited the second claim and its attendant inference that apathy and inertia explain the Mexican condition.[1]

Although the inconsistency on the subject of Mexican politics may have reached a satisfactory resolution in our times, I encountered a similar dilemma in my research on the Mexican worker from Texas. Most contemporary observers and recent scholarly works ignore or minimize Mexican self-organization during the early 1900s, a period that witnessed one of the most impressive Mexican mobilization efforts of the twentieth century.[2] We thus find Texas employers informing a Department of Labor researcher in 1908 that Mexican workers were docile and tractable about the same time that a union composed of approximately one thousand of them were conducting a strike against the railroad shops in Laredo.[3] Similarly, some scholars continue to deny or downplay the importance of long-standing grievances held by Mexicans in South Texas as a principal cause of the irredentist movement of 1915–16, despite documented claims to the contrary by the *revoltosos* themselves.[4]

Another example that demonstrates the fallacy of a disinterested and apathetic population includes the basic work on Texas labor history by Ruth Allen.[5] Allen's study depicts Mexicans as unorganizable workers and potential strikebreakers, suggesting that they were the principal cause of disunity among the working class in the state. Allen's focus on Anglo trade unionism prevented her from acknowledging the statewide orga-

3

nizing campaigns among the Mexican working-class population; she ignored the 1911 effort by El Congreso Mexicanista to build a regional federation of Mexican community organizations, and she overlooked the organizing work by the one of the most important exiled groups of the time, the Partido Liberal Mexicano (PLM).[6] Allen also omitted a review of Mexican participation in the Texas Socialist Party and its economic arm, the Land League of America, two organizations that otherwise drew her interest.[7]

Although it is not my intent to explain why historians have depicted Mexicans in such an unfavorable light, a review of some possible reasons would be helpful.[8] These reasons include: 1) the uncritical use of biased documentary evidence, that is, the historical record left by employers seeking unrestricted Mexican immigration by promoting the image of a docile and tractable Mexican worker; 2) the failure to make use of the large amount of documentary evidence in Spanish that carries the disaffected voice of the Mexican community; and 3) the theoretical assumption that Mexicans, particularly immigrants, represented a by-gone preindustrial era and that as such were generally content with their relatively improved condition in the United States and were disinterested in the more modern ways of industrial struggle.[9]

The abundant archival material on working conditions and on Mexican workers' organizations within and outside the trade union movement first led me to study Mexican workers' political responses to three major issues of the day: poverty, social discrimination, and inequality in the work place and in the union halls. Consequently, I have included in this study a focus on the topics of work and labor organizing among skilled and unskilled workers and on the experiences of Mexican workers' organizations seeking incorporation into the Texas labor movement. By so doing, I seek to demonstrate that Mexican workers actively sought to improve their condition as a minority, and a bottom segment of the working class, by forming the organizations and regional and interethnic alliances necessary to accommodate varied aspirations and group interests within the community.

Further research into the 1920s led me to broaden the scope of my work in several ways. First of all, I contend that Mexican labor, both outside and within the fold of the labor movements in Mexico and Texas, represented only one dimension of a broader socio-political movement that generated various organizational forms and a complex mix of political visions and ideologies including nationalism, internationalism, and class consciousness.

An examination of the expansive world of Mexican workers provides an opportunity to study their social, political, and cultural environment.

The need to understand the larger context has made it necessary also to treat such issues as political culture. I propose that the unifying cultural elements were an all-inclusive Mexicanist identity and a popular ethic of mutuality with its constituent working-class values of fraternalism, reciprocity, and altruism. A blend of cultural tradition and social exigency reinforced a sense of community and spawned various political strategies, including labor organizing. My underlying argument is that Mexicans were active participants in the making of their own world and that popular concerns and aspirations regarding living and working conditions found expression in the labor struggle. In other words, I also examine the social and cultural world of the Mexican worker in an attempt to cross what the social historian Herbert Gutman called the "traditional imperial boundaries" that have enclosed the exclusive trade union focus in U.S. labor history.[10]

Approach and Perspectives

This study is in part a critique of the traditional and narrow trade union approach associated with the "old" labor history. Consequently, it is necessary to describe the "new" labor history that this work represents.[11] Following the lead of such scholars as Edward P. Thompson and Herbert Gutman, the "new" labor historians have challenged the conventional focus of the Wisconsin school associated with the late John R. Commons.[12] They have replaced Commons's focus on trade unions, collective bargaining, and the "pure and simple philosophy" of the American Federation of Labor (AFL) with new studies "from below" that incorporate social and cultural experiences in the world of work and community, including the historical record of previously neglected groups of workers such as women and racial minorities. The Mexican worker is still not an integral part of the tentative synthesis that "new" labor historians are elaborating. This book offers a broad treatment of Mexican work, community, and struggle as a contribution to the field.[13]

Labor economist Ray Marshall offers a trade union framework for the study of the emergence, growth, and development of labor in Texas that has served as a conventional point of departure.[14] Marshall claims that Texas labor followed a historical pattern evident in the rest of the United States. According to this reasoning, industrialization accounted for the emergence of the labor union, an organizational form that was suited to the adversarial demands of a new industrial reality. Moreover, unions increasingly replaced preindustrial organizations of a benevolent or fraternal type because the latter were unable to address new needs and problems effectively. The AFL extended its influence into the South during the late nineteenth century with its focus on craft workers. The guiding idea was that workers with scarce and specialized skills were best equipped to challenge the power of employers. This narrow organizing strategy effectively excluded the primarily unskilled minority work force. Unintended exclusion, however, also combined with more active and racially motivated attempts to deny union membership to minority workers. The AFL and its state affiliates thus reflected and reinforced racial divisions in the labor market.

The urban-based Anglo trade unionists, like their kin in the rest of the South, benefitted greatly from segregation and exclusion in the unions and in the work place. Although they often forced employers to concede to their demands or to sit at the bargaining table on the basis of their specialized skills or their strategic location in the production process, the predominantly Anglo unions also maintained job control by barring African-American workers from the skilled occupations. Racist policies, however, also impaired working-class unity by excluding blacks or assigning them to separate locals in the AFL and the Texas State Federation of Labor (TSFL). Moreover, segregation and exclusion denied African Americans an important opportunity to share in the benefits of unionization.

Marshall's schematic treatment of Texas labor history is incomplete partly because it excludes Mexican workers and their struggles. A void in the literature that he examined in 1971 helps explain this problem. Subsequent studies in Mexican labor history, particularly the works on Mexican labor in Texas, provide the initial basis for amending his observations and for constructing a more complete historical picture of labor in Texas.

For instance, racism was a far more important factor than Marshall supposes. Mexican workers, too, shared in the discrimination experience. This means that our first adjustment to Marshall's blueprint requires that we also examine the case of the Mexican worker to determine the role that race played in shaping the state's occupational structure, the job consciousness of Anglo labor, the political motivations and decisions of minority workers, and race relations in the work place and in the union movement. Moreover, the story of the working-class struggle included more than Anglo trade unionists, their job and wage concerns, and their relationship with minority workers in the labor market and in the labor movement. It also involved the organizing experiences of both skilled and unskilled Mexicans, including their relations with the homeland, political culture, and the larger socio-political movement in their communities.

Although my study responds to key revisionist concerns in the "new" field of U.S. labor history, it is more at home with the literature on Mexican labor history produced since the early 1970s.[15] Mexican labor history has made singular contributions to our knowledge of the Mexican community in the United States. This new knowledge presents an unequivocal challenge to the long-standing myth that Mexican workers were incapable of self-organization, and were therefore the principal cause of disunity among the working class. Despite the vast amount of work that has been produced, important gaps remain, including the study of Mexican labor in Texas during the early 1900s.[16]

I have found the works of historian Juan Gómez-Quiñones, especially his article on southwestern Mexican labor during the 1900–20 period, useful in writing this history.[17] My findings, particularly those related to the cause and nature of labor organizing and the influences of Mexican exiled politics, confirm some of his contentions. Gómez-Quiñones points out that Mexican labor in the Southwest mirrored a resurgence of left-wing as well as pure-and-simple unionism in both Mexico and the United States. Mexican workers raised the issue of labor within the larger context of Mexican political life in the Southwest. Labor activity, therefore, accompanied and was a part of broader socio-political actions designed to ensure survival, combat poverty, social discrimination, and inequality, and gain a measure of acceptance in the institutional life of the dominant society. Gómez-Quiñones also points out that workers' organizations from Mexico and the United States influenced Mexican labor in the Southwest ideologically and organizationally. This occurred as Mexico's 1910–17 social revolution, which threatened to overflow into Texas heightened social tensions over the issues of immigration and Mexican politics in Texas. The attendant diplomatic and military crisis, and the decisions that labor groups took as they sought to gain a political foothold in their respective countries, also constitute parts of the historical backdrop.

Two other studies form part of this work's frame of reference: David Montejano's study of ethnic relations in Texas and Stanley Greenberg's work on race relations in South Africa and the American South.[18] I incorporate Montejano's discussion on the development of commercial agriculture and the segregated order that it established in the early 1900s. Moreover, I examine the issue of immigration as a point of contention among workers in the cities and give an emphasis to the disaffected Mexican worker which is generally absent in Montejano's work. One of Montejano's underlying implications is that growers prevented unionization by controlling the movement of Mexican workers. Although this may have been true to an extent, Montejano also points out that labor repression was never complete. The act of withholding their labor was only one of many initiatives that Mexicans took in their rural and urban-based labor struggles.

Greenberg's study of race relations confirms my findings that Anglo workers inside and outside organized labor reacted racially to the prospects of facing large numbers of Mexican job competitors and strikebreakers when increasing numbers of U.S.-born and immigrant Mexicans began to arrive in the cities. According to Greenberg, racism in the American South and in South Africa intensified as dominant workers defended their privileged position in the labor market with exclusionary practices in the work place and in the unions. Dominant workers situated in the bottom occupational levels and in large industrial settings were most apt to feel threatened and to respond to their perceived threat with defensive measures intended to control the labor supply. Although Greenberg's analysis of the dynamics of exclusion is very instructive, it leaves out the collective responses of the subordinate workers—in this case, Mexicans. Again, as with the Montejano study, I add an examination of the Mexican labor struggle and the issue of race relations from the perspective of the Mexican worker.

This more inclusive conceptualization of the history of Mexican labor incorporates the varied experience and meaning of work and mobility held by groups differentiated by job standing and skills, nativity, citizenship, generational differences, time of arrival from Mexico, and class identification. It also encompasses a unified sense of community and the activities of such working-class organizations as mutual aid societies, cooperatives, Masonic orders, and unions that gave expression to popular sentiments and concerns associated with the homeland and life in the United States. Additionally, such a perspective suggests that the use of "preindustrial" organizational forms did not necessarily imply that Mexicans practiced a backward or even a wholly tradition-bound type of political activity. The indifference of Anglo labor, for example, often left them no other option but to express their views and concerns independently through familiar and popular organizational forms.

Faced by worsening conditions, widespread discrimination, and an indifferent and at times hostile Anglo labor movement, Mexicans often looked inwardly or towards Mexico for support and inspiration in building a largely autochthonous and trans-border labor struggle. Some Mexican workers' organizations bridged the stubborn racial divide and recorded the first instances of affiliation with the Texas Socialist Party, the AFL, and the TSFL. Although these early instances of interethnic unity failed to materialize fully, they nevertheless provide a legacy that tell us much about the minority position of the Mexican community, the impressive organizing activity and bid for incorporation by Mexican workers, and the ambivalent response by organized and unorganized Anglo workers.

Chapter One

Discrimination and Inequality in the Towns and Countryside

Industrialization during the last half of the 1800s shaped the Mexican's subordinate position in the socio-economy. Territorial expansion into the northern frontier of the newly independent Mexican nation initially made industrialization possible. The Texas War for Independence, the U.S.-Mexico War, and the annexation of Mexico's tier of northern states led to continued violence and to the incorporation of the Southwest into the U.S. national economy. As regional economies followed the general developmental march, predominantly rural and often self-sustaining locales became urban, industrialized, and interlocked areas. This economic process included changes in the use of land, a shift in land ownership away from Mexican hands, and the proletarianization of the Mexican people.[1] The early years of the twentieth century manifested historical continuities evident in southwestern regions like South Texas.

Although the wars provided boosts to local economies, South Texas remained isolated and underdeveloped until the turn of the century when the railroads opened up new markets and drew the region into a process of economic development sweeping the entire state. Moreover, as the pace of development quickened and such labor-intensive industries as agriculture, railroads, and construction grew, the demand for cheap labor increased and drew multitudes of immigrants from Mexico.[2] Large numbers of Anglos who made use of improved employment and investment opportunities benefitted greatly from economic development. Mexicans, however, did not share equally in this new-found prosperity. This was particularly true for the immigrants, who were welcomed or rejected as low-wage labor depending on the ebb and flow of the business cycle. Although some Mexicans in places like deep South Texas, the Nueces County area, and San Antonio managed to maintain ownership over their land and businesses or to obtain skilled jobs, the great majority worked as laborers in the farms, railroads, and urban-based low-wage industries throughout the state.[3]

Population

As a result of Mexican emigration during the wars with Mexico and the arrival of large number of Anglo immigrants, the Mexican population lost its majority standing in the San Antonio area and became completely engulfed in the old frontier settlements of Nacogdoches and Victoria by the late 1880s. Mexicans continued to dominate numerically in the border region during the early 1900s. Industrialization, especially the growth and expansion of agriculture, resulted in the first large-scale immigration of Mexicans and, as employment opportunities increased in areas beyond deep South Texas, immigrants and U.S.-born Mexicans began the process of demographically reconquering the state. By the 1910s the cotton belt area rivaled the border region of the Rio Grande Valley in the number of permanent Mexican residents. Anglo immigrants also entered Texas in significant numbers and traveled in the opposite direction.[4] The result was a significant population increase during the early 1900s. Barely above one million in 1900, the state's total population increased to almost four million in 1910 and to a little over four and one-half million in 1920.[5]

Despite impressive increases, population growth was not continuous, nor was it evenly distributed during the early 1900s. The permanent outmigration of large numbers of workers to better-paying jobs in the nation's northern industrial centers, coupled with decreases in the number of entries from other states during the second decade, reduced the rate of Anglo population growth. This was especially evident in the eastern and western sections of Texas, where Anglo residents registered a significant outmigration pattern. The population movement from the south, on the other hand, continued unabated.[6]

As a significant result of these uneven patterns of growth and dispersal, the Mexican became more salient in the ethnic makeup of the state's work force. Anglo population losses accounted for the state's slower rate of population growth as well as for absolute decreases in selected areas. An important exception to this trend was the Rio Grande Valley, where both the Anglo and Mexican populations increased significantly during the 1910s and 1920s. This exception notwithstanding, as Anglo communities experienced slow growth or losses, Mexican communities continued to expand at a faster rate throughout South Texas, in such cities as Corpus Christi, San Antonio, Austin, Houston, and Dallas, and in areas like West Texas. The growing demand for agricultural labor maintained these sharply contrasting patterns throughout the 1910s and 1920s.

The dramatic demographic growth and expansion of the Mexican population was especially evident in the larger cities such as San Antonio. The Alamo City experienced sudden growth as a result of a growing demand for Mexican labor in the interior of the state and beyond. When the railroads connected Texas with the interior of Mexico, the immigrant population significantly increased. The new additions of economic refugees and political exiles made San Antonio a bustling Mexican population center. The city became known for the concentration of a large number of destitute working-class families in the west side. A muckraking journalist who reported on urban congestion and squalor in the state's major cities concluded that San Antonio Mexicans lived in deplorable conditions. Their homes reminded him of tenement dwellings in New York. People lived in long one-story structures called *corrales* extending for approximately one hundred yards and containing numerous overcrowded "stalls." The occupants, many of whom worked as laborers in the city until the cotton season began, paid ninety cents a week for a bare apartment and $1.25 for one with a stove. The landlord usually charged $250 a month in rent for each of the corrales. Unstable employment and low wages often made it necessary for several families to crowd into each structure in order to meet the rent payment.[7]

Immigrants engulfed other long-established Mexican communities in places such as Corpus Christi, Laredo, and Brownsville. The result was further congestion and poverty. Beyond South Texas, cities like Austin, Houston, Dallas, and Lubbock, however, saw their Mexican communities spring up where few had lived before. The Mexican community from Houston, for example, grew from a small population of several hundred at the turn of the century to well over fifteen thousand in 1930. Here, as in San Antonio, the Mexican urban population was overwhelmingly working-class, with impressive representation by the Mexico-born. Social differentiation, however, was also evident in the emergence of Mexican businesses and such skilled workers as teachers, journalists, and doctors who catered to the community. Mexican nationals were more numerous in the developing rural areas along the cotton belt that extended to the vicinity of Corpus Christi and in the new towns that appeared in the Rio Grande Valley. Although increasing numbers became permanent residents, especially along the border and in cotton belt towns, the large Mexican agricultural work force swept through the area during harvest time. They usually lived in makeshift quarters provided by farmers or in tents and wagons set up near work sites. The primarily ranching corridor that extended north from Rio Grande City and Laredo to Freer and Alice did not attract large numbers of workers from the border area and the interior of Mexico. As

A Mexican basket vendor and customer in San Antonio, ca.
1915. *Courtesy Daughters of the Republic of Texas Library,
San Antonio*

a consequence, the area's population did not grow suddenly like that
of the cities and rural areas. Many of the older residents belonged to
a ranch- and farm-owning class that survived dispossession with a measure of political influence, often through a system of political bossism.[8]

It is difficult to determine the size of the Mexican population, because of the inconsistent methods used by the U.S. Bureau of the Census. Prior to 1930 the census categorized the general population according to nativity and parentage. Accordingly, Mexicans were classified
under the white category and by the nativity of their parents. U.S.-born
Mexicans of the U.S.-born parents were tabulated as whites. Thus, the
numerical size of this sector of the Mexican population is unknown.
Moreover, the census may have undercounted the Mexico-born population, since large numbers of them periodically crossed the international
border without the benefit of legal status and, presumably, escaped the
reach of census tabulators. Given this probable undercount, total estimated Mexican population figures must be regarded as minimal.

Roberto Villarreal, a historian in the field, has developed a useful quantitative model for estimating the total Mexican population in Texas (see Table 1). The significant population increases that appear in 1890 and that reappear in 1910 and 1920 parallel high points in Mexican immigration. Also, the larger U.S.-born figures indicate that an increasing number of Mexican nationals were setting permanent quarters and raising families in the state. Although U.S.-born Mexicans were a numerically larger portion of the total Mexican population beginning in 1890, the immigrant group registered impressive increases. Mexican nationals increased their numbers by seventy-six percent in 1910 and by one hundred percent in 1920. The Mexico-born population increased its proportional representation in the resident community at a slower rate, from 43 percent in 1900 to 45 percent in 1910 and 49 percent in 1920. Their proportional increase among the state's foreign-born population was equally striking. They constituted 40 percent of the foreign born in 1900, 52 percent in 1910, and 63 percent in 1920. Early expectations that Mexican immigrants would return to Mexico at the end of the agricultural seasons dissipated with time, in part because immigrant families increasingly decided to stay. A sizable number of U.S.-born Mexicans—150,000—claimed in 1920 one or both parents born in Mexico. The absolute and proportional increases of the Mexican immigrant population also made Mexicans more noticeable, especially among Anglo urban workers who increasingly saw in the unregulated immigrant flow and the growth of the Mexican population a threat to their privileged position in the labor market.

Although most immigrants may have failed to seek U.S. citizenship, it became increasingly clear that they were not temporary sojourners. According to a 1919 study of 15,785 emigrés that crossed at El Paso, twenty-nine percent, thirteen percent, and four percent had lived in the United States between five and ten years, ten and twenty years, and twenty or more years, respectively.[9] Presumably, the remaining fifty-four percent had been residents for as many as four years. Undoubtedly, many of these long-term residents had raised families and were returning with U.S.-born youngsters. Long-term residency did not change their immigrant status. They and their children were as expendable as the more recent arrivals during the periodic economic and political crisis that the state witnessed during the early 1900s.

The Mexican population of South Texas was concentrated in two general areas: along the international border from Cameron County, at the mouth of the Rio Grande River, to Valverde County; and in the southwestern portion of the cotton belt region extending from East Texas to the area south of Austin and San Antonio, and to Nueces County. With the expansion of the state's cotton economy and the concomitant rise in Mexican immigration, the Mexican population dispersed in a northeastern direction. Large numbers from the border counties and northern Mexico traveled to the cotton belt region in the upper portion of South Texas.[10] Others settled in the border counties.

Immigration

Aside from increasing the size of their host Mexican communities in the Southwest, Mexican immigrants enlarged the cheap labor supply required by an expanding economy. This gave rise to what some social scientists have called a segmented labor market or a colonized labor force. Although conditions in Mexico forced workers of varied occupational backgrounds to join the northward migrations, the southwestern economy generated a special demand, that is, it called for workers to fill low-wage laboring occupations in the agricultural, railway, and mining industries. The expansion of Mexico's economy had lured industrial workers and agricultural laborers to the north. Increased railroad construction and other industrial activity beginning during the late 1800s encouraged and directed these migrations toward the northern Mexican region. Better job opportunities and wages in the Southwest influenced Mexicans to continue on their northward trek. The Mexican Revolution of 1910 also contributed to the immigrant flow.[11]

One of the rarely acknowledged yet prominent features of Mexican immigration during early 1900s was the movement of significant numbers of workers back to Mexico. Return migrations reinforced a pattern of cultural and political interactions between communities on both sides of the border. These interactions resulted from shared levels of industrial development in Texas and the Mexican states of Tamaulipas, Nuevo León, and Coahuila.[12] The railroad connections that were established during the 1880s as well as major American investments in mining, railroads, and agriculture joined the future of the northern Mexican economy with U.S. developmental patterns. Growth and expansion was evident throughout the northern Mexican region: in the vast commercial agricultural enterprises of La Laguna district that included the area where the states of Durango, Coahuila, and Zacatecas meet; in the oil, petroleum, and shipping industries of the Tampico area; in the mining operations of Coahuila; in the trade, service, transportation, and light industrial activities of the major border towns; and in heavier industry, trade, and finance located in the larger cities of the interior, Monterrey, and Torreón.

The northern Mexican region also witnessed the growth and expansion of its industrial work force. It became a reserve pool of labor that met the fluctuating needs of Texas industries, especially agriculture. This international work force traveled back and forth, its direction depending on the availability of jobs on both sides of the border. The migration of workers between the cotton-producing regions of La Laguna area and South Texas illustrate the degree of economic interdependence that existed. The development of commercial agriculture in La Laguna district, as in South Texas, began in the 1880s. La Laguna growers almost immediately attracted large numbers of workers and their families from the interior of Mexico. During a thirty-year period ending in 1910, La Laguna's population increased from fewer than twenty thousand to more than two hundred thousand. A major portion of its industrial work force of approximately thirty thousand workers began to migrate to and from Texas during the 1890s as the cotton crop matured in a northeasterly direction. Many of these workers returned to La Laguna to await the early maturation of cotton in Mexico.

An interdependent relationship became especially evident in the corresponding measures that La Laguna and Texas growers took to regulate the flow of workers. These measures often resulted in a competitive relationship that favored the Texas growers. When faced with the problem of labor shortages, for instance, La Laguna growers often enlisted the help of local authorities to discourage workers from leaving and to prevent Texas labor agents from recruiting in the area. This was a recurrent problem that was difficult to resolve, primarily because workers usually left before the local harvest was over. They migrated to capitalize on maturing crops and better wages in Texas. Periodic downturns in the world cotton market and anti-immigration campaigns in Texas, on the other hand, increased the numbers of unemployed workers in Mexico. The efforts by La Laguna growers to encourage or assist workers to migrate to Texas under these conditions often failed. Depressed wages and high unemployment in the labor-congested area of La Laguna led to agrarian discontent, a development that coincided with the emergence of socialist labor activity among Mexican farm tenants and laborers in South Texas.

Workers also left Mexico to escape political conflicts and economic dislocations associated with the Mexican revolution. Beginning in the first decade, many of these immigrants returned to fight in the revolution. The politically charged interaction that resulted from this type of back-and-forth migration reinforced a historic attachment with Mexico and an interest in political developments in the northern region that had been evident among Mexicans from South Texas at least since the middle 1800s. A long history of close relations fostered by familial, economic, and political ties spanning the border line had always drawn political exiles to Texas and had encouraged the participation of Texas-Mexican border residents in Mexican political affairs.

Although the migration experience may have served to link communities from both sides of the border, it also fostered impermanence and economic insecurity even for those who remained for extended periods of time in the United States. This was evident in the lives of two old-timers that attracted the attention of the labor economist Paul Taylor when he conducted his research in Nueces County during the late 1920s. One of them had come to Texas from the state of Tamaulipas in 1890. He worked as a cowboy, trackman, miner, and candy maker in his travels through Oklahoma, Missouri, and Pennsylvania. The second worker had been a trackman, miner, stevedore, and sugar beet worker in California, New Mexico, Colorado, Pennsylvania, and New York. When Taylor interviewed them, they had made a complete circle in their work lives and were still picking cotton for low wages in their old age.[13]

The size of the immigrant work force was large. In 1908 the U.S. government calculated that between sixty thousand and one hundred thousand Mexicans were entering the country every year. According to a study that examined the rates of Mexican immigration to selected states in the United States, the largest number of Mexican immigrants chose Texas as their preferred point of destination until 1915. Immigration peaked during the second decade with an estimated annual average of around fifty thousand crossings into Texas. Between fifty to seventy-five percent of the new arrivals in Texas returned to Mexico every year.[14]

The social and economic impact of immigration was often greater than the numbers indicate because the census did not take into account the large undetermined number of undocumented, or officially unde-tected, crossings. Immigration officials clearly undercounted the number of persons in 1918, 1919, and 1920 with their approximations of 17,602, 28,844, and 50,852 entering immigrants. Spirited debates between restrictionists and antirestrictionists added to the confusion and tensions. The latter, usually employer representatives, used conservative figures to buttress their arguments for the continued admission of immigrants.[15]

Restrictionists, on the other hand, often quoted inflated figures in opposing such progrower measures as the amendment to the Immigration Act of 1917, which allowed for the temporary admission of Mexican workers. John Box, U.S. Representative from Texas and an avid restrictionist, for example, pointed out that as many as two hundred thousand Mexicans were recruited on the Texas-Mexico border in 1920. Box and other restrictionists utilized exaggerated numbers to underscore their xenophobic arguments of racial, cultural, and economic peril. The economic arguments were sometimes the most effective because they were based on the well-substantiated claim that Mexicans were traveling to the cities in increasing numbers and were contributing to the dramatic growth of the urban work force. Restrictionists argued that Mexican immigrants refused to stay on the farms, thereby depressing wages and displacing Anglo workers in urban areas throughout the state.[16]

Although restrictionists, including organized labor, waged an impressive campaign during the latter part of the second decade, immigration continued relatively unchecked, primarily because growers successfully maintained that Mexican immigrant labor was critical to agricultural production. Despite guarantees that the cotton economy would naturally attract workers from the border area and Mexico, farmers continued to recruit workers from Mexico to meet the insatiable demand for low-wage labor. These recruitment efforts often involved collaboration between railroads, farmers' organizations, and labor recruiters. Recruitment contracts offered to Mexican workers on the border usually guaranteed them railway transportation to a predetermined destination in Texas or in other parts of the Southwest. From there they were either shipped to fill prearranged contracts, or they were amassed and distributed according to on-the-spot secondary orders. Contracting costs varied, although these were always eventually deducted from the workers' earnings.[17]

Fred Roberts, a farmer from Corpus Christi and member of the South Texas Cotton Growers' Association, described a common labor contracting arrangement that supplied Nueces County with approximately sixty-five hundred Mexican workers during the 1919 cotton picking season. Roberts reported that it cost him four dollars in labor agent fees for each of the sixty-seven workers that he contracted. He also paid the Texas-Mexican Railroad two cents a mile, or a total of $2.60 per worker, to transport the crews to a point close to his farm. Roberts supplied the workers with such essentials as beans, bacon, pots, and pans from his commissary for an average cost of $2.00 to $3.50 per worker. He calculated a total average cost of between ten to fifteen dollars to secure one adult. Roberts always deducted from the worker's first week's earnings an average of twenty dollars for a family composed of a husband, a wife, and two children.[18]

Labor recruiters were most active in El Paso, one of the major crossing points at the turn of the century. They were instrumental in directing the immigrant flow in a fan-like fashion to various points in the interior. Between January and September of 1907, for example, six employment agencies operating in the city supplied 16,479 workers to railroad companies throughout the country.[19] Labor recruiters usually freighted Mexicans to the railroad lines outside of Texas. Other crossing points down the river supplied labor to railways, mines, ranches, and farms located mostly in South Texas. Some of these workers that crossed at Eagle Pass, Laredo, and Brownsville traveled throughout Texas and beyond. Laredo, one of the most important crossing points in South Texas, registered an increasing number of immigrants; the monthly total rose to nearly fifteen hundred in 1914. The immigrants often converged in San Antonio, the most important labor distribution center in Texas outside of El Paso.[20]

Immigration authorities usually reported that the great majority of Mexican immigrants were unskilled. Although this classification may have held true for most of the immigrants, authorities on the border generally made these determinations based on the kinds of jobs that awaited the Mexicans, rather than on the actual skills that the workers possessed. Trade unionists and other restrictionists who were more inclined to notice such differences often pointed to skilled workers among the immigrants. An Anglo trade unionist from El Paso, for instance, reported to the 1910 TSFL convention that Mexican immigrants were, "entering the United States at the rate of more than one thousand per month, many of whom are partially skilled as musicians, carpenters, painters, tinners, etc."[21]

Occupations and Wages

Railways employed the largest number of Mexicans in the United States during the early 1900s. They mostly worked as laborers on the railroad lines and shops throughout California, Texas, New Mexico, and Arizona, as well as in places within Nevada, Colorado, Wyoming, Illinois, and Iowa. Cotton farmers and ranchers employed the second largest number. Seasonal work in cotton attracted workers who welcomed the opportunity to optimize their low earning power with the help of the entire family. Consequently, the largest number of women and children working outside the home were usually found on the farms, as well as in the packing sheds that processed vegetables. Different seasonal schedules for vegetable farms and preharvest work and tenancy in cotton production often increased the employment period. Farm laborers worked in Texas, Oklahoma, Colorado, and southern California as well as in the irrigated sections of New Mexico and Arizona. Many of the older immigrants and U.S.-born Mexicans became intrastate and interstate migrant workers when new immigration waves pressured them out. They were most numerous in the cotton fields and vegetable farms of South Texas. The largest number of Mexican miners worked in New Mexico,

Farm and packing shed workers in the Rio Grande Valley, ca. 1920. *Courtesy Institute of Texan Cultures, The University of Texas at San Antonio*

Colorado, and Arizona. As in the railways and farms, Mexicans were the principal source of cheap labor for copper, silver, and coal mines. They were assigned the lowest paying, most hazardous, and least skilled jobs in the industry. In the cities, employment for Mexicans varied per industry, although they were generally placed in the lowest occupational levels.[22]

A study of the occupational distribution of foreign-born workers in New Mexico, Arizona, and Texas during the 1900–20 period provides additional information on the position and status of Mexican workers.[23] Roden Fuller, a student of southwestern labor markets, used general occupational figures attributed to persons that were foreign-born or of foreign parentage. He reasoned that the data generated by the census applied to Mexicans because they constituted between 70 and 79 percent of the immigrant work force in the three-state region. We can further assume that Fuller's findings apply to U.S.-born Mexicans, since they usually worked alongside the immigrant workers (see Table 2).

The numbers of foreign-born workers increased significantly in Texas agriculture. They increased their representation from 5 percent in 1900 to almost 11 percent in 1920. The absolute and proportional increases were primarily due to the influx of Mexican immigrants. Agriculture played a less important role in increasing immigrant occupational figures in New Mexico and Arizona. Foreign-born workers from New Mexico and Texas decreased in importance as farmers, planters, and overseers. This suggests that Mexican nationals did not generally enter these occupations. They became merchants and dealers to the same low extent as other foreign-born groups between 1900 and 1910. This changed significantly by 1920 in New Mexico and Arizona and, to a lesser degree, in Texas. Mexicans fared worse in the ranches. The number of foreign-born stockraisers, herders, and drovers decreased from 2,968 in 1900 to 2,300 in 1920. Texas recorded the largest numbers and a steady decline in percentage figures, from 18 percent in 1900 to 11½ percent in 1920. The largest concentration of foreign-born laborers from New Mexico and Arizona worked in the mines and quarries. In Texas, miners and quarrymen represented one of the smallest group of foreign-born laborers.

Fuller did not provide a count for the number of foreign-born railroad workers, although he claims that the proportional increase involved the displacement of U.S.-born workers. Contemporary observers often made similar claims of a queuing process in which newer immigrants displaced older immigrants, blacks, and U.S.-born Mexicans. What very often remained unclear, however, was the extent to which the U.S.-born workers experienced upward mobility as they made room for the recent arrivals. This was an important question that was lost in the debate over immigration. The popular view was that Mexican immigrants were coming into the cities and threatening to displace Anglo workers. This claim often served as a barrier to most Mexicans, including the older immigrants and the U.S.-born who were attempting to leave agriculture or the laboring occupations in urban-based industries.

Foreign-born carpenters and joiners decreased in representation, while their counterparts in domestic service increased proportionally between 1900 and 1920. This comparative finding once again raises the issue of displacement and the organization of work according to nativity. A downward trend in the numbers of foreign-born workers in the more promising occupations like farm operator, merchant, or carpenter accompanied a corresponding motion in the opposite direction among U.S.-born workers. In other words, as foreign-born workers entered the labor market largely as laborers, native-born workers faced increased competition and lost traditional sources of employment. With regard to workers from Mexico, we can further surmise that they contributed significantly to the process of displacement, with a disproportionate concentration in the more menial occupations.

Mexican workers from Texas exhibited the general occupational trends evident throughout the Southwest. They constructed the railroad lines that criss-crossed the South Texas area. When construction was completed, they worked with maintenance crews throughout the state and in the railroad shops. Mexicans had also participated in the cattle and

Railroad workers on the line in the Cotulla area, ca. 1890.
Courtesy LaSalle County Historical Museum, Cotulla; and Institute of Texan Cultures, The University of Texas at San Antonio

sheep industries of South Texas since the late eighteenth century. They cleared much of the land of South Texas for the expansion of agriculture during the turn of the century. Labor demands also attracted large numbers from Mexico and Texas to the cane fields in Louisiana during the 1890s, to the cotton fields of West, Central and North Texas in the 1910s, and to the farms and factories in Wyoming, Nebraska, Idaho, New York, Pennsylvania, Illinois, and Indiana during the 1920s.[24]

Mexicans held a variety of occupations in urban areas. They participated in the building trades, railroad shops, smelting plants, public works projects, and construction, as well as in pecan-shelling, garment work, laundries, retailing, and in other small industries involved in candy, hat, and cigar making. Border towns like Laredo and Brownsville registered a high number of Mexican workers with such specialized skills as teachers, typographical workers, taxi drivers, clerks, electricians, and carpenters. However, in urban areas away from the border the social structure was more racially defined and employers generally denied Mexicans the more attractive positions. Both U.S.-born and Mexico-born skilled workers faced occupational discrimination and earned depressed wages. Although an increased number of Mexican workers acquired employment in industrial establishments throughout the state, especially after 1910, they usually filled lower-waged and lower-skilled positions.[25]

An electrician and three carpenters in the Rio Grande Valley, ca. 1910. *Courtesy Harry Lund Collection, Archives Division, Texas State Library, Austin*

The construction and maintenance shops of the Ferrocarriles Nacionales de Mexico, or the Mexican National Railroad, for example, concentrated Mexican shop workers in the laboring positions. The better paying and more skilled jobs were reserved for Anglos. The Freeport Sulphur Works and the Freeport Chemical Works placed its Mexican work force in the laboring occupations. The former company paid its approximately one hundred Mexican employees thirty-six cents an hour to load crude sulphur on railroad cars. Mexican dock and construction workers in Galveston and oil workers in Fort Worth also worked as laborers for a lower wage. Mexican railway workers from Big Spring were largely laborers receiving low wages. In San Angelo, Mexican railway laborers earned $1.75 for a ten-hour work day, while Anglos earned $2.00 for an eight-hour day.[26]

Mexican job earnings were the lowest in the state, partly because Mexicans were consistently placed in the lower-paying laboring occupations. Low earnings were also due to a dual wage system that granted Anglo workers higher pay for the same work. As a general rule, wages for Mexican workers were lower in Texas than in California. Within the state, Mexicans could earn more the farther north they migrated, though skilled job opportunities were better in the towns along the border.[27] Mexican workers earned low wages and their earnings increased at a slow pace (see Table 3). The largest single group of workers, Mexican laborers, earned the lowest wages in the state. Ranchers and farmers paid them an average daily wage of fifty-five cents during the first decade and seventy-five cents during the second. Railroad workers, particularly shop employees, earned slightly higher amounts during both decades and registered significant increases that ranged between fifty and sixty-five cents per day. The other category of urban laborers, the public works employees, also earned more than agricultural workers. However, their wages remained relatively unchanged at $1.35 per day. Mine workers, the smallest numerical group, earned the highest wages, an average of $1.60 a day.

A 1926 survey study of Mexicans from San Antonio by William J. Knox, a local school teacher, indicates that they improved their earnings by the third decade at the same time that they remained impoverished and concentrated in the lesser-skilled occupations (see Table 4). By 1926 close to fifty percent of them were classified as common laborers, or transients, who usually earned less than $14 a week when work was available. Unable to secure permanent employment in the city, most of them searched for jobs in farms throughout the state or in the industrial establishments of the northern and eastern parts of the United States. Laborers with more permanent sources of employment, or regular

Mexican leather workers and Anglo employers in Laredo, 1900. *Courtesy Laredo Public Library*

job holders, included railroad workers, store clerks, truck drivers, and employees of the city's public works system, the most numerous in the group. Stable employment for these 270 workers meant that they could earn approximately one-half more than the irregularly employed laborers.

The significantly fewer number of businessmen such as small store owners and butchers, on the other hand, exceeded the earnings of the permanently employed laborers by a small amount. Skilled workers, including barbers, shoemakers, plumbers, tailors, painters, mechanics, cement workers, and carpenters, represented over twenty-one percent of the Mexican work force, a figure that was comparable to the one registered by the regularly employed laborers. One of Knox's most suggestive findings is that businessmen and skilled workers did not earn appreciably higher incomes than the permanently employed laborers. Businessmen most probably registered low earnings because they depended on an impoverished clientele. The low earnings of skilled workers, however, suggest a wage ceiling. The professional group which was composed mostly of musicians, printers, and journalists was the highest in average earnings yet the smallest in number.

Knox also examined the nativity of Mexican male heads of households to explain earning variations (see Table 5). His hypothesis was that longer residence in the United States and the knowledge of English resulted in continuous and better paying work. According to this logic, the recent arrivals, regardless of skills or prior job experience, disadvantaged the entire community. In accordance with his proposition, Knox found that a larger portion, or sixty-five percent, of Mexico-born male workers that he surveyed were concentrated in occupations that commanded lower wages. Sixty-three percent of the U.S.-born Mexican workers, however, also worked in the laboring occupations. This finding undermines his argument and suggests that Mexicans as a whole were denied upward mobility. Knox's assumptions are more tenable when he points out the greater concentration of Mexico-born workers in the transient occupations. On the other hand, the U.S.-born did not record an appreciable proportional advantage over the Mexico-born in the business, skilled, and professional ranks.

Mexican Women

While Mexicans as a whole faced a racially defined labor market experience, Mexicanas had to contend with the added gender division of labor. Most married females with U.S.-born and Mexico-born husbands remained in the home to fulfill work responsibilities that sustained and reproduced the Mexican family. Some of them took in boarders, made "drawn" work, did washing, sewing, and ironing for other families, or periodically joined the rural work force to supplement the income of their working-class families. Young single women, on the other hand, joined the work force outside the home in increasing numbers throughout the early 1900s. Despite this mobility experience, they represented a bottom working segment with lower-status and poorly-paying jobs that were extensions of home work.[28]

Mexican women working outside the home were concentrated in agriculture, primarily in cotton and vegetable farms. They usually worked alongside other family members, including children, in order to make use of the family's full earning power. Male immigrants at first made the trek to Texas alone; however, they began to bring along their entire families during the early 1900s. Farmers encouraged the migration of family units because it made workers less mobile, that is, less prone to move in search of better wages and working conditions on other farms and in nearby towns or cities. By the 1910s improved job opportunities in places like Corpus Christi, San Antonio, Houston, and Dallas encouraged the movement of Mexicana workers into industrial occupations that included laundresses, garment workers, maids, and pecan shellers.

Mexican women doing drawn work in Brownsville, ca. 1910.
Courtesy Brownsville Historical Association

A survey conducted by the Texas Bureau of Labor Statistics among Mexican and Anglo female workers employed by industrial establishments in El Paso provides a basis for making some determinations concerning the racial division of labor among women during the second decade.[29] The survey was based on a sample of 1,787 female workers employed by the leading urban-based employers of women (see Table 6). We are unable to say much about the problem of occupational stratification because the bureau researchers failed to distinguish between the various occupations in each of the six industrial sectors. We can tell, however, that the single largest concentration of Mexican and Anglo female workers was in the mercantile stores. Other sources indicate that Mexican women usually filled lower-status jobs in Mexican-owned stores that catered to a poor Mexican clientele. The second largest number of Mexican female workers were laundresses, while a comparable group of Anglo female workers were telegraph and telephone operators. This underscores the view that Mexican women assumed the lower-status, lower-paying jobs and that Anglo women filled the higher-status, higher-paying ones.

The El Paso survey reveals a significant wage disparity overall and within six types of industrial establishments that employed women. Mexican women (843) averaged a weekly income of $8.69, while Anglo women (944) earned around $18.56 each. The aggregate difference in

Garment work in Brownsville, 1926. *Courtesy Brownsville Historical Association*

pay totalled $9.87. The disparity was particularly evident in the miscellaneous industries, a general and occupationally undefined category.

The El Paso survey also generated educational data that allow us to determine the relationship of schooling to occupational and wage disparities. One possible explanation for the disparity is that a lower educational standing among the Mexican women accounted for the differences. Race, however, was the primary determinant of inequality when the women were grouped according to education and industrial sectors (see Table 7).

The fourth-to-eighth and high school categories are the most useful because they provide sizable comparative sets of data for Mexican and Anglo women. According to these general data and the accompanying data by industry that the bureau provided we can conclude that even when Mexican women registered a comparable grade level they still obtained significantly lower weekly salaries than Anglo females. The bureau also found that Mexican women were on the average younger, single, and lived at home. This indicates that Mexican women had a higher labor market participation rate primarily because Mexican families, in contrast to Anglo families, expected their women to take a more active role in meeting a greater economic need. In other words, a dual wage system made it necessary for a larger number of Mexican workers to maintain their families.[30]

Conclusion

When seen within the context of the entire Mexican work force, the Mexican women from El Paso studied by the Bureau of Labor Statistics researchers earned less and more frequently assumed lower-status jobs than their male counterparts. Racial discrimination compounded their problems and helped define the farthest reach of occupational mobility allowed Mexicans during the early 1900s.

Industrialization in South Texas did not generally involve Mexicans in the skilled and better-paying jobs. They usually worked as laborers in the mines, farms, ranches, construction sites, public works systems, service and food establishments, and railroads. Also, they suffered from wage discrimination and the refusal by landowners to rent them land. The subordination of the Mexican community began during a period of U.S. territorial expansion during the middle 1800s. It reached a southern limit with the development of the Rio Grande Valley in the early 1900s. Landed Mexican families, merchants, and artisans suffered significant losses. Further, the increasing numbers of Mexicans traveling from Mexico were concentrated in the laboring occupations alongside earlier arrivals and U.S.-born Mexicans. Discrimination that denied Mexicans occupational mobility and better wages reinforced their subordinate position in the labor market.

Chapter Two

Race and Work
on the Farms and in the Cities

Expanded job opportunities accompanying the growth and development of the economy must have given Mexicans reason for hope. These developments, however, were also sources of frustration. Not only did discrimination deny Mexicans equal access to most of the new better-paying skilled occupations, but the massive entry of Mexican nationals created a labor surplus in the lower ranks that depressed wages, intensified conflict, and undermined workers' organizing potential. The development of agriculture exemplified the discouraging set of affairs. Land developers drove up the price of land beyond the reach of agricultural workers and encouraged midwestern and northern farmers to expect and exploit low-wage Mexican labor. The accompanying negative portrayals of Mexican workers justified and reinforced their exploitation and gave racial definition to social relations. Adding to the racial tensions were accusations by displaced Anglo farmers that Mexican labor gave the large growers an unfair competitive advantage over them.

One of the major requirements of commercialized agriculture was to maintain efficient recruitment efforts to meet the critical demands for mass labor. Recruitment, however, was only half of the farmer's problem. Farmers also worried about regulating the labor force, because Mexicans were prone to travel from farm to farm and from rural areas to nearby towns in search of better wages. Mexicans were neither bound to their employers by contractual agreements nor encouraged to remain in one location by uniform wages. Consequently, farmers responded with measures to immobilize the work force. Farmers may have had the upper hand, but they were never able to completely control the mobile work force. They constantly searched for more efficient measures of labor control, while Mexican workers persisted in their attempts to informally bargain improvements in their condition by seeking the highest wage in neighboring farms and towns. Whether seen as a response or as an initiative, the migration strategy mirrored self-organization and defiance.[1]

Although lacking a formal organizational base, individual and collective decisions to seek the highest wage in neighboring farms and cities sustained an oppositional force in the fields of South Texas. Such challenges, including spontaneous work stoppages and sabotage, contributed to a major political crisis in the farms as well as in urban areas. As Mexicans traveled to the cities, Anglo workers began to accuse farmers of exporting the problem of unregulated low-wage labor into their domain. Fearing depressed wages and job displacement, they responded with their own measures to control urban labor markets and to help farmers restrict the labor force to the farms. Racial tensions became especially pronounced as increasing numbers of immigrant and U.S.-born Mexicans traveled to the cities.

A racial tone characterized the debate over Mexican immigration to the extent that defenders of the status quo often failed to make a distinction between U.S.-born and Mexican nationals. Another indication of the seriousness of the racial conflict was that organized labor resisted the idea of organizing Mexicans. Although the state federation eventually decided to incorporate U.S.-born and naturalized Mexicans, despite appearances of magnanimity this new policy represented yet another method to control Mexican labor.[2]

Conflict in the Farms

Much of the racial thinking that justified the subordination of Mexicans originated in the wars with Mexico and in the propensity by large numbers of Anglo immigrants to transfer their anti-black and anti–Native American sentiments to the Mexican. With time, however, new stereotypes that depicted Mexicans as docile and obedient workers joined with older disparaging views to justify their exploitation. Such antipathies obtained special economic importance as a rejuvenated form of "race thinking" that historical sociologist David Montejano associates with immigration and the development of commercial agriculture.[3] Land companies and newspapers, for instance, contributed to the new racially defined occupational structure in agriculture with advertising campaigns that promoted farm sales to midwestern and southern farmers by promising an ample supply of cheap Mexican labor in Texas. As early as 1885, for instance, the *Corpus Christi Caller* announced that investments in the production of cotton promised profitable returns due to the "abundant" and "cheap labor at hand."[4]

The *Galveston News* added that cheap Mexican labor in Bee County assured farmers profits even for harvests that would ordinarily produce losses in other parts of the state.[5] The confident and suggestive announcements by local labor agents cast aside whatever fears a prospective farmer might have about securing an adequate supply of cheap labor. As one of these agents noted, "Plenty of Labor: I secure Mexican labor-

This is an actual photograph
MEXICAN LABOR—Cheap and plentiful—wages $1.50 per day,
ten hours—efficient, loyal and plentiful. Note this wonderful
cabbage field.
"Personally conducted tour every week by Valley Developments, Inc.,
Harlingen, Texas. Write for information."

Advertising cheap and plentiful Mexican labor in a promotional brochure for Valley Development, Inc., a farm development company from Harlingen, ca. 1928. *Courtesy Harlingen Public Library*

ers for all kinds of work at reasonable prices in any number."[6] Another publication added that Mexican labor was "practically unlimited, while the nearness of Mexico guaranteed to forestall the evolution of a 'problem' in the labor question for many years to come."[7] A land development company located in Pharr painted an even more alluring picture that farmers could expect: "The great advantage of Mexican labor is its dependability. The men are expert farmers, competent, willing and contented. They hold their place without attempting to mingle socially with the Americans, and are segregated in their own districts and have their own schools and churches. The Mexican women assist the housewives with their work. These conditions assure ready help at all times of the year at small cost."[8]

The high cost of farming and the instability of the market also encouraged the new farmers to expect low-wage Mexican labor. Intense speculation during the early 1900s contributed to skyrocketing land values and prompted farmers to shift down the burden of the cost of production by restricting Mexicans to a relatively fixed occupational position as poorly paid laborers. At the same time, speculative buying eventually boosted the price of land beyond the means of Mexicans entering in succeeding waves from deep South Texas and from across the border.[9]

During the late nineteenth century land companies bought South Texas farm land for fifty to seventy-five cents an acre. By the turn of the century speculators bought this same land for seven or eight dollars an acre and sold it to midwestern farmers for twenty-five or thirty dollars an acre.[10] The price of land continued to increase. By the middle of the second decade the average cost of an acre of undeveloped land in the Rio Grande Valley ranged between one hundred and three hundred dollars. What followed was predictable. Farmers compensated for inflated land prices and production costs by paying low wages to farm laborers.[11]

Conditions were most exacting on Mexican laborers who in 1914 and 1915 cleared Rio Grande Valley land for a fraction of the total value of new farms. According to one estimate, they averaged $110.05 in total wages for making productive fifty-nine acre properties that reached average land values of seventeen thousand dollars each. Mexicans were responsible for clearing the land of mesquite, huisache, ebony, cactus, and chaparral bush, for leveling the ground, and for digging numerous irrigation ditches throughout the farms. They received between seventy-five cents and one dollar per day for clearing and leveling the land and for planting, transplanting, hoeing, and harvesting the crops.[12]

Mexicans who traveled to the cotton belt area south of Austin and San Antonio also bore a major portion of the cost of overproduction and deflated cotton prices. Periodic drops in the price of cotton forced many small farmers to sell their land, equipment, and stock to larger enterprises. They either became tenant farmers or moved to nearby towns in search of better opportunities. Some Mexicans also became renters and sharecroppers; however, farmers usually preferred to hire them as laborers. The unstable and highly competitive market resulted in low wages and periodic unemployment for the burgeoning Mexican work force on the farms.[13] The concentration of land ownership, the rise in land tenancy, and the accompanying downward pressures on Mexican workers accelerated by the second decade. In 1880 renters operated 37.6 percent of the farms in the state. By 1920 the figure rose to 53.3 percent. Mexican farm laborers, on the other hand, registered depressed wages and high unemployment, especially during the 1907 and 1914 economic downturns in cotton.[14]

In addition to bearing a major cost of production, Mexicans served the political function of scapegoats. They entered the cotton economy as laborers at a point when Anglo farmers were severing their ties with a rural social order previously characterized by relatively self-sustaining

Female tomato pickers in the Rio Grande Valley, 1912. *Courtesy Hidalgo County Historical Museum, Edinburg*

and culturally homogeneous land-owning producers. As a result, displaced Anglo farmers directed their aggression towards one of the many features of the developing cotton economy, mass Mexican labor. The case of Keglar Hill from Caldwell County throws light on this process.[15]

Keglar Hill was established in 1860. Between 1860 and 1890 Anglo farmers experienced relative prosperity. Some became farm owners while others turned to tenancy with the intention of eventually becoming land owners. Although they were disturbed by the statewide increase in tenancy, a favorable price for cotton and good harvests in Keglar Hill in 1887 and 1888 helped to maintain a sense of harmony and good will among them. Economic growth and shared cultural values caused Anglo farm operators to enter "the affairs of community life on a basis of fundamental equality."[16]

Mexican laborers arrived in large numbers beginning around 1887. By 1897 every large planter from the area was employing Mexican sharecroppers and laborers. Before long, the large enterprises had increased production and contributed to a rise in the value of land and a drop in the price of cotton. Anglo farmers from Keglar Hill fell victim to this process. According to an observer, "of three hundred odd white Americans who composed that robust community in 1895, not one remained in 1910."[17] Although Mexicans did not voluntarily contribute to this state of affairs, former Anglo farm owners saw Mexicans as the key element in the deterioration of their way of life and adopted a racist view of Mexicans as a consequence. The result was increased opposition to Mexican immigration and a further justification of discrimination against Mexican laborers, sharecroppers, and tenants, regardless of nativity.[18]

Mexicans were said to be the most exploitable workers primarily because they were accustomed to harsher working conditions in Mexico and demanded less of their employers in the United States. Restrictionists and antirestrictionists agreed with this assessment. A University of Texas sociologist who opposed immigration, for example, noted that "the Mexican [immigrant] works for less, he can be supervised more easily, and the problem of labor is solved by his working the whole family and living under conditions which the American farmer would not tolerate."[19] Antirestrictionist Congressman Carlos Bee also pointed to the exploitability of the Mexican worker, although with a different purpose in mind. He sought to convince a congressional committee that continued immigration made economic sense. The Mexican worker, according to Bee, was "especially fitted for the burdensome task of bending his back to picking the cotton and the burdensome task of grubbing the fields." Testifying before the same committee, Roy Miller, a Corpus Christi official of the Rural Land Owners' Association and the Texas Cattle Raisers' Association, added that the numerous Anglo farmers who had come from the North and Midwest expected this kind of low-wage and tractable labor in order to effectively develop the region.[20]

The numerous observers who described the Mexican immigrant as an easily exploitable worker pointed to a type of newcomer mentality that had some basis in fact. Despite the impressive resolve exhibited in their decision to immigrate, they were no different from European-origin immigrants who saw the new world through the eyes of newcomers. They accepted the terms of their employment as an improvement to their lives in Mexico, an established fact prior to their arrival in Texas, and a new-found opportunity waiting to be exploited. However, they were also like other immigrants in their propensity to adjust their expectations to the new possibilities for improving their condition.[21] This was especially true for Mexican immigrants, who were more familiar than their European counterparts with the world that awaited them and presumably were better prepared to respond to labor problems in the United States.

The back and forth migrations gave them the opportunity to accumulate experiences which they subsequently shared by word of mouth with other newer immigrants. Moreover, Mexican presidents and northern Mexican governors, municipal authorities, and journalists throughout the 1910s and 1920s led vigorous public campaigns that informed immigrants of the discrimination and exploitation occurring in the United States. Governmental agencies, including officers attached to the Secretary of the Interior, the Secretary of Foreign Relations, and the Consular Service, also advised workers to challenge discrimination, seek formal contracts with U.S. employers, and report cases of contractual violations and other disputes. Although governmental intercession was often weak and inconsistent, it did keep immigrant workers abreast of their rights and encouraged them to protest discriminatory practices.[22]

When Mexicans responded in ways that denied their image as docile and tractable workers, Anglo perceptions hardened with equal legitimating force. Victor Clark, a Department of Labor researcher who conducted a study of Mexican labor in 1908, intimated this when he pointed out that farmers also described Mexicans as intractable workers. In numerous instances, employers called them insolent, inefficient, and highly irregular or undependable workers, alleged attributes that may have involved decisions by workers to slow down or quit work.[23] Antirestrictionist Miller likewise indicated a concern over the tractability of the highly mobile Mexican workers when he suggested measures to regulate "this labor and at the same time protect ourselves against its detrimental effects, if there be such."[24] A railroad supervisor from southern Kansas, who directed the recruitment of Mexican labor along the Texas border, expressed similar concern: "Though they are used to low pay at home, they want as much as anybody when they get to this country."[25] According to an Anglo cotton picker interviewed by Paul Taylor in 1929 for his study of Nueces County, "It's mainly the wets [recent undocumented arrivals] who work for less; after they've been here a while they want more money."[26]

Most farmers, however, insisted that the U.S.-born and older immigrants were more prone to challenge their employers. A farmer, frustrated with Mexican workers' demands, complained that "the Texas-Mexicans and Old Mexicans work differently. Texas-Mexicans don't work as good. They strike, they don't like the water, etc." Others underscored their penchant for striking: "The Mexicans always strike. Every Monday morning they want to know if they aren't going to raise the price. They have anarchists—agitators—who go around and tell them what price to pick for," and "they are highly sensitive and will leave you if you show you are dissatisfied. They will leave without a dime, and with no place to go."[27]

Immigrant and U.S.-born Mexicans also withheld their labor and joined the migrant work stream. For the immigrants, traveling in search of better cotton pickings or improved wages involved an enterprising spirit that led them to make the decision to cross the international bor-

Onion workers from Cotulla, ca. 1905. *Courtesy LaSalle Historical Museum, Cotulla; and Institute of Texan Cultures, The University of Texas at San Antonio*

der in the first place. Their willingness to hazard the distant and unfamiliar world of work in the United States for the sake of economic improvement revealed a form of proletarian daring and tenacity that found continued expression in Texas. This was evident in the numerous instances when they broke labor contracts with railroad and farmer representatives as they were being transported to their work sites. Many of them apparently entered into these contracts to reach cotton and vegetable farms that promised them better wages. Once they arrived at their destination, many began their trek in search of better wages in the area. This was such a serious problem that labor agents often locked railroad car doors and posted armed guards on train platforms to prevent desertions.[28]

Clearly, farmers enjoyed a formidable bargaining advantage with their large and, to some extent, regulated labor supply. The low wages in the industry and the lack of formal union organization suggests that this important edge limited the organizing potential of agricultural workers. Farmers, however, were not able to prevent Mexicans from taking important organizing initiatives. Although large numbers and constant migration undermined organizational and formal bargaining possibilities, laborers did conduct slowdowns, sabotage, contract violations, and spontaneous walkouts.[29] Farm workers often refused to work for some farmers, or they left unexpectedly when they heard that newly maturing crops in other regions to the north promised them better pickings and higher wages. This placed farmers in a highly vulnerable position especially when changing climatic conditions and unstable cotton prices dictated a quick harvest and a sudden need for more workers.[30]

Large corporate farms like the Coleman-Fulton Pasture Company located in Taft, Gregory, and Portland were the most efficient in responding to the mobility of Mexican workers due to the almost absolute control that they had over their work forces. Workers depended on Coleman-Fulton for everything, including company-owned homes and food and tools from the company store. Isolation, indebtedness, physical threats, and lack of legal recourse discouraged them from joining the migrant stream in the middle of the harvest, but workers nevertheless took organizing initiatives. This prompted company representatives to institute added measures to discourage and undermine labor organizing. For instance, Coleman-Fulton purposely hired both Mexicans and Anglos on the assumption that the language barrier would prevent them from forming a union. Aside from preventing interethnic alliances, the company assigned Anglos to the tenant positions and Mexicans to the laborer occupations, partly to more effectively single out English-speaking organizers and Mexican labor "agitators." The idea was to quickly remove them from the company properties before they had a chance to organize workers.[31]

Smaller corporate farms and individual farmers also sought to reinforce social relations by immobilizing Mexican workers. They used indebtedness among sharecroppers and tenants as well as intimidation and physical force among the migrant workers. Mexicans, however, continued to evade these constrictions, leading farmers to seek more formal and efficient methods of control. The state and federal governments responded to the pleas for help with measures to supply added immigrant workers, oversee the migrant flow throughout the state, and regulate private employment agencies that were exporting migrant labor from the state.

The expected wartime demand for increased agricultural production first led agribusiness to call for unrestricted immigration. The U.S. Department of labor responded by granting Texas farmers exemptions from the literacy and head tax requirements of the 1917 immigration law. When thousands of Mexican workers began to emigrate because they feared being drafted and possibly forced to fight against Mexico, Texas farmers requested the intercession of chambers of commerce, Mexican consulate offices, and local law enforcement and military leaders. The response was overwhelming during the spring of 1917. Civic leaders in places like San Antonio and Laredo rushed to the aid of the farmers with public rallies and announcements in the press intended to counter the rumors allegedly circulated by German agents.[32] Requests for assistance in resolving the problem of throat-cutting competition also brought results. In 1918, for instance, the Nueces County Council of Defense issued a directive to local representatives that read: "You shall inform the farmers of your community that efforts and schemes on the part of farmers to get labor away from their neighbors by offering them higher prices or other inducements, will not be tolerated by this organization. You will let it be known in your community that such underhanded action on the part of any person will be considered as an unpatriotic and disloyal act."[33]

The state government intervened in 1918 when the legislature appropriated money to the Bureau of Labor Statistics for the establishment of an alternative to independent employment agencies. The new creation was a farm labor distribution program involving "free employment agencies" in Waco, Fort Worth, Amarillo, Dallas, San Antonio, and El Paso. State labor agents normally conducted surveys prior to the beginning of the season, in anticipation of labor needs in selected agricultural areas. They then directed migrant workers to areas of high demand in cooperation with members of the Federal Farm Labor Service, a companion labor distribution program operating during the war under the U.S. Employment Service.[34]

The state legislature also passed an Emigrant Labor Agency Law in 1929 to regulate the operations of private employment agencies that were directing the movement of Mexicans towards better job opportunities in the Midwest and the North. The Bureau of Labor Statistics described its efforts to regulate the flow of farm labor through its labor distribution program and the Emigrant Labor Agency Law as an attempt to regularize the labor market for the benefit of both the farmer and the farm laborer. This was expressed in terms of bringing together the "jobless man" and the "manless job" without the intrusion of private employment agencies that allegedly deceived both.[35]

Despite this expressed purpose, it was evident that the primary intent was to immobilize Mexican labor. Neither the Emigrant Labor Agency Law nor the labor distribution program, however, prevented Mexicans from traveling to the cities, a strategy that Mexicans increasingly adopted. Consequently, the calls for immobilizing farm labor also originated in the cities. Anglo urban workers claimed that farmers had lost control, allowing immigrants to travel into the cities where they depressed wages and threatened to displace the native-born. The reaction by Anglo urban workers reinforced the general climate of social discrimination characterized by school segregation, the refusal of service in public establishments, and even lynchings, which according to one estimate occurred at the rate of one a week during the years following the first world war.[36]

Conflict in the City

The dramatic growth of the labor force on the farms, along with increased competition and the seasonal nature of agricultural production, may have served to push increasing numbers of Mexican laborers into joining the migrant stream. But it was the lure of improved job possibilities in the developing urban economies that channeled the movement into the towns and the cities. Many workers established permanent residency, while others became itinerant laborers who periodically traveled to the outlying agricultural areas or to places outside the state in search of employment.[37] The move to the cities constituted one of the most significant human migrations witnessed in the state. It combined the surplus immigrant labor with the U.S.-born Mexican portion of the state's rural-to-urban flow, producing one of the fastest urban population growth rates evident at the time.

Urbanization exacerbated racial conflict when Anglo workers reacted to the growing Mexican work force as a threat to their privileged position in the labor market. The added numbers of Mexicans placed in question the familiar custom of reserving skilled jobs for Anglo workers. This became an especially serious problem for lesser-skilled Anglos, who feared that their employers would lower their wages or replace them. Fear became widespread and reinforced occupational discrimination. Although unfavorable market conditions at times prohibited the employment of some Mexicans, racial employment barriers established with the consent and support of Anglo labor became the major obstacles to mobility.

A sense of racial superiority often expressed by a refusal to work alongside Mexicans imbued the job consciousness of Anglo workers and permitted them to think of skilled jobs as their exclusive domain. Taylor witnessed this attitude among Anglo farm workers in Nueces County during the late 1920s.[38] They made the familiar and at times substantiated arguments that Mexicans undercut wages and drove Anglos out of work. Others, however, expressed disdain against working with Mexicans because they feared a loss of status. This perception also found expression in urban areas. In 1901 Anglo female garment workers from Corpus Christi, for instance, compelled their employer to discharge Mexican females by refusing to be in the same room with them.[39] A similar arrangement between employers and workers that involved organized labor was in operation in the expanding garment industry of

Detail from a panoramic photograph of Mexican workers from San Antonio waiting for job assignments at an employment agency, 1924. *Courtesy Photography Collection, Harry Ransom Humanities Research Center, The University of Texas at Austin*

San Antonio by 1910. During that year's TSFL convention one of the federation's vice-presidents reported the exclusionary practice with noticeable approval: "The Garment Workers of San Antonio consist of girls from the best families and no Mexican girls are allowed to work in the factory."[40]

Labor reformers also expressed racial motivations when they sought to protect the moral virtue of "helpless" Anglo women who were entering the industrial work force. At the urging of TSFL leaders, the Bureau of Labor Statistics and the Bureau of Industrial Welfare called for a minimum wage for women, to keep Anglo females from falling prey to the alleged immorality that labor exploitation made evident among Mexican women.[41] The call for protective legislation led to the establishment of a minimum wage law in 1919. The legislature, however, repealed the law in 1921 because the original proponents opposed its uniform nature. They insisted on a system that fixed and enforced minimum wages according to prevailing customs, that is, a racial-hierar-chical wage system. The editor of the Austin newspaper *La Vanguardia,* an ever watchful critic of the Texas legislature, pointed out that people like T. C. Jennings, past president of the TSFL, director of the Texas Bureau of Labor Statistics, and a member of the Bureau of Industrial Welfare, had publicly opposed the law because it did not guarantee a higher wage for Anglo women. The editor's criticism demonstrated the kind of justified response that such blatant discrimination ordinarily evoked among Mexicans: "More importance should be given to the value of women's work on the basis of what they produce. That is the only way to insure justice. The woman who is clearly dedicated to her work has the right to the same wage given to a man who does the same work. The woman that works with the same efficiency, whether she is Black, Mexican, or 'white,' has the same right to the same wage."[42]

Although Anglo workers offered unadulterated racial justifications to support wage and occupational barriers, they often expressed their concerns over job control in economic and political terms. This became apparent among the least-skilled Anglo workers, who were most fear-ful of the growing number of Mexican workers during periodic eco-nomic downturns. The more skilled and organized workers may have had greater job security; however, they, too, were drawn into the con-flict when economic crisis and the open-shop movement made them equally sensitive to the alleged immigrant threat.

The large supply of labor in the cities granted employers a bargain-ing advantage over workers dangerously situated a mere notch above the bulging bottom sector. These included Anglos in public works, con-struction, and the service industry. The growing immigrant work force and wage reductions in some occupations made it increasingly apparent to Anglo workers that employers were in a favorable position to replace them or to depress wages further with the mere threat of displacement. To state this in another way, lesser-skilled Anglo workers were witness-ing the erosion of traditional employment barriers, the familiar mode of exclusion that protected them and the more secure skilled workers as privileged sectors in the labor market.[43]

The vulnerability of lesser-skilled Anglo workers, however, is not sufficient to explain the widespread opposition to immigration and the continuing denial of upward occupational opportunities to Mexican workers. Economic downturns in the economy, disruptions in the ex-isting relations of power between labor and employers in a plant or an industry, the mass character of a particular work force, and the size and skill structure of the threatening group of workers in a given locality also shaped a perception of vulnerability among Anglo labor. Although this conclusion may have involved actual cases of displacement or strike-breaking activity by Mexicans, the possibility that job control could be lost was enough to cause serious concern.

Examining variations in the conflict experience sheds light on the type and intensity of Anglo reactions. For instance, Anglo workers in the Corpus Christi building trades were especially sensitive to the uncertainties of the labor market by virtue of their lesser-skilled status. They avoided a prolonged conflict with possible racial overtones, however, because they were well-organized, using their predominantly Anglo union to successfully assume control over their jobs. They simply excluded Mexicans from the unions and from most of the nonunionized skilled positions. Consequently, Mexicans remained relatively isolated in the small-scale construction sites and lower-paying jobs. The union continued to exclude Mexicans without resorting to overt racial justifications and accusations.[44]

Anglo unions in San Antonio were also successful in segregating the work force, although they had a harder time doing it. San Antonio drew a larger number of immigrants and domestic migrants in part because the city was a major distribution point for workers traveling throughout the country. Moreover, the building of military bases in the city increased the number of low-wage jobs and drew a large number of workers from Mexico and South Texas. Employers thus gained a bargaining advantage, suggesting the possibility that the organized, yet lesser-skilled, Anglo carpenters, painters, and sheet metal workers might have to accept the low wages that were customarily given to Mexicans. This partly explains why the conflict over jobs in construction was pronounced in San Antonio. It accentuated local racial tensions and became a special source of concern for the TSFL in its campaign against immigrant labor.[45]

Anglo musicians, garment, and typographical workers from San Antonio, although highly specialized and unionized and theoretically secure in their positions, faced a similar problem as a result of the influx of Mexicans. Mexican musicians and printers that catered to the large Mexican community charged lower prices for their services and consequently contributed to depressed wages and job uncertainties.[46] Anglo garment workers increasingly found themselves in a vulnerable position as large numbers of women with training and experience in Mexico's needle trades began to offer services for a lower wage. The immediate response by the garment unions was to exclude the women because they accepted the lower wages customarily offered in Mexico and in the Mexican-owned establishments of the west side of town. Typographical and garment workers eventually invited some Mexican skilled workers into their ranks when the unions undertook strike actions during the early 1920s.[47] Skilled railroad workers—conductors, engineers, firemen, and machinists—on the other hand, generally remained indifferent to the threat of competition from below in San Antonio and in other places throughout the state. They were the most secure, primarily as a result of their highly specialized skills and the exclusion of Mexicans from the large and politically influential railroad unions or brotherhoods.[48]

At Galveston Anglo longshoremen had less job control, in part because of difficulties in effectively organizing such a large industrial work force. Furthermore, ethnic and skill divisions occasionally hampered organizing and strike activity. To make matters worse, the union faced a formidable problem in the open shop campaigns of the 1920s. Anglo workers also became especially sensitive to Mexican competition during the 1920 strike. Longshoremen accused employers of attempting to break the strike with imported Mexican workers who were reportedly deceived into thinking that they had been contracted to pick cotton in the area. Another serious concern was the presence of untold numbers of Mexican workers who had recently become unemployed upon the completion of an extension to the sea wall.[49]

Mexican immigration also appeared as a particularly serious threat in industries experiencing major setbacks. A painters' union from San Antonio, for instance, claimed in 1917 that it was "confronted with cheap labor from Mexico," at the same time that "the brunt of war has advanced the price of material to such an exorbitant price that it makes it hard on the ordinary house owner to have such work done."[50]

The economic slump of the post-war period, resulting from a decline in industrial production and a drop in the price of cotton, accentuated tensions and extended the conflict. Unable to accommodate an already burgeoning work force, city labor markets faced the arrival of additional workers that included Anglos from other states and from rural areas. Despite the presence of Anglo migrants, Mexicans were most visible because of their large numbers and their seeming propensity to accept whatever job was available. This provoked deeper fears among Anglo workers who had experienced or had come close to experiencing a major economic setback. Mexicans also contributed disproportionately to the ranks of the unemployed. Anglos who had just arrived from the farms or who had lost their jobs as a result of the economic crisis displaced Mexican workers, forcing additional numbers of them to join the unemployed or to migrate to rural areas, the border region, and Mexico.[51]

The Fort Worth delegation to the TSFL convention of 1920 revealed the nervous state of Anglo labor during the postwar period. Unionists from Fort Worth had never reported any serious problems with Mexican labor. Now, however, the local railroad shops and meat packing plants had released a large number of workers. Anglos feared that employers would use the thousands of unemployed Mexicans to displace them and to depress wages. Although no evidence was offered to support the claim, the threat seemed real enough to motivate the federation to lobby for immigration restrictions.[52]

Problems continued in Fort Worth the following year. According to welfare officials, the city's Mexican work force registered a ninety percent unemployment rate. Anglo and African-American workers, some of whom may have belonged to local unions, subsequently began to agitate for employment restrictions and deportations. A group of 263 workers sent an anonymous letter to the chamber of commerce threatening violence and general mayhem unless civic leaders "rid the city of cheap Mexican labor." Anglo and African-American workers next marched on city hall to underscore their grievance. The city's commissioner of streets responded to the pressure with a request to local paving companies to replace their Mexican workers. Local authorities were equally responsive. They began to arrest large numbers of unemployed Mexicans on vagrancy charges and to jail them by the truck load.[53]

One of the most extreme postwar reactions to Mexican workers occurred during February, 1921, in the oil fields of Eastland County. The large industrial work force included lesser-skilled workers who were exposed further to competition by the declining wages of the post-war depression. Many of the oil workers were young men from rural areas, men with fresh memories of family farm losses. They were prone to see Mexicans as threats to their livelihood. The oil workers' union leadership reinforced this view with a policy that excluded Mexican workers from the organizations. In 1920 the *International Oil Worker* revealed the degree of opposition to Mexican workers when it commended the "international officers [who] have done everything in their power to eliminate this undesirable element from the oil fields." The oil companies contracted Mexicans allegedly "to reduce wages and lower the standard of living." The oil unions subsequently submitted complaints to the Department of Labor and the Department of Justice which resulted in a finding that seventy-five percent of the workers were Mexican nationals. Following this investigation, authorities deported "quite a number" of the Mexican workers. The conflict continued despite governmental intervention.[54]

The following year, when the oil companies introduced into the work force a group of Mexican workers, 250 residents of Eastland County petitioned a senator for the removal "of every Mexican laborer from the State of Texas to his home in Mexico," so that "the native laborers may have work to support his family and to live like a white man should."

When the Mexican workers refused to heed posted warnings of violence unless they and their families left the area, a group of apporoximately fifteen masked men entered the Mexican community, dragging men, women, and children from their homes and beating some of them severely. The next day three hundred of them left for Fort Worth to submit a complaint with the Mexican Consul, Francisco Pérez. Although local authorities and Governor Pat Neff intervened at Pérez's request, the Mexican families did not return to the area. The consul later recalled that they left for Mexico without their wages and before their contracts had expired. He expressed his anger to the readers of *The Nation,* noting that the violent reaction against Mexicans was widespread and the cause of great concern in his country.[55]

Two important themes became evident in the ensuing conflict. First of all, Anglos within and outside organized labor consistently associated the threat from below with the immigrant workers although their competitors also included older immigrants and U.S.-born Mexicans. Second, they claimed that Mexicans depressed wages, displaced Anglos, and crossed picket lines. Although the claims against immigrants had some validity, it is also true that employment barriers remained relatively secure, suggesting that Anglo workers exaggerated the problem of displacement. Also, the wholesale criticism of Mexican workers meant that Anglo workers were not only reacting against actual competition but against the prospects of far-reaching disruptions to social relations.

The Department of Labor offered some of the more convincing evidence in 1920 that Anglo urban labor was exaggerating its claims against immigrants. The Secretary of Labor had appointed a committee to investigate the matter in response to charges by restrictionists that immigrants were displacing native labor. The committee visited twenty-five towns and cities in ten states and reported no evidence that Mexican immigrants had displaced Anglo workers. Instead, Mexicans had filled a need created by the wartime demand on agriculture. A dramatic decline in European immigration, a population drain in rural areas occasioned by migrations to the cities, and a general reluctance by Anglos to accept employment as common laborers explained why Mexicans had not displaced Anglo workers to any noticeable degree. The report added that "white men are adverse, and refuse to accept employment (as they have a right to do) as unskilled or common laborers, except, perhaps, where that employment is within the limits of towns or cities."[56]

A labor agent from San Antonio confirmed the Department of Labor findings when he informed Taylor that the railroad industry in the Fort Worth area excluded Mexicans until the early 1920s, when they were accepted but confined to track maintenance work. Another of Taylor's informants reported that Mexicans in the railroad lines south of El Paso worked as maintenance crews and in the shops. An onion grower from Carrizo Springs added: "The labor unions are trying to stop Mexican immigration but the Mexicans aren't competing with them at all; they aren't doing any work that the Union men [would] want to do."[57] A 1916 study of farm labor in Travis County made a similar observation about the alleged threat that Mexicans posed for Anglo labor: "Cities offer greater opportunities and better wages in trades where there is less competition with the unskilled Negroes and Mexicans and the rural white laborer drifts to the cities."[58]

Former Congressman James L. Slayden had the opportunity to personally witness a debate in 1920 between San Antonio's labor federation, the Trades Assembly, and the chamber of commerce that convinced him that workers were too quick to blame the immigrants for depressed conditions. Approximately two thousand immigrants who entered the city after the cotton picking season became stranded because they were unable to find employment. Labor immediately claimed that they were displacing skilled workers. The chamber denied the charge, noting that many of the Mexicans were already being referred to nearby farms. Chamber representatives, however, were known for leading local efforts for the unrestricted entry of Mexican laborers to work in cotton. Anglo workers thus held the officials partly responsible for the growing Mexican work force in the city. Although the chamber was no great friend of organized labor, as its open-shop campaigns so amply demonstrated, there is no evidence that it intended to use the Mexican workers to undermine unionism in San Antonio. Slayden sided with the chamber since the Trades Assembly never substantiated its charges.[59]

Racial thinking coupled with hard times magnified the real or imagined immigrant threat and encouraged a wholesale reaction against all Mexicans, a reaction that reinforced further the traditional employment barriers. Anglo labor reflected and reinforced this public reaction. The predominantly Anglo unions within the TSFL had previously confined their exclusionary practices to the work place and the union hall. Beginning in the 1910s they broadened their strategy by appealing to the state and the AFL for job protection from Mexican immigrants. Anglo unions thus joined with a public demand to confine Mexicans to the farms, deny them government employment, and regulate immigration.

Labor's move against immigrants can be best understood in light of the battles that it was waging and the alliances that it was establishing as it faced the formidable open-shop campaigns of the early 1900s. Popular antiunion campaigns led by chambers of commerce and citizens' alliances first appeared during the pre-1910 period and then reappeared during the postwar years. Almost every city with a labor organization had an antiunion organization. Theoretically implying that employers had the right to hire whomever they chose, unionized or not, the open-shop movement sought the destruction of unionism in the state. In addition to the spirited antiunion campaigns in the media and the widespread introduction of Anglo strikebreakers from the farms and from other states, organized labor also faced an unfriendly state government, particularly during the strike wave of the 1920s. The reactions that labor elicited from unfriendly forces included the popularly backed decisions by governors William P. Hobby and Pat Neff to break the strikes of the longshoremen and railroad workers in 1920 and 1922. When the longshoremen struck against the shipping companies in Galveston, Hobby responded by declaring martial law. Neff sent troops to numerous cities, including Denison and Kingsville, to protect the right of employers to hire scab labor. He also placed Sherman and Childress under the open-port law, the equivalent of the open-shop law that operated in ports facilities.[60]

Facing a hostile opposition and eventually a dwindling membership during the 1920s, organized labor searched for a protective alliance with the influential Farmers' Union and the railroad brotherhoods. The TSFL first sought the help of the Farmers' Union to discourage Anglo farm boys from coming into the cities as strikebreakers.[61] Based on this initial experience of cooperation, the Farmers' Union and the TSFL joined with the railway brotherhoods in 1907 to form the Joint Legislative Board in an attempt to promote a legislative program that served the interests of labor.

The TSFL was one of the main beneficiaries of this alliance. Its association with the Farmers' Union attracted the support of a legislature that was controlled by rural interests and that favored legislative appeals from two of the most critical industries in the state, agriculture and railroads. Labor managed to secure numerous legislative concessions, among them the establishment of the Labor Bureau within the Bureau of Labor Statistics on the eve of the First World War. The Bureau of Labor Statistics and the cooperative relations that the TSFL established with the legislature and its allies served well when time came to address the issue of Mexican labor competition.[62]

The TSFL did not express concern that the Mexican worker would become a job competitor or strikebreaker prior to 1910, primarily because occupational discrimination effectively barred Mexicans from the skilled occupations that served as the organizational base for the state federation. Labor was more preoccupied with the threat posed by immigration from southern and eastern Europe, a fear that was shared with organized labor throughout the country.[63] This began to change in 1910 when James Murray, a union official from Galveston, warned that skilled workers, too, would have to face competition from foreign-born labor: "There is no guarantee, my friends, but that we may have to face similar conditions sooner or later. In fact, I am sorry to state that we have today in Texas corporations and municipalities, who will employ non-English speaking foreigners in preference to American citizens."[64]

The TSFL treated the issue of Mexican immigration during 1910–12 primarily as a problem confined to agriculture and the border area. As long as immigrants remained on the farms, labor did not worry much about the prospects of a conflict in the inland cities. The problem, of course, existed in border towns and cities that began to draw large number of Mexican immigrants at the turn of the century. While some officials began calling for immigration restrictions in 1910, the federation's membership did not seem to worry that the immigrant flow would soon reach the interior and that the permanent Mexican population would increase significantly.[65] They still shared a sense of self-assurance expressed by a delegate to the 1912 Convention: "The peon Mexican does not make an American citizen, and he seldom naturalizes. He remains in this country long enough to earn some money, living cheaply, and returns to his fatherland when he has accumulated a small capital."[66]

During the same convention, the TSFL delegates endorsed a statement on the history of Texas that revealed labor's conventional frame of reference. Mexicans still represented a culturally inferior people and not yet the economic threat that Anglos would soon claim: "When first discovered, Texas consisted mostly of cosmic junk, including cactus, rattlesnakes, horned toads, tarantulas and four kinds of climate. Later, the greaser, a species of human invented by the Spaniards moved in and the rattlesnakes moved north in search of a better society. In the past seventy years, however, great improvements have been made."[67]

As Mexicans entered the inland cities, local unions of San Antonio, Austin, Houston, Galveston, Waco, and Fort Worth began to complain about Mexican labor during the annual TSFL conventions. Some of these complaints took the form of resolutions that committed the federation to seek assistance in resolving an issue that seemed to be growing worse every year. The decision to seek assistance from outside sources represented a more determined attempt by Anglo labor to regain control over the labor market. Expanding the arena of struggle against Mexicans involved strategies that sought the intercession of the local authorities, the state government, and the AFL.

The El Paso and Houston central labor councils took the lead during the early part of 1914 in the first major effort to pressure city, county, state, and federal governments to stop hiring Mexico-born workers in their public works projects. The antialien campaign soon spread to other union strongholds like San Antonio, Waco, and Fort Worth. Although there is little evidence that the campaigns succeeded, the unionists were able to improve the negative public image promoted by antiunion forces and regain some influence in their communities. They had the backing of the central labor councils and appealed through the press and public meetings to popular anti-immigrant sentiments. Moreover, their campaigns occurred during economically depressed periods when arguments in favor of using tax monies to provide first for unemployed citizens had a major effect.[68] Anti-immigrant campaigns had a particularly detrimental effect on Mexican workers who depended on public employment.

An untold number of Mexicans throughout the state had come to depend on federal military camp construction and on city-county road, park, and bridge construction. The work had been the preserve of Mexicans primarily because it was low-status, low-waged, and unskilled. Economic downturns during the 1910s and the 1920s forced them out as Anglo workers began to compete for jobs that they had traditionally rejected as "Mexican work." The determining element in this fight was, according to the editor of *La Prensa*, "the exclusivity of labor" that promoted "subversive propaganda against the foreign-born."[69]

Labor's offensive outside the work place and the union hall also influenced the state government to regulate the flow of farm labor. As indicated earlier, organized labor played a critical role in the establishment of a farm labor distribution program. The program placed the state government in the position of a labor contractor to solve "the Mexican problem," that is, to supply labor to commercial farmers and discourage farm labor from coming to the cities. Labor thus encouraged the government to assume control over the independent labor agencies and the unpredictable farm labor force. Organized labor maintained its influence over the program primarily through the Labor Commissioner, a governmental appointee often drawn from the ranks of labor. The commissioner directed the Texas Bureau of Labor Statistics, the agency responsible for overseeing the farm labor distribution program and, beginning in 1929, the implementation of the Emigrant Labor Agency Law. Labor also influenced the U.S. Employment Service, the office that collaborated with the Bureau in regulating farm labor and private employment agencies. Its Farm Division Director in Texas during the 1920s was C. W. Woodman, a prominent Fort Worth unionist and labor journalist who prided himself in securing for Texas the largest allotments of federal monies designated for state labor distribution programs.[70]

Despite impressive efforts to control the market, labor continued to worry over the increasing numbers of Mexicans entering the urban areas. Consequently, the TSFL in combination with the AFL, began to actively lobby for immigration restrictions. The TSFL became one of the most active proponents of regulating immigration restrictions within the AFL, primarily because immigrants were selecting Texas as the final point of destination during the early 1900s. Texas unionists joined with other federations from the southwestern states in alerting the AFL to the threat that immigration posed and in supplying the parent organization with the necessary arguments and information to lobby in Congress. Contributing to this was the important role that the avid restrictionist Congressman Box played in drawing attention to his home state.[71]

Although the TSFL usually allowed the AFL to take the lead in the fight against immigration, its members also took their own initiatives. As early as 1911 the TSFL, at the insistence of the El Paso Central Labor Council, submitted a complaint to the U.S. Immigration Bureau with the result that "several inspectors" visited the border. During the 1912 TSFL convention, the El Paso delegation reported that they had successfully demonstrated to governmental officials that labor agencies were violating the Foreign Contract Law which prohibited the recruitment of labor on foreign soil.[72]

The TSFL also reacted strongly to a decision by Congress to allow the Secretary of Labor to exempt Mexico from the 1917 Immigration Law. Agricultural interests had claimed that the wartime demand on the industry required the relaxation of the head tax, the literacy tax, and the contract labor provisions of the law. Texas farmers recruited a large number of contract workers between 1917 and 1921 as a result of the exemption. Unwilling to challenge the farmers' claim of a greater labor need during the war, the TSFL instead argued that Mexican workers remained in Texas after the harvest and traveled to the cities. The war ended, yet immigration continued primarily because the immigration laws of 1921 and 1924 did not set quotas on the western hemisphere countries. The TSFL also continued to entertain the view that the government favored the development of agriculture at the expense of Anglo urban workers.[73]

The TSFL expressed its position clearly to AFL Secretary Frank Morrison in a telegram intended for his use in the congressional deliberations of 1920 over the pending immigration legislation. Morrison was to advise Congress that Mexican workers brought into Texas "ostensibly for the purpose of assisting the farmers are being recruited by various interests to displace American labor, and are being employed by the oil interests to displace white labor, by railroads to displace maintenance of way men, by the packing houses and thousands have been shipped north, all for the purpose of displacing Americans."[74]

The TSFL sent numerous other resolutions and messages to the AFL with the hope of influencing immigration policy and stemming an immigrant flow that was growing larger every year. Neither the TSFL nor the AFL, however, effectively counteracted the clout of agribusiness in Washington. Moreover, Congress and the president did not wish to restrict immigration, for fear that such a policy change would impair relations with Mexico.[75]

In the meantime Samuel Gompers, the head of the AFL, was planning to establish a Pan-American alliance of labor to extend the federation's sphere of influence into Latin America. The AFL was also beginning to implement a plan to selectively incorporate Mexicans as a concession to gain the support of its counterpart in Mexico, the Confederación Regional Obrera Mexicana (CROM), in discouraging Mexican immigration. CROM, on the other hand, entered into its own collaborationist relationship with the Mexican government and sought to use the newly created Pan American Federation of Labor to legitimize its position as an important actor in diplomatic relations with the United States. After a period of acrimonious debate, CROM conceded to the AFL by declaring support for the "principle of self-restraint" whereby CROM promised to pressure the Mexican government to restrict immigration. Part of the agreement involved a plan of cooperation between the national federations and their affiliates along the border to share information on labor needs and to discourage Mexicans from crossing when labor demands in agriculture waned. The plan placed the TSFL in an even broader political arena.[76]

The TSFL thus entered into the final phase in its attempts to regain control over the labor market. This era was distinct in two ways. First, the state federation entered the larger world of labor that was not entirely of its own making, one that minimally encouraged public and meaningful demonstrations of support for the binding principle of working class solidarity. Second, and in line with its new responsibility, the TSFL began to welcome the incorporation of Mexican nationals and U.S.-born Mexicans into its unions—an acceptable trade-off since it could now declare its opposition to Mexican immigration as a legitimate expression of international labor cooperation. The plan to selectively incorporate Mexicans represented an important opportunity for organized labor to build unity and expand its organizational strength in Texas. The logic behind the idea of diffusing the perceived threat by incorporating Mexican workers had been difficult to see in the racial conflict. Ironically, this breakthrough was made possible by an interest in regaining racial control over the labor market.

Conclusion

Economic change and immigration during the first three decades of the century transformed social relations on the farms and in the cities of Texas. Mexican workers played a central role in this transformation by shouldering a major portion of the unwelcome cost of economic change as laborers. In addition to bearing stereotypical images as exploitable workers, they became the object of discontent among displaced farmers in the rural areas and insecure unionized and nonunionized workers in the cities. Moreover, farmers and Anglo urban workers reacted unfavorably as Mexicans threatened to upset labor market understandings with their propensity to take to the road in search of the higher wage. Other informal initiatives that included sabotage and strikes also contributed to the stereotype of the insolent and intractable worker. The resulting antipathies justified and reinforced their subordination. During the 1910s formal and informal efforts by planters and organized labor to control the labor market also contributed to the Mexican's position as an exploited worker with little prospects for mobility.

Tensions in the agricultural industry followed the displaced Anglo farm owners and renters into the cities. These tensions evolved during the second and third decades around the issue of immigration and the economic fears that it engendered among Anglo workers. The arrival of large numbers of immigrants most probably contributed to depressed wages in the lower-skilled occupations. They did not, however, appear to have displaced Anglo workers to any appreciable degree. Anglo fears and the resulting antipathies were frequently based on perceived, rather than actual, threats, and they appeared when increased immigration created a labor surplus that overflowed into the cities.

Sectors within the Anglo community directed their anger against all Mexicans regardless of nativity, though the central issue became Mexican immigration and the alleged threat that it posed for Anglo workers. The TSFL joined the agitation for racial hiring policies and immigration restrictions in 1912 when it shifted its attention from southern and eastern European labor to Mexican immigrant workers. The state federation played no small part in influencing the national federation to focus its attention on Mexican immigration and to lobby for control and restrictions. One of the results was the tendency by organized labor to view the issue of labor control in racial terms, although it also began to selectively incorporate Mexican workers in line with the AFL's plan for hemispheric influence. Despite private agendas that sought to control Mexican labor and extend trade unionism in Mexico and along the border, organized labor opened its back door and allowed Mexican workers to begin entering in significant numbers. This was a costly proposition for Mexicans, considering the added control over immigration and, later, the divisions that deepened as U.S.-born Mexican trade unionists set themselves apart on the basis of their U.S. citizenship.

Chapter Three

Mobilizing
the Mexican Response

To what extent did Mexicans respond organizationally to their condition as an exploited working class and minority group? The conventional assessment is that they formed numerous organizations of a mutualist type that sought to meet the immediate material interests of their poor and often destitute members. This chapter seeks to demonstrate that Mexican workers responded with a wide array of actions that were defensive and combative, informal and formal, spontaneous and sustained. This new approach combines the various political initiatives by Mexicans that historians have heretofore examined in isolation from each other, with additional ones that have been discovered. Withholding one's labor, organizing spontaneously, establishing mutual aid societies and unions, forming regional federations of workers' organizations, and waging armed action represent important parts of this story. Instances of self-organization and evidence of political influences emanating from Mexico underscore the fact that despite seemingly insurmountable obstacles, Mexicans managed to issue an impressive response.[1]

Among the many concerns addressed by Mexican mobilization efforts were the conditions and experiences of Mexicans as poor and exploited workers in rural and urban settings. Although they demonstrated a noteworthy resolve and capacity to organize, they most often bargained from a position of weakness against normally recalcitrant employers. As a result, they suffered numerous defeats and disappointments. These setbacks, coupled with the persistence of economic hardship and discrimination, however, contributed to more determined and broader efforts to mobilize.

With some important exceptions, which will be examined in subsequent chapters, Mexican workers generally remained outside the fold of the major U.S. labor federations. This was not because Mexicans lacked interest in building and sustaining organizations which under more favorable circumstances could have served to bridge the racial divide. In early and isolated cases when Anglo workers' organizations welcomed Mexicans, they joined or participated in important strike actions. However, since Mexican workers generally remained apart from the major labor federations, they either took spontaneous actions or built their own separate workers' organizations to ameliorate or challenge the difficult conditions under which they lived and worked. Although organizations adopted union-like identities and functions, they most often served as multipurpose community organizations. Their relative isolation from organized labor, along with the pressing expectations from communities with varied needs, contributed to their adoption of more general outlooks and functions. As a result of immigration, racial conflict, and estrangement from Anglo institutions, Mexican workers' organizations looked southward to Mexico for support and inspiration. The work of exiled groups in Texas and binational interactions involving labor groups constituted important unionist influences during the early 1900s. Mexican workers and their organizations, however, continued to operate in a relatively independent manner and ultimately fended for themselves.

Cooperation in the State and across the Border

Mexican workers participated in some of the earliest labor struggles recorded in Texas. Participation, however, was restricted to areas outside of deep South Texas, where the incorporation of Mexicans was most often incidental to other organizing policy decisions by Anglo unions. In other words, Mexicans participated when Anglo unions organized areas and industries that included them. Rarely were Mexicans specifically recruited. Limited interactions consequently minimized the possibility of Anglo unionist influences.

One of the first recorded cases of interethnic unity occurred during the first large strike by approximately three hundred West Texas cowboys in 1883. A Mexican named Juan A. Gómez assumed a leading role in this historic and successful cowboy strike. His name was among the signatures on the ultimatum sent to managers of the seven Panhandle ranches being struck. Gómez's name points to the participation of Mexicans, who were numerous in the work force at the time. Mexican cowboys, welcomed for the skills that they had developed in the cattle industry of South Texas and in the cattle drives into Missouri and Kansas, usually worked as separate groups with a single cowboy designated as their representative. Gómez may have been of these work crew leaders.[2]

Three years after the cowboy strike, Mexicans from Galveston joined one of the earliest industrial organizations in Texas, the Screwmen's Benevolent Association. The association included dock workers attracted to the island by the growing trade and shipping business in cotton. At least three Mexicans joined the organization during the 1880s. Although

Mexicans continued to travel to Galveston to secure employment as dock workers, few may have participated in the association because of the racially charged atmosphere that always accompanied labor organizing on the Galveston docks. The reaction to Mexican immigration mentioned previously, plus the recurring conflicts between Anglo and black workers, indicates that Mexicans did not find a friendly reception in the association.[3]

The Knights of Labor was the first national labor federation to express an official interest in incorporating Mexican workers. This industrially based federation, which had preceded the A F L, had formulated an all-inclusive strategy of organizing that attempted to include African Americans and Mexicans. The Knights first entered Texas while attempting to implement a national plan to organize railroad workers. The federation made a strong bid to establish its influence among Texas workers during the late 1880s. In 1886 a shoemaker named Manuel López presented the closing speech during the Texas Knights of Labor State Convention held in San Antonio. The fact that López spoke in Spanish strongly suggests that Mexicans were present at this convention and that the Knights of Labor was seeking to incorporate Mexican workers. This may have been a temporary relationship, however, because there is no evidence that the Knights continued to recruit them.[4]

Northeast of San Antonio Mexican miners from Thurber participated in organizing and strike activity between 1893 and 1926. Officials of the United Mine Workers sent a Mexican organizer to Thurber in 1903 to encourage the participation of Mexicans in a planned strike against the mine operators. Shortly after arriving, the organizer disappeared. Union officials speculated that employer agents killed him. Mexicans reappeared in the 1910s and 1920s as workers and unionists. Their participation ended in 1926 when the union, weakened by a strike and a reduction in the work force occasioned by a production slump, decided that some members had to leave in order to relieve the financial pressure on the union. The union apparently decided that its entire Mexican work force of one hundred and sixty-two Mexicans, including unionists and their families, were the most expendable; they were placed on railroad cars and shipped to Mexico.[5]

Thomas Hagerty, a Catholic priest, one of the founders of the Industrial Workers of the World (I W W) and the T S F L, and a popular organizer among Spanish-speaking workers in Chicago during the first decade of the century, had a temporary association with Mexican workers in Texas. As a rector of Catholic churches at Cleburne and Paris, Texas, between 1897 and 1902, he used his pulpit and his standing in the community to speak out on behalf of Mexican railroad workers who had apparently organized in close association with the church. He translated German, French, and English socialist literature into Spanish and made these translated documents available to the local Mexican population.[6] Hagerty left after a five-year stay. There is no evidence that the railroad workers continued operating as an organization in association with the local churches.

Bill Haywood, another founder and leader of the I W W and the Western Federation of Miners (W F M), appeared in South Texas in 1909. Accompanied by a Mexican interpreter, Haywood traveled on a lecture circuit throughout the region.[7] Haywood's reputation may have preceded him; local papers had provided full coverage to the work of the W F M and the I W W among Mexican workers in New Mexico, Arizona, and California. Although he used the opportunity to promote industrial unionism, Haywood and his notable companions, Mary "Mother" Jones and James Murray, visited Texas in support of Mexican exiled leaders accused of violating United States neutrality laws. The jailed exiles were members of the Partido Liberal Mexicano (P L M), the political group responsible for planning, in Texas, the first armed uprisings of the revolution in northern Mexico. The Political Refugee's Defense League led the campaign that included the W F M, the I W W, the Texas Socialist Party, and the Carpenters and Joiners of America No. 640, of San Antonio.[8] Much of the public support generated in Texas was channeled through Mexican community organizations that sympathized with the P L M. This socialist alliance was one of the earliest instance in which political influences from Mexico and the United States met and overlapped in the Mexican community of South Texas.[9]

The I W W reemerged in 1912 during a strike by Mexican onion clippers from Asherton. The workers, who were mostly permanent residents from the area, struck for an improved wage. The growers, however, defeated the strike by contracting a group of strikebreakers. The editor of a local newspaper reminded its readers that "there was some I.W.W. activity in the country in connection with its support of the Zapata revolution, led by Charles Cline."[10] The newspaper editor was making reference to a P L M group arrested in Dimmit County as a result of a shootout with local authorities. The group, known as *Los Mártires de Texas* to P L M sympathizers who waged an international campaign for their release, was one of many groups organized by the P L M to stage the initial armed revolts in northern Mexico. One of the leading P L M organizers in Texas, Jesús M. Rangel, led the group.[11]

The editor of the paper attempted to discredit the strikers by associating them with the I W W and with the revolution brewing in Mexico. He demonstrated his opposition in disparaging terms:

Some Asherton Mexicans got the idea that onion clipping was skilled labor, and that they ought to be fashionable and strike. Likewise they thought they had the onion growers where they couldn't kick. . . . The onion growers couldn't see the raise. They offered to come through with half the extra money, but the clippers said it was a whole loaf or no crust, and they were pretty crusty about it too. The onion men simply sent out for more Mexicans, and now the former clippers are in the soup, no money, no job, and no strike fund in the treasury.[12]

Five years after the strike the paper reported that the Mexican onion clippers, "mostly the ones who live in the country," were once again asking for a higher wage. The story ended with a threat of violence and a repeat of the red-baiting tactic that the paper used against the workers in 1912. The paper's editor described one of the principal organizers as "some copper fronted gentleman from the south [who] tries to do a little IWW propaganda among the working force."[13] Although Anglo IWW leaders traveled into Texas, the references to the PLM and the organizer from "the south" leaves little doubt that the IWW influence originated in South Texas or in Mexico.

In contrast to a distant and conflict-ridden relationship that generally prohibited cooperation between Mexican and Anglo workers, Mexican communities from both sides of the border reinforced their historic ties with an increasing number of interactions involving economic refugees, political exiles, immigrants, and emigrants. Economic factors contributed to such interactions. Instead of severing community ties with the establishment of the border in 1848 the United States and Mexico had initiated a process of development that increased the region's population and encouraged a larger back-and-forth migration of workers and their families between Texas and the Mexican states of Tamaulipas, Nuevo León, and Coahuila.[14]

Most of the immigrants were preoccupied with capitalizing on job opportunities in Texas and with building a better life for their families. Although these migrants were responding to immediate and personal motivations, they collectively broadened and reinforced the historic cultural identity of the border region.[15] Other migrants gave these interactions political meaning as they cross-fertilized the different and often opposing camps of Mexican organized labor on both sides of the border. Although labor influences originating in Mexico may seem more probable, given the marked growth of organized labor on the Mexican side of the border and the large number of immigrant workers in Texas, they also traveled in the other direction. An excellent example of this involved a railroad worker named Silvino Rodríguez. Rodríguez is best known for the singular role that he played in the formation of the Chihuahua chapter of La Unión de Mecánicos (machinists) Mexicanos in January, 1903. Rodríguez achieved national prominence that same year when he assumed command of the federation and began to direct successful organizing and strike campaigns against the Central Mexican Railroad.[16]

Rodríguez had assumed his first leadership position in labor when he migrated to San Antonio during the 1880s. While at San Antonio, he witnessed the practice of occupational and wage discrimination directed against Mexican workers at the Missouri Pacific shops. Moreover, the racially exclusive railroad brotherhoods of Anglo workers functioned as job cartels. Since there was little hope of cooperating with the brotherhoods, the Mexican workers adopted what became a familiar strategy throughout the state—they established their own alternative to the brotherhood, a mutual aid society, La Sociedad Ignacio Zaragoza. Rodríguez served as an official orator and officer of the organization for at least one year. He returned to Chihuahua in 1898 and joined a circle of workers intent on waging an organizing campaign in response to the same problems he had encountered in San Antonio, the racial hiring and wage policies of the railroads and the exclusive organizing practices of Anglo brotherhoods.[17]

Other individual unionists, for example Sabas Hernández, traveled from Mexico and joined with labor in Texas. Hernández, a native of the border town of Piedras Negras, Coahuila, served four years as a carpenter's apprentice and five as a mechanic's apprentice at the shops of the International and Great Northern Railway. He became a carpenter for the railroad in 1910 and subsequently worked for at least two years as a coal miner. Hernández returned to the shops for a short while and then crossed over to Eagle Pass and continued working as a union carpenter for the railroad shops. In 1919 he moved to Galveston and he once again worked as a carpenter, maintaining his union membership in a carpenters' union until his death in the 1950s.[18]

Others came from Mexico as official representatives of unions for the expressed purpose of organizing workers and establishing relations with workers' organizations in Texas. In 1913 the Nuevo Laredo chapter of the Aguascalientes-based Unión Ferrocarrilera y Gremios Confederados del Trabajo sent an organizer named Arnulfo G. Gómez to Laredo, Kingsville, Raymondville, Mercedes, and Brownsville. Gómez apparently planned the trip in collaboration with local voluntary organizations. His hosts helped Gómez organize an unknown number of pacifist organizations and unions among Mexicans in the area. One of these may have been La Unión Local de Trabajadores, a Kingsville-based rail-road workers' organization that obtained an AFL charter soon after the visit by the Nuevo Laredo organizer.[19]

The early 1900s witnessed even more substantive interactions involv-ing railroad workers employed by the Ferrocarriles Nacionales de Méx-ico, or the Mexican National Railroad, between Nuevo Laredo and Saltillo. La Unión Nacional de Fogoneros (Firemen) initiated a strike to protest the racial wage and occupational policy. This action ultimately spread across the border along the Texas Mexican Railroad line extend-ing from Laredo to Corpus Christi. The strikers eventually met defeat in Mexico, but not before demonstrating that they had open commu-nication with and mutual support from railroad workers in Texas. There is no evidence to indicate the numbers of strikers on the Texas side nor their ethnic makeup, although it is clear that Mexican workers had es-tablished binational ties as early as 1902.[20]

Mexican labor influences also evolved across time. One such story began with Nicasio Idar, the patriarch of a politically prominent family from Laredo. He was born in Port Isabel and migrated to Mexico to work with the Mexican National Railroad during the 1880s. Idar became a cofounder of one of Mexico's earliest national unions of railroad workers, La Orden Suprema de Empleados Ferrocarrileros Mexicanos. Workers on this line, which extended from San Luis Potosí to Nuevo Laredo, established the union in 1890. Idar started his unionist career as early as 1887 when the railroad workers from Nuevo Laredo formed the short-lived La Sociedad del Ferrocarril Mexicano. He played a key organizing role in the formation of La Orden Suprema in San Luis Potosí while working as a messenger for the railroad company.[21]

Soon after the demise of the union Idar traveled to Laredo, where he established residence and became especially well known as a civic leader and editor of *La Crónica,* a weekly newspaper that continually attacked class and racial discrimination in Texas. Nicasio maintained an active interest in Mexican politics, evidenced by his association with the PLM in 1904 when the exiled group's leadership arrived in Laredo. He also assisted his son Clemente and his daughter Jovita in organizing the famous 1911 statewide meeting, El Congreso Mexicanista, which brought together delegates from throughout the state and from some places along the Mexican side of the border to discuss the numerous problems confronting Mexicans in Texas and to arrive at some consen-sus for their resolution.[22]

According to a Mexican railroad historian, Idar also continued to work "in favor of the labor struggle and singularly in defense of rail-road workers" in Laredo.[23] Although he was personally and ideologi-

Nicasio Idar and sons, Clemente and Eduardo, 1906. *Courtesy Institute of Texan Cultures, The University of Texas at San Antonio*

cally opposed to the socialist leadership of the local AFL–affiliated union of railroad workers, Federal Labor Union No. 11953, Nicasio consistently expressed support for the unionization of Mexican workers. Idar's lasting influence in the area of labor organizing was most evident in the career of his son Clemente. By the 1910s Clemente had established his own reputation as a young man on the political rise by his impressive writing and oratorical skills in both Spanish and English. Like his father, he became known as a champion of the Mexican working class through the family newspaper and El Congreso Mexicanista.[24]

In 1918 Clemente rose to international prominence when Samuel Gompers, president of the AFL, named him official AFL organizer with the primary responsibility of organizing Mexican workers in the United States. Gompers announced the appointment soon after the Pan American Federation of Labor conference, an international labor meeting held in Laredo ostensibly for the purpose of unifying workers on a hemispheric basis. In a sense, Nicasio's influence now joined a new binational interchange involving the leadership of the major labor federations from Mexico and the United States, CROM and the AFL.[25]

By the 1920s Nicasio's prior union experience in Mexico and his active support for labor organizing in South Texas reached a new level of fruition in the work of his son. Clemente made use of an opportunity made possible by other interactions involving organized labor from Mexico and the United States. This opportunity involved a major change in the AFL's organizing policy, a change prompted by the insistence of Mexican organized labor that the AFL organize Mexican workers. An important consequence was the chartering of numerous Mexican workers' organizations by the AFL and the TSFL. Idar played a key role as an organizer in this first significant case of incorporation by the federations.[26]

Mexico's most important social upheaval of the twentieth century—the Mexican Revolution of 1910—also contributed significantly to binational ties and interactions. This was especially true in reference to political exiles such as PLM agitators who escaped persecution, recruited sympathizers in Texas, and returned to join in the fighting in northern Mexico.[27] The PLM originated as an anti-Díaz group at the turn of the century. Political repression eventually forced the leadership to leave Mexico in 1904 and to establish its headquarters in Laredo and in San Antonio. They left for St. Louis and then moved to Los Angeles because of constant harassment by Mexican and U.S. government authorities and agents. In 1906 the PLM developed a plan of action calling for armed struggle and the radical transformation of Mexican society. The plan was notable for its progressive position on labor and for its call for a working-class revolution of world-wide proportions. It also addressed the rights of Mexicans outside the homeland.[28]

Historians generally acknowledge that PLM leaders were the primary intellectual precursors of the Mexican revolution. The critical social analysis and views of leading theorists such as Ricardo Flores Magón eventually found their way into the Mexican constitution of 1917. Equally significant was the PLM's success in establishing liberal clubs throughout Mexico and the southwestern part of the United States in a network that promoted the cause of labor and organized the initial armed actions against the Díaz dictatorship. Within this network Mexican labor on both sides of the Texas-Mexico border made some of the more consistent connections between 1901 and 1917.[29]

The area south of San Antonio and Austin was a PLM stronghold that contributed to the precursory activity of the revolution. The PLM's organizational network provided recruits and material support for the first anti-Díaz revolts between 1906 (Jiménez) and 1908 (Viesca and

Female revolutionaries at Matamoros, ca. 1915. *Courtesy Hidalgo County Historical Museum, Edinburg*

Las Vacas, Coahuila; and Palomares, Chihuahua) that occurred in northern Mexico. In 1909 and 1910 distinctly P L M armed activity in northern Mexico subsided, quelled by the repressive military and legal measures taken by Mexican and U.S. authorities. In addition, the broader-based movement headed by Francisco Madero eclipsed the work of the more revolutionary P L M. *Magonistas,* however, continued to travel into Mexico as small armed groups to join in the fighting along the border.[30]

P L M revolutionary activity along the border, like that of other exiled movements that operated in Texas, struck a responsive chord. Although historic ties with Mexico, as well as the natural attention attracted by the revolution, contributed to a popular interest in political developments in Mexico, it was the back-and-forth movement of immigrants that linked communities and reinforced this interest at the turn of the century. The immigrant flow between La Laguna, in northern Mexico, and the cotton belt area south of Austin and San Antonio, for instance, involved early political P L M interactions and labor agitation.

La Laguna agricultural workers who began to wage strikes against planters at the turn of the century often joined the migrant stream into Texas. Although some of the earlier strikes may have involved unorganized groups of workers who simply withheld their labor, these actions nevertheless imparted an experience that encouraged workers to take similar measures against farmers, labor agents, and authorities in Texas. The circularity of struggle was evident when these workers returned more determined than ever to challenge their employers. By the early 1900s La Laguna planters began to notice that returning immigrants were somewhat more belligerent. They made stronger demands on their employers or simply refused to work. A planter lamented this change in 1905: "In the last five years everything has changed with regard to workers in the Laguna. Before then, the peon was content with his reed hut and with 32 centavos per day. Today he demands a house of adobe and a salary of two or three times more. All the haciendas are now forced to construct new housing for workers and if not, we will not be able to secure good working people."[31] By the following year Mexican workers, returning from Texas with a heightened social and political consciousness, were contributing to unrest in La Laguna with "anarchist and socialist ideas." By this time many, if not most, of the agitators had been allied with the P L M in Texas. One such P L M group called the "Mexican cotton pickers," who came from the cotton belt, led the armed revolt against the military post at Viesca.[32]

Binational interactions involved important mutually reinforcing influences. Though there was distant influence by Anglo labor, these interactions suggest that Mexicans in Texas were closely attuned to political change in Mexico and thus were subject to its influence. Although more research is needed on the nature and the process of cross-fertilization, there is no doubt that it was extensive and that it involved labor organizing.

Spontaneous and Independent Labor Activity

Outside influences notwithstanding, most Mexican workers generally remained isolated from organized labor. Individuals and groups of workers who faced immediate and often urgent problems without the benefit of outside help consequently responded by initiating independent and sometimes spontaneous efforts at self-organization. Often without assistance or guidance from established and experienced groups, Mexicans most often relied on their own means to improve their condition. Self-reliance was especially evident in isolated areas where Mexicans waged individual or group acts of resistance as well as spontaneous strikes against their employers.

The most popular expression of self-reliance and initiative involved the decision by workers to withhold their labor. This was especially evident among the large number of farm workers who essentially bargained for improvements in working conditions by moving from farm to farm and from rural areas to towns and cities in hope of securing better wages. Although such actions by individuals, families, and groups of workers often lacked formal organization or sustained coordination, they represented a useful strategy that played on the farmers' need for large number of workers during short harvest periods.[33] As indicated earlier, the strategy of withholding labor was pervasive. Farmers contributed to this mobility by continually flooding the market to assure themselves an improved bargaining position. Successful attempts to maintain a surplus of labor, however, did not necessarily mean that farmers were able to retain control.

When picking cotton, Mexican workers employed other methods to gain an advantage over the farmer. According to Paul Taylor, they mixed dirt and rocks with the cotton that they picked, or they left cotton in the sacks after the weighing to maximize the credit that they received. These actions led farmers to fix their scales to compensate for the losses that they incurred. Other such initiatives and the corresponding responses were evident when workers demanded better wages and threatened to walk off the farms. On more than one occasion farmers in Nueces County reacted by replacing workers with new arrivals or by threatening to introduce new farming methods and technology such as cross plowing and tractors.[34] At the Coleman-Fulton Pasture Company, in San Patricio County, a group of between fifteen and twenty Mexican farm laborers also walked off the fields in 1914 when they were refused a fifteen-cent increase on the picking rate of sixty cents per one hundred pounds. According to the superintendent of the large corporate farm, "they said if we didn't pay them they would go where they could get it [a better wage], and my man told them to go, and they went."[35]

Using a technique popular among immigrants who sometimes came as self-organized groups, sheep shearers, cowboys, and farm laborers also organized themselves into work crews and selected from among them one English-speaking person to act as their contractor or intermediary. Labor economist Ernesto Galarza defined these incipient bargaining units as an independent form of organization that resulted naturally throughout the first half of the twentieth century from the need to strengthen workers' bargaining power. An alternative to the labor contracting form of organization, the work crews were based on ties of acquaintance, kinship, and common experience that built confidence and trust. Mexican sheep shearers who migrated from Mexico and from South and West Texas at the turn of the century often traveled under the direction of a group leader that the workers selected and called *capitán*. The capitán usually assumed the responsibility of negotiating contracts and paying the workers according to predetermined agreements reached by the group.[36]

Farm laborers also adopted this work crew strategy. Groups of Mexican nationals occasionally secured the assistance of Mexican consuls in writing and negotiating formal work contracts.[37] The workers, however, usually acted independently in selecting a contractor from the group. The contractor normally assumed responsibility for negotiating contracts, overseeing work, purchasing food and supplies, and disbursing wages at the end of the picking season. A researcher from the University of Texas astutely described one of these groups in 1916 as a "kind of labor union in which collective bargaining is substituted for individual bargaining."[38]

A large group of workers from San Antonio adopted a similar ad hoc organizing strategy in 1917 while preparing for the start of construction work in the new military establishment named Camp Wilson. Camp officials expected to hire around five thousand workers, including carpenters, blacksmiths, masons, painters, and plumbers. Most of them already worked as the lowest paid laborers in the other military camps. Approximately two thousand of them met at the meeting hall of a popular Mexican organization and established a "transitory organization" for the purpose of circumventing unscrupulous labor recruiting practices in the area. They hoped to negotiate a fair wage, adequate working hours, and good working conditions with the camp's contracting agency. They also resolved to begin negotiating favorable contracts at the other camps by dealing directly with the corresponding contracting agencies. The supportive newspaper *La Prensa* ended its last report on this impromptu action by describing the workers' goal as an informal union-hall arrangement: "The contracting of workers through a center that will defend their interests and that is responsible to its obligations."[39]

The 1914 slump in the cotton economy led to a different form of bargaining at Gonzales. This time the unemployed workers lacked credit and had no recourse but to appeal to area farmers for jobs. The one hundred laborers suggested a separate purpose to their appeal when they reprinted their petition in *La Prensa*. They sought to demonstrate that Mexicans were bearing a major burden during the crisis and that they deserved better treatment. The condition called for a humanitarian response from farmers since the entire community "has been especially hard-hit by the current crisis that is affecting this country." They added another compelling argument when they pointed out that Mexicans had made an important contribution to "the material development and growth in this large state, particularly in agriculture."[40] The editors of *La Prensa* used the occasion to critique discrimination in agriculture and to encourage further organizing.

Such organized public appeals were not exceptional occurrences, particularly during times of economic difficulties and antialien campaigns. A group of twenty-three workers from Waco, for instance, reported in *La Prensa* the following year that unionized and nonunionized Anglo workers were waging a campaign to deny Mexicans employment in the city's public works system and to drive them out of town.[41] Such reports were not simply meant to inform the public about the hard times that Mexicans faced, a fact that the readers of the San Antonio paper understood all too well. Their primary purpose was to publicize their mutual resolve to confront racism openly and thereby offer an example that others could emulate. They monitored the anti-Mexican rallies and the antialien petitions before the county commissioners' meeting where one of their own, Agustín Sierra, a U.S.-born tenant from Oglesby, spoke for the aggrieved Mexicans. Sierra pointed out that while it was understandable for Anglos to seek to protect their own, they were mistaken in blaming Mexican job competitors for their misfortune: "The war in Mexico is the primary reason why many of my compatriots are coming to the United States, and the war in Europe is also in part responsible for the hard times that we are experiencing. But more than all of that, it is due to the fact that some individuals who monopolize many things have been at liberty to determine the price of items of primary necessity."[42]

Thousands of immigrant and U.S.-born Mexicans facing repatriation during the 1920s also took collective measures intended to influence public opinion and safeguard their interests. Bearing public criticism as potential job competitors, groups of unemployed Mexicans appealed to local organizations and consulate offices for assistance. One result was the formation of organizations such as the Unión Colonizadora Mexicana, which obtained financial and logistical assistance from the Mexican government and the AFL to transport to the border an untold number of Mexican families from Fort Worth, San Antonio, and Houston.[43] As in the Gonzales case, Mexicans were in no position to negotiate in the adversarial fashion associated with labor unions. Their position at the bottom of the occupational structure, coupled with their minority status, meant that some of them would periodically have to face extreme hardship and adopt independent organizing strategies for the purpose of shaping public opinion and surviving the economic crisis.

Mexican workers also took spontaneous strike actions in rural and urban areas. Workers usually took such sudden initiatives in response to pressing problems that required an immediate solution. One of the earliest such strikes occurred at Austin in 1877. An undetermined number of Mexican and black workers employed in the local waterworks, brickyards, and construction sites walked off their jobs, demanding that wages be increased to at least $1.50 a day. Approximately four hundred workers and sympathizers convened at a well-known street corner. No doubt intending to provoke a public reaction, a local newspaper reported that some of the strikers were carrying guns and sending couriers to the outlying areas to recruit agricultural laborers. Presumably, the employers wanted to recruit strikebreakers from among the laborers in the area, and the strikers sent their representatives to forestall these efforts. Employers may have succeeded in defeating the strike; the local papers did not offer further commentary on it.[44]

At least three independent and spontaneous strike actions occurred during the early 1900s among railroad workers. As in previously mentioned cases, the strikers operated independently, and employers gained an upper hand by importing strikebreakers from Mexico. The first strike occurred in 1904 among track laborers working on the new line between Corpus Christi and the Rio Grande Valley. The Mexican construction crew included approximately one hundred workers and their families, who camped alongside the railroad on their desolate march through the chaparral. When operations reached Combes, the employer decided to reduce by twenty-five cents the daily wages of $1.25 and $1.50. The proximity of the border where prevailing "Mexican wages" were low and labor was plentiful may have prompted the labor contractor to suddenly cut the pay. The workers probably understood that their bargaining position had deteriorated as they neared the border, but they struck anyway and demanded the old wage rate. The contractor responded by releasing the strikers and replacing them with newly recruited workers from Mexico.[45]

Dissension among Mexican construction workers continued to plague railroad building in the Rio Grande Valley. Dissenting workers, however, seem to have avoided strike actions as a strategy. Instead, they simply withheld their labor and moved from employer to employer in much the same manner as did agricultural workers. The informal bargaining process between Mexican workers and railroad labor contractors mirrored agricultural labor relations in other ways. One of the leading railroad labor contractors, for example, resolved the "great turn-over" problem by regularly dipping into the inexhaustible labor pool of the border region. Railroad representatives also offered disparaging cultural explanations for dissident worker behavior. A railroad developer made one of the most interesting observations when he reasoned that "the more the peons made, the less they worked." Some immigrants from isolated Mexican rural areas may have exhibited such preindustrial work habits. Employers, however, also sought to justify low wages and to misinterpret expressions of discontent with negative portrayals of the Mexican work force.[46]

Mexican railroad workers from Cotulla met an even quicker defeat when they struck in 1906 for a daily wage of one dollar. Within hours of their spontaneous strike call, employers brought in seventy-five new workers from Mexico to replace them. When the strikers attempted to block the strikebreakers, the local sheriff intervened and ended the strike with violent threats. The new work crew began earning fifty cents a day, a twenty-five cent reduction from the wage rate that the strikers had contested. Three years after the Cotulla strike, 150 railroad workers in nearby Artesia Wells also went on strike; they, too, were immediately fired. The subsequent events are unclear, however, they were serious enough to require the intervention of the Mexican consulate, which reported a shootout among the workers.[47]

Mexicans also worked more deliberately to build their organizations and sustain localized campaigns as workers. These generally unassisted actions normally involved such groupings as mutual aid societies that initially assumed multiple functions to meet varied community needs. With time, some of them adopted specialized, or union-like, functions. This was the case with several Mexican workers' organizations that appeared in the Nueces County area between 1897 and 1913.

Increased agricultural production beginning at the turn of the century attracted large numbers of workers from the Rio Grande Valley and Mexico to Nueces County. With time, the workers and their families became permanent residents in the small towns and in the new isolated rural communities that they established. In some cases, they migrated from the same general area or from the same Mexican village as small transplanted communities. In 1912, for example, everyone in Villa Acuña, Coahuila, fled across the border into Del Rio to escape an advancing revolutionary army led by Pascual Orozco. The following year, eight thousand residents from Piedras Negras, Coahuila, arrived in Eagle Pass. Some of them may have continued traveling into the interior of the state. These kinds of migrations may explain why almost immediately upon arriving some of them began to manifest an impressive sense of unity by establishing religious confraternities and mutual aid societies. This initial form of organization often evolved into unionlike associations, that is, collectives that adopted adversarial methods and expressed concern for the condition of Mexicans as workers.[48]

Some of the first Mexican arrivals in Nueces County during the middle 1880s worked as gang laborers responsible for clearing land devoted to cotton production. Soon after establishing their communities, they began to form mutual aid societies. Between 1897 and 1905, for instance, Mexican tenant farmers organized three of these groups. The more numerous laborers residing in the growing communities formed seventeen similar organizations between 1900 and 1920. Mexican sharecroppers established three saints' societies in 1898, and gang laborers formed one religious confraternity in 1904 and many more in 1914 and 1915. A more aggressive form of action eventually accompanied this basic organizing practice. In 1911 Mexican farm laborers formed a "defensive league." This same league—which may have been affiliated with the Texas Socialist Party—staged a strike in 1913 against a cotton farm. Demands included a wage and hour contract that called for improved working conditions. Earlier economic actions included a 1907 strike by gang laborers working on clearance projects and a 1910 work stoppage by Mexican teamsters. There is no evidence that these strike actions succeeded; however, they do indicate a higher level of labor organizing that involved independent formal organizations and deliberately planned initiatives, a pattern that was evident throughout the state.[49]

Independent Workers' Organizations

Informal, ad hoc, spontaneous, and organization-building responses by Mexicans to conditions and experiences associated with work point to an incremental process of mobilization. Although this process suggests a succession of developmental phases that measure growing intensity and complexity, these stages in fact coexisted as parallel efforts throughout the state. This can be best illustrated with a review of selected working-class organizations that were representative of the rich organizational life in the Mexican community of the late 1800s and early 1900s. The wide geographical distribution of these groups as well as their federated organizational forms and cooperative relations indicate more than just coexistence—they also demonstrate a form of minority and working-class unity based on common concerns and grievances.

The numerous organizations that emerged during the early 1900s included mutual aid societies, protective associations, Masonic orders, and patriotic organizations that expressed, either directly or indirectly, a working-class focus and orientation. This focus and orientation were characterized by: 1) a predominantly working-class membership and leadership; 2) low dues and such basic economic services as death and health insurance benefits; 3) critiques, both formal and informal, of general social, economic, and political problems affecting Mexicans; 4) recurring references in patriotic terms to an improved, and often idealized, socio-economic order in both Mexico and the United States; 5) participation in cooperative organizational endeavors; and 6) a broadly based method of organizing that encouraged Mexican workers to join on patriotic, moral, and rational grounds, regardless of occupation, gender, or nativity.[50]

Independent workers' organizations appeared throughout the state in significant numbers beginning in the 1870s. The larger towns like San Antonio, Corpus Christi, Laredo, and Brownsville registered the largest number, although smaller places like Alice, San Diego, and Eagle Pass also claimed some of their own. Drawing their members from among the growing number of poor workers, voluntary organizations like the more popular mutual aid societies included both U.S.-born and Mexico-born men and women. Although the community registered all-female and mixed gender organizations, most of them were predominantly male. This reflected the subordinate status of women and a prevailing patriarchal order.

Mutual aid societies usually offered their membership illness and death insurance, loans, and job-seeking assistance as well as a sense of belonging and identification with their rapidly growing communities. They also assumed a central position in the life of their communities by sponsoring important public events and by establishing other key institutions like newspapers and private schools. The focus on the homeland and on problems associated with racial discrimination that Mexicans faced in Texas made these organizations highly representative of popular interests and concerns in their communities.[51]

Officers, members, and visitors of a women's organization
from Brownsville, ca. 1905. *Courtesy Harry Lund Collection,
Archives Division, Texas State Library, Austin*

One of the earliest organizations established in the fledgling Mexican community of Houston was El Campamento Laurel No. 2333. This Woodmen of the World chapter began offering its working-class members life and death insurance benefits and a focal point for entertainment and fraternal companionship in 1908. Although far removed from areas of high Mexican concentration, Mexicans from Houston were not distanced from statewide political activities. A Methodist minister and teacher, Profesor J. J. Mercado, represented the local Mexican community at El Congreso Mexicanista. Delegates representing the Houston chapter of La Agrupación Protectora Mexicana, a federation of approximately twenty-five organizations headquartered in San Antonio, accompanied him to the Laredo meeting. Another Houston organization established in 1914, La Sociedad Mexicana "Vigilancia," maintained fraternal relations with sister organizations throughout the state and occasionally expressed serious concern over the fighting in the homeland. In 1915, the officers of the organizations pledged their support for the embattled president of Mexico, Venustiano Carranza.[52]

The city of Austin, located on the northern fringe of South Texas, produced fewer organizations than the older and better-established Mexican communities in San Antonio and deep South Texas. Early organizations may have been short-lived; only three organizations of note existed during the 1910s. La Liga Mexicanista Berriozabal No. 10, clearly a member of a regional federation, appeared between 1912 and 1914.

The use of the popular organizational self-referent, Mexicanista, denotes a nationalist and all-inclusive orientation that welcomed immigrant and U.S.-born Mexicans as members. Based on the name of the organization, it may have been an affiliate of La Liga Mexicanista, the state federation established by El Congreso Mexicanista. It was probably aligned with organized labor in Austin; it met regularly at the local trades council hall. A more independent organization with a distinctly working-class name, El Gran Círculo de Obreros, was active in the Mexican community of Austin between 1913 and 1915, while La Liga de Protección Mexicana, a possible branch of a federation associated with the Catholic Church, appeared in 1914.[53]

In San Antonio, the center of exile politics, the appearance and growth of numerous Mexican organizations accompanied organizing activity that focused on political developments in Mexico. Political exiles representing different camps often directed the attention of the Mexican community away from local issues. Homeland politics, however, also reinforced local concerns and efforts. Opposing political groups from San Antonio, for example, often found it necessary to increase their following by advocating material improvements for local Mexicans. This is evident in the case of La Gran Liga Mexicana.

La Gran Liga Mexicana was formed in 1909 to "bind the Mexicans together for mutual protection and benefit."[54] In that same year, the San Antonio headquarters announced plans to install branches in New Braunfels, Seguín, and Elmendorf. Eventually La Gran Liga established chapters in San Marcos, Texas, and in California, Colorado, New Mexico, and Arizona. La Gran Liga demonstrated a marked political focus on Mexico and support for President Porfirio Díaz. It also collaborated with local workers' organizations. In September, 1910, the *San Antonio Daily Express* noted under the headline "Mexicans Cheer Díaz" that La Gran Liga had joined other organizations in a patriotic celebration. The other participants included El Gran Círculo de Obreros, La Sociedad de la Unión, La Sociedad Benito Juárez, El Campamento Bernardo Reyes, El Campamento Servando Canales, and El Club de Trabajadores.[55]

Other San Antonio organizations also adopted names that explicitly referred to their working-class membership and orientation. These included El Concilio Obrero Mexicano and Sociedad Mutualista Artes Gráficas. Others made explicit reference to their special makeup as artisans and skilled workers: Sociedad Morelos Mutua de Panaderos (bakers), Sociedad de Albañiles (masons and bricklayers), Sociedad Mutualista de Zapateros (shoemakers) "Porfirio Díaz" and Sociedad Mutualista Mexicana de Sastres (tailors). In some cases, workers formed separate organizations according to their place of employment. The Unión

Public ceremony of a San Antonio Woodmen of the World or-
ganization, ca. 1917. *Courtesy Photography Collection, Harry
Ransom Humanities Research Center, The University of
Texas at Austin*

Fraternal Mexicana de Cementville, for example, included several hundred workers who lived in a company town owned by the San Antonio
Portland Cement Company on the northern edge of the city. A lodge
of the Woodmen of the World appeared in Cementville earlier and waged
an unsuccessful strike for an eight-hour day. Its defeat may have led the
workers to form the new organization in 1925.[56]

Cooperation among San Antonio organizations was extensive. They
co-sponsored community events such as Mexican patriotic celebrations
and exchanged delegates to maintain close contact and ensure continuing collaboration. Close communications were also maintained with
sister organizations in Mexico. For example, La Sociedad de la Unión,
one of the largest in the city, corresponded with fifteen mutualist organizations from Mexico. Exchanges most probably involved formal ties
that extended across the border. This was evident when Joaquín C. Martínez, representing the Gran Círculo de Obreros, of Monterrey, visited
several organizations in the city and delivered a speech during the anniversary celebration of the Sociedad Benevolencia Mexicana.[57]

Among the most important services offered by these organizations was legal assistance to persons who faced discrimination in the work place. La Alianza Hispano Americana Lodge 167, for instance, established a center in 1895 that handled such complaints. La Sociedad Protectora de Mexicanos en los Estados Unidos had lawyers readily available to handle complaints against railroad companies, city railways, and other corporations. La Liga Protectora Mexicana, on the other hand, maintained contractual relations with local attorneys and offered legal advice and representation to its members for a nominal fee. One of the founders of La Liga, Manuel C. González, played an important role in advising the members on the state's tenant law, work contracts, interest rates for loans, the constitutional rights of assembly and free speech among the foreign-born, workmen's compensation, and due process. La Liga also extended its legal service by publishing a regular column in *El Imparcial de Texas* and by compiling a handbook of Texas laws which gave emphasis to workers' rights and landlord-tenant contracts.[58]

Some of the San Antonio–based federations extended their operations into the rural area south and east of the city. In 1913 La Sociedad de Amigos, Beneficiencia Mutua, established a chapter in Guadalupe County.[59] By 1922 it boasted six member organizations extending as far south as Weslaco.[60] One year later La Sociedad Benefectora Mexicana registered at least one affiliate at Leesville.[61] El Club Cooperativo Mexicano, on the other hand, established its headquarters in Floresville and a chapter in San Antonio. The membership of this federation totalled thirteen hundred.[62] El Club Cooperativo adopted a specialized function, while La Gran Liga, Los Amigos del Pueblo, and La Sociedad Benefectora focused on educational, legal, and job-related issues. El Club Cooperativo established a food cooperative to meet an immediate and special need of destitute Mexican families.

Mexicans in rural areas also established numerous organizations in order to survive difficult times. In 1913, for instance, agricultural workers from Gonzales established a mutual aid society called La Sociedad Agrícola Mexicana, Benito Juárez y Sebastian Lerdo do Tejada. Members of this organization may have participated in the previously-mentioned public appeal for jobs. A similar organization of Mexican agricultural workers from Hochelin was active in 1914 as La Sociedad Mutualista de Agricultores Mexicanos.[63] Three other agricultural workers' organizations appeared during 1915 in nearby New Braunfels, Falls City, and in an undetermined locale in Guadalupe County. These were La Unión de Sembradores Mexicanos, La Sociedad Beneficiencia de Agricultores Mexicanos, and La Unión de Agricultores Mexicanos. La Unión de Agricultores Mexicanos was an independent labor federation that established various locals throughout Guadalupe County in 1915.[64]

The town of Seguín registered one of the largest of these agricultural unions in 1915, one which possibly may have been a Socialist Party local. It consisted of approximately two hundred Mexican tenants, sharecroppers, and laborers who came together in response to the passage of a state law that set new and improved land rental rates in agriculture. The union decided to test the law by urging Mexican renters to refuse the old arrangement that required a third of their cotton harvest as rental payment. It also called on farm laborers to demand a minimum wage of $1.50 a day. Other agricultural unions like La Union de Sembradores Mexicanos, at New Braunfels, also urged Mexican tenants to favor contracts that observed the new law.[65]

Southwest of San Antonio, Stockdale claimed a voluntary organization, Sociedad Ignacio Zaragoza, that frequently sponsored patriotic holidays for Mexicans in Wilson County. A few miles east of Stockdale, Mexicans from Nixon formed La Sociedad "Unión de Obreros," a mutual aid society with a clearly manifested working-class identity. Mexicanas from Pearsall, Kingsville, and Brownsville established all-female organizations: La Sociedad Mutualista Benito Juárez, W.O.W. No. 1003 Ignacio A. de la Peña, and La Sociedad Carmen Romero Rubio de Díaz de Señoras y Señoritas, respectively.[66]

Women also participated prominently in pacifist organizations that sought an end to the fighting in Mexico. Jovita Idar and Leonor Villegas de Magnón, members of the Laredo chapter of the Junta Femenil Pacifista, brought attention to their organization when they volunteered as nurses to care for the wounded after the 1914 military conflict between constitutionalist and Villa forces in Nuevo Laredo. The following year, the president of the statewide organization, María de Jesús Pérez, gave wide publicity to pacifism when she headed a committee of women that traveled into Mexico to confer with political and military leaders. The pacifist movement, however, was not without its internal differences. Idar and Villegas de Magnón, although in favor of peace, declined participation in this effort until Carranza obtained official recognition from other governments. Obviously concerned about the widespread rumors of possible U.S. intervention and the fledgling condition of Carranza's government, Villegas de Magnón kept the Mexican president informed about support for his administration within her organization. The Laredo group kept an eye on other political developments that could help the Carranza administration or at least ease political pressures. Villegas de Magnón, for instance, also transmitted to Carranza a copy of an insurrectionist document that sought the independence of Texas and its possible annexation by Mexico. The Laredo pacifists may have been secretly allied with this group, which made its declaration a full year before the celebrated armed uprising in South Texas known as the San Diego revolt.[67]

Mexican associations in Laredo also displayed a high degree of cooperation in matters related to the Mexican worker. The proximity of Mexico plus a concentrated population may account for the numerous instances in which Mexican societies combined organizing efforts throughout the city and across the international border.[68] Laredo groups that took part in El Congreso Mexicanista included La Sociedad Mutualista, Hijos de Juárez; La Sociedad Mutua de Trabajadores; La Sociedad de Obreros, Igualdad y Progreso; and three local Masonic lodges named Benito Juárez, Ignacio Zaragosa, and Caballeros de Honor, No. 14. Some of these organizations also participated in the 1916 cornerstone ceremonies of El Instituto Domínguez, a private educational institution headed by the popular Mason and educator Simón G. Domínguez. La Sociedad de Obreros, Igualdad y Progreso and La Sociedad Mutualista, Hijos de Juárez led the list of participants. La Unión de Albañiles (masons) and a local chapter of the Woodmen of the World, as well as the work crew responsible for building the school, participated in the ceremonies.[69]

Local societies often demonstrated a popular spirit of cooperation when they joined together to celebrate important community events. In September, 1907, for instance, at least twelve local groups with a minimum aggregate number of one thousand workers participated in a Labor Day parade. The participants included AFL-affiliated unions, some of which had been organized by Federal Labor Union No. 11953, as well as the always reliable La Sociedad de Obreros, Igualdad y Progreso; La Sociedad Mutualista, Hijos de Juárez; and the local Masonic lodge, Caballeros de Honor, No. 14.[70]

Local preparations for the 1918 Pan American Federation of Labor conference also produced a joint organizing project. Clemente Idar called a public meeting two months before the convocation date and managed to bring together "several presidents of Societies and Unions." He sought to encourage some of the existing workers' organizations to join the AFL. Although no one noted the names of the associations that were present at this meeting, a local paper declared that fifteen agreed to seek AFL membership. Besides those previously mentioned, other unaffiliated groups such as La Unión de Pintores (painters); El Club Centenario de Carpinteros y Albañiles (carpenters and masons); La Sociedad Unión de Jornaleros (day laborers), Protección y Trabajo; and La Unión de Impresores (typographical workers) may have been present, as they were popular and active at the time.[71]

Down the river from Laredo, Brownsville recorded a number of orga-

Groundbreaking ceremonies of El Instituto Domínguez, 1916.
On platform, left to right, are Jovita Idar, "profesor" Simón
Domínguez, and Domínguez's daughter. *Courtesy Institute of
Texas Cultures, The University of Texas at San Antonio*

nizations including El Gremio de Panaderos (bakery workers), La Agrupación Protectora Mexicana No. 25, La Fraternidad Obrera de Brownsville, La Liga Protectora de Obreros Mexicanos, La Sociedad Cristóbal Colón, La Unión Mexicana, and La Sociedad Mutualista Hidalgo y Costilla. A local hall, El Salón Sociedad de Obreros, served as a meeting place for the local organizations. Union organizing may have occurred in 1911 when the editors of *La Crónica* urged workers, especially coachmen, to seek improvements by forming unions and securing charters from U.S. labor federations, "the only ones that can supply the necessary financial support" to resolve their problems.[72]

Brownsville residents also initiated a recruiting campaign for Masonry that eventually produced fifty-seven Caballeros de Honor lodges throughout the state. The first lodge was established in Brownsville around 1906. Others followed in close succession in a northern and northwestern direction. This growth pattern reached its northernmost points in San Marcos and New Braunfels in 1915.[73] The names of some of these lodges reflect a Mexican working-class identity. The Kingsville lodge, for instance, was called La Logia Obreros de Monte Libano. The Corpus Christi lodge was known as La Logia Benito Juárez, Hijo No. 3, de la Orden de Libres y Unidos Obreros del Universo.[74]

Masons indirectly contributed to the establishment of another type of organization, mutual aid societies associated with the Catholic Church. According to an Oblate priest from Del Rio, parishioners decided to form a mutual aid society when local Masons and "liberales rojos," possibly P L M members, levelled strong criticisms against the local clergy and church members. The Liga de Protección Mexicana took legal action and boycotted the two local newspapers that were responsible for the attack. True to its origins and sponsorship, the organization presented itself as a defender of the Catholic Church and its religion. The association's constitution, however, left little doubt that the Liga was primarily a mutual aid society that sought to provide basic services for its members and assume a prominent position in local civic affairs. The Liga grew with the assistance of the Catholic Church. A succession of mutual aid societies appeared in close association with parishes in Uvalde, Eagle Pass, Mission, and Mercedes between 1908 and 1915.[75]

The establishment of federations of Mexican organizations owed much to a popular sense of unity that community leaders successfully harnessed for greater effectiveness. These networks, however, could not have emerged, much less prospered, if not for effective communications and coordinated activities in the regional community of South Texas. One of the earliest recorded campaigns, one which resulted in the formation of numerous loosely affiliated organizations, involved Catarino Garza.

Garza is best known for organizing and leading an armed group of Mexican ranchers and vaqueros in 1891 to depose Mexican president Porfirio Díaz. Garza also was a widely respected journalist who built a reputation as a fearless leader when he denounced racial discrimination in South Texas and despotic rule in Mexico. Prior to this more controversial phase in his life, he had traveled the area bordered by Brownsville, Laredo, and Corpus Christi as a sewing machine salesman during the 1880s. During these travels he helped local groups form organizations and communicate on political issues pertaining to South Texas and Mexico. In the process he not only accumulated the necessary experience for his budding political career, but also contributed to building formal ties among Mexican organizations.[76]

Mexicans also sought to formalize existing ties for more effective coordination of activities on a regional level. The West Texas Mexican community of San Angelo issued one of the earliest invitations to form a statewide federation of Mexican organizations. La Sociedad Latino Americana de Auxilios Mutuos, which made the 1906 appeal for unity, does not appear to have succeeded.[77] The first successful attempt that left a documented record was El Congreso Mexicanista.[78]

Nicasio Idar, along with his son Clemente and daughter Jovita, planned and organized El Congreso Mexicanista to establish a federation of community organizations that could lead a unified struggle against discrimination and inequality in Texas. The call for the conference appeared in *La Crónica* at the same time that its editors were giving wide publicity to a number of issues associated with discrimination, including the lynching of a young Mexican boy in Thorndale.[79] Mexican organizations that included mutual aid societies, Masonic orders, and protective associations from throughout the state and some border Mexican towns sent approximately twenty-four delegates to convene at Laredo during the week of September 16, a date that had symbolic value as Mexican Independence Day.

We can only speculate on the possible success of the federation that resulted from El Congreso, La Gran Liga Mexicanista de Beneficiencia y Protección, since it suffered a premature death of yet unknown causes. Its demise, however, does not minimize the significance of El Congreso Mexicanista as a representative organizational and ideological response of the Mexican community acting on its own independent behalf. The subject of workers' rights was a central concern, and nationalism and a sense of moral and historical purpose guided this important mobilization effort.[80]

La Revolución de Texas

While efforts to build regional unity through federated forms of organization revolved around the conventional idea of waging cooperative and protest activity, others opted for armed action that mirrored insurrectionist trends in Mexico. The San Diego revolt, named after the South Texas town where the call to arms originated, erupted in 1915 when roving bands of Mexican insurgents carried out a formally declared plan to reconquer the territory lost during the U.S.-Mexico War. The insurgents issued a plan of action that detailed long-standing grievances and that called upon sympathizers to join in an armed struggle to establish separate independent republics for Mexicans, blacks, and Native Americans.[81] The revolt initially involved as many as fifteen guerilla groups carrying flags that read "Libertad, Igualdad, e Independencia," and "El Ejercito Libertador de los México-Texanos." The largest guerrilla group included as many as sixty men led by Aniceto Pizaña, a PLM sympathizer native to the San Benito area, and Luis de la Rosa, a former deputy sheriff from Rio Hondo. The insurgent force eventually adopted the more conventional form of warfare that involved amassing troops and positioning them for face-to-face fighting in the field in order to accommodate the growing numbers of adherents to the cause, an increasing number of whom lived on the Mexican side of the border. Between

National guardsmen at Mercedes with captured flag of the "sediciosos," 1915. The flag's inscription reads, "Ejercito Libertador de los Mexico-Texanos." *Courtesy Hidalgo County Historical Museum, Edinburg*

three and five thousand eventually joined the revolt in preparation for an invasion of the United States during the latter part of 1916. The insurgency eventually met defeat in 1916 when President Venustiano Carranza, prompted by a desire to obtain U.S. recognition for his regime, ordered his military to arrest the leaders of the insurgency and to take other punitive measures to keep them from using Mexico as a refuge and base of operations.[82]

Despite ample documented evidence surrounding the San Diego revolt, historians have generally denied or minimized its importance as part of a more general political response to discrimination and inequality by Mexicans in Texas. Instead, they have credited sources often far removed from the fighting.[83] There is no doubt that the revolt intersected in important ways with political developments in the larger political arena of international relations. In attempting to describe the bigger picture, however, historians have overlooked one of the essential points in the matter, that the revolt was what it purported to be, an attempt to reclaim the Southwest and to initiate an armed movement of liberation among oppressed people in the Americas.

A more recent examination of the San Diego revolt by David Montejano acknowledges the influence of international tensions as a contributing factor. He places the cause of the insurgency on the replacement of the old ranch order by the modern farm society, with attendant violent dislocation and proletarianization of the Mexican population.[84] This study comes closest in explaining why Mexicans from South Texas lent a receptive ear to insurrectionist politics. Like other histories of the revolt, Montejano's work, however, does not view "la revolución de Texas" as an integral part of a general and increasingly intense activist environment in the Mexican community of Texas.

The revolt officially began on January 6, 1915, when the formulators of the Plan de San Diego sent out organizers to form revolutionary juntas, or affiliated organizations, throughout South Texas. These juntas were to select delegates to convene on February 20, the date when the armed struggle was to begin. Then the delegates revised the original Plan de San Diego, giving the revolutionary program a more anarchistic stamp that was similar to the language in PLM documents. The revolutionary congress expanded its focus with the second plan by calling for the liberation of all the oppressed people of the Americas:

> Yankee arrogance has reached its limits; it is not content with the daily lynching of men, it now seeks to lynch an entire people, a whole race, an entire continent. And it is against this arrogance that we must unite; and it is against this insolence that we must unite; and it is against this insolence that we must energetically fight a cause without political or religions distinctions, nor ethnic and social differences . . . in order to vindicate with torrents of blood our prerogatives as humans, our rights as men, men that feel, think, love and work like any of those arrogant "white men" to whom we feel superior though our skin may be black, brown, yellow or red.[85]

It was impossible to continue disregarding the lynchings and the labor exploitation that victimized Mexicans especially in Texas, according to the delegates to the revolutionary congress. The time, therefore, was ripe for an "Emancipating Revolution of People and Races of the Americas" that would seek war with no quarter, abolition of racial hatred and labor exploitation, establishment of the Social Republic of Texas, establishment of "Modern" schools guided by the principal of universal love, and communalization of property.[86]

Though unable to calculate accurately the number of Mexicans directly or indirectly involved in the San Diego revolt, we can say that the numbers were substantial enough to create a crisis of international proportions. They included once "friendly" Mexicans who submitted to the spirit of rebellion with a muted sense of bitterness as well as others who openly participated in the discussions and debates on the Mexican condition that the revolt encouraged, or who secretly supported the revolt and participated in the fighting. More importantly, the revolt gave radical expression to popular ideas and sentiments in the Mexican community of the border region.

The plan and subsequent manifestos issued by the Mexican revolutionists expressed concerns similar to those voiced earlier by the delegates to El Congreso Mexicanista. However, the plan went beyond the political formulations of the Laredo conference by calling for an anarcho-syndicalist order in revolutionary alliance with oppressed peoples from throughout the Americas. The San Diego revolt was exceptional in the sense that it was one of the most dramatic formal expressions of discontent registered during the early 1900s. If placed within the progressive sequence of mobilization events, it represents an ideological peak in protest activity. The revolt underscored the fact that Mexicans entertained radical political outlooks that emerged from their condition and mirrored Mexican revolutionary thought and action.

Conclusion

The foregoing examination of the varied and extensive organized responses of Mexicans to work and related issues broadens the narrow understanding of labor offered by the conventional trade union and immigrant history approaches. It also gives balance and added perspective to the view that Mexicans were unorganizable or players of secondary importance in the historical process.

Mexicans adapted nonconventional means to address work-related issues for various reasons. First, racial divisions and conflicts isolated them from the Anglo trade union movement and from influences that could have led to the adoption of a union structure as their primary vehicle of struggle. Second, Mexican workers often took informal and spontaneous actions or formed ad hoc organizations because they faced pressing issues and lacked sufficient resources to take more deliberate and sustained actions. Third, workers who established organizations and regional alliances adopted a broad outlook in keeping with the numerous issues that their communities faced.

This broader view of the world of Mexican labor reveals an impressive level of organizing that manifested a unifying set of working-class and minority concerns. Interactions with groups in Mexico represented an added dimension in the story of mobilization. The revolution and exiled politics, in particular, reinforced nationalism and led to radical critiques and actions in community struggles.

Much of early twentieth century Mexican political life evolved around the mutual aid societies. *Mutualistas* were numerous and as such gave expression to the collective Mexican identity as well as to popularly held beliefs and concerns. These organizations thus provide an opportunity to study the political culture that defined what was valued and desired in the larger community. Further examination will reveal an encompassing ethic of mutuality and a popular brand of nationalism that guided these organizations.

Voluntary Organizations and the Ethic of Mutuality: Expressions of a Mexicanist Political Culture

The Mexican community was by no means homogeneous in cultural identity or political outlook. Mutual aid, pacifist, Masonic, and union organizations, for instance, at times reflected broadly defined civic outlooks, highly specialized interests, or narrow instrumental views. Moreover, the agitational, self-help, and economic strategies adopted by Mexican organizations suggest ongoing tension between collectivist and individualist orientations. These variations resulted from evolving homeland politics, changing economic conditions, and the attendant development of class differentiation. The impressive amount of collectivist political activity that evolved around mutual aid societies, the most popular form of voluntary organization at the time, however, points to a unifying cultural frame of reference that gave impetus and meaning to Mexican organizational life.[1]

Despite opposing class and ethnic organizing appeals, calls for unity openly adhered to a Mexicanist,[2] or all-inclusive, nationalist sense of community and a popular ethic of mutuality, or the collective idea that Edward P. Thompson attributes to English working-class culture and its politics. A Mexicanist orientation, based on grievances against racial discrimination plus the influence of nationalist thought from Mexico, often blurred differences in the community. Mutualism incorporated such values as fraternalism, reciprocity, and altruism into a moral prescription for human behavior, a cultural basis for moralistic and nationalistic political action that was intended to set things right, as Juan Gómez-Quiñones points out.[3]

Voluntary organizations expressed the clearest visions of mutualism and a Mexicanist orientation in their conscious working-class endeavors. The fundamental concern among the members was to help each other survive the very difficult conditions under which they lived and worked. Mutualista organizations, however, did not always confine their attention to the immediate and pressing material interests of their largely working-class membership, nor did they simply embrace a narrow self-

Centro Latino, a meeting hall for Brownsville organizations,
with sign reading, "Labor Omni Vincint," ca. 1910. *Courtesy
Harry Lund Collection, Archives Division, Texas State
Library, Austin*

help outlook. Mutual aid societies also reinforced a collectivist spirit
with resolute statements of purpose in support of nationalist principles
and moral values, an active civic role, and strict rules that disciplined
their members into conscious Mexicanist proponents of the ethic of mutuality. Intellectuals, in turn articulated these principles and values into
different calls for unity and collective action, including unionism. Consequently, even different and at times opposing groups adhered to the
same legitimating set of fundamentally unifying principles and values,
as an examination of ethnic and homeland politics will demonstrate.

Social Divisions

Any discussion of political culture must address the presence of class and generational divisions associated with the emergence of a U.S.-born Mexican middle class and its organizations. Luis Recinos, a researcher assisting Manuel Gamio in the preparation of his highly acclaimed study of Mexican immigration, noted such divisions between the immigrant and U.S.-born Mexicans during the late 1920s. He was careful to point out, however, that voluntary organizations included everyone regardless of nativity.[4] In other words, a Mexicanist identity and organizational style predominated at the same time that divisions and an incipient ethnic outlook began to emerge.

Underlying the class and generational divisions was a popular tendency in Anglo society to view Mexicans as a homogenous group. Mexicans were, as Texas Congressman James Slayden stated, "'Mexicans' just as all blacks are Negroes though they may have five generations of American ancestors." Nemesio García Naranjo, an exiled politician living in San Antonio, added that "from the legal point of view, they were citizens of the great north american union. However, the racial sectarianism of the Anglo Saxons condemned them to an inferior place." Finally, Johnny Solís, one of the founders of the Hijos de América and the League of United Latin American Citizens (LULAC), confirmed this racially-defined division and the negative meaning associated with the term Mexican: "The biggest drawback which the Texas-Mexicans face is that no matter how we behave or what we do or how long we have been here we are still 'Mexicans'."[5] Solís inferred that racism was especially onerous because it denied U.S.-born Mexicans the opportunities ordinarily extended to other upwardly mobile citizens.

The issues of immigration and denial of occupational mobility accentuated tensions among Mexicans. Immigration intensified job competition and depressed wages while occupational discrimination denied the U.S.-born and older immigrants the chance to escape their condition. Class and generational differences were often expressed in cultural terms, with Mexican nationals accusing the U.S.-born of being *agringados* and ashamed of their Mexican identity, and the U.S.-born charging that the new arrivals depressed wages and encouraged further exploitation with their alleged backward customs of extreme deference and reserve. The erosion of a unified Mexicanist identity became more noticeable among upwardly mobile U.S.-born Mexicans who felt the pressure of competition from below and social discrimination from above. Many of them sought to disassociate themselves from the immigrant population, giving emphasis to their nativity and citizenship as a way to challenge discrimination, improve opportunities for mobility, and gain a measure of acceptance in the larger world. Such an ethnic strategy of incorporation also challenged discrimination, although its proponents increasingly saw their association with the Mexican nationals as a source of their problems and not as a point of unity or common cause.[6]

The very racism that strengthened bonds among Mexicans thus also led to the development of a distinct ethnic style of politics that gave special emphasis to citizenship. Historians generally associate this development with the emergence of a small Mexican middle class and the appearance of L U L A C in 1929. A recent publication by Carole E. Christian suggests that the "Mexican American mind," a popular acculturated outlook, held by the upwardly mobile U.S.-born, that allegedly gave rise to L U L A C actually originated during the First World War.[7] Although this may be true, the expressions of wartime loyalty that she recounts did not necessarily signify a fundamental cultural transformation and the abandonment of collectivist cultural values. José de la Luz Saenz, one of L U L A C's founders and author of a war memoir, provides useful observations on the persistence of a Mexicanist identity in the 1920s.

De la Luz Saenz acknowledges that he joined the military to counter accusations of disloyalty brought on by the San Diego revolt and Mexican draft resisters and to challenge discrimination and segregation with a record of wartime contributions. He did not describe his loyalty in patriotic or acculturated terms, but he spoke rather as a Mexican seeking equality and an opportunity to demonstrate "to the entire world our dignity as a people."[8] When told by his superiors to write his last letters that were to be delivered to his loved ones in case of death, he informed his wife that he had fallen "fighting with honor in support of the inalienable rights of humanity and for the future well-being of our children."[9]

In a statement to his *conraciales,* or fellow Mexicans, de la Luz Saenz expressed a highly nationalist identity: "Don't forget that we have fallen fighting solely in honor of our good name. To live without the guarantees that are extended to people that are free is not to live. Let us once and for all demonstrate that we are worthy of fighting for those rights so that in the future we may enjoy them."[10]

The community, according to de la Luz Saenz, needed mature persons prepared "to fight for the common good of our people."[11] Two of L U L A C's predecessors that appeared during the 1920s, the Hijos de América and the Hijos de Texas, also expressed de la Luz Saenz' views and concerns. Although such organizations entertained an identity based on citizenship, they did not exclude Mexican nationals. Instead, they adopted the Mexicanist, or all-inclusive method of organizing, and co-operated fully with the more popular mutual aid societies.[12] As important as class and generational divisions may have been in everyday experiences, they had not yet given rise to the ethnic form of politics associated with L U L A C. A Mexicanist outlook predominated at least until the late 1920s.

Homeland rather than ethnic politics reflected a more serious source of divisions during the early 1900s. Homeland politics included numerous exiled groups, pacifist organizations, and other community institutions whose interest in Mexico and its politics guided many of their community activities. A number of factors contributed to the ascendancy of homeland politics. Population growth in northern Mexico along with increasing immigration strengthened historical and cultural ties with the homeland throughout the last half of the nineteenth century and the beginning of the twentieth. These demographic changes alone were sufficient to draw Mexicans further into the orbit of Mexico's politics. Another important factor was the proximity of Mexico. Also, the revolution encouraged numerous economic refugees and political exiles to join the immigrant stream. Political exiles, refugees, and consular offices played an especially important role in politicizing homeland ties. The result was the transfer of divisions from the Mexican revolution to the political world of the Mexican community of Texas.

Texas was a major staging area for exiled politics. Thousands of Mexicans along the border and in areas as far north as San Antonio, Austin, and Waco actively supported the various revolutionary groups operating throughout the state in 1915. Divisions were so deep that supporters of regimes in power in Mexico secretly collaborated with the Mexican consuls in identifying opposition groups operating along the Texas border. Journalists and former office holders also debated their support for opposing revolutionary groups active in Mexico and Texas. These divisions were equally pronounced among less prominent individuals. A Mexican foreman of a work crew that labored in the delta of the Rio Grande Valley, for example, recalled that between 1912 and 1917 he supervised groups of up to eighty workers including battle-hardened veterans representing different revolutionary camps.[13]

The revolution, however, also reinforced a sense of nationalist identity. At one level, this identity involved a widespread and unifying concern for the well-being of the motherland. The revolution was taking a high human and economic toll, and it was making Mexico highly vulnerable to U.S. intervention. Immigrants felt this concern more closely, lamenting the diaspora and worrying about kin and friends they had left behind. For Querido Moheno, an exiled politician who wrote extensively on Mexico and the revolution for such papers as *La Prensa,* Mexicans overlooked their differences and focused their attention on the motherland once they reached the familiar and spiritually unifying surroundings of Texas: "The mere crossing of the border has been enough to make us agreeable with each other. If we were still there we would be fighting each other. But since we are here, in this land where the remains of our grandfathers rest, all of us raise our hearts to bless the motherland."[14]

Pacifists also captured the attention of Mexicans who became increasingly concerned that the revolution had lasted long enough. In the process, they strengthened a popular identification with Mexico. More partisan individuals may have offered opposing visions and approaches to change. However, they also energized public discourse on such issues as workers' rights, nationalism, and class consciousness, encouraging added numbers to join the world of politics. The PLM, for instance, increased the numbers of active participants in the political life of their communities and promoted a nationalist identity within a developing anarchist programme of action. On the other hand, when Mexican officials like president Venustiano Carranza sought and utilized public support in Texas to advance their diplomatic interests, the results worked to the advantage of Mexicans in Texas. In such instances, according to a student of border history, the ideology of the Mexican revolution inspired and strengthened a belief in egalitarianism, social justice, and anti-imperialism, ideas that were integral to an idealized and exalted Mexican identity.[15]

One of the best indications that the revolution influenced Mexicans was the San Diego revolt. Exiles representing various ideologies and focusing on the Mexican revolution invariably directed the attention of their newly organized forces to their own condition in the state. According to Alonzo B. Garrett, U.S. Consul in Nuevo Laredo, exiles organized in the area of South Texas, "supposedly to invade Mexico in the interest of the faction with which they are affiliated, but there have been unscrupulous leaders who have been industrially preaching the Plan of San Diego."[16] The rank and file responded favorably, he noted: "Many of the lower classes of Texas Mexicans have joined this movement, and they have a considerable following in Laredo and vicinity."[17] Despite attempts by such political exiles as Ricardo Flores Magón to attribute the revolt to local grievances, there was sufficient reason to believe that the revolution inspired the *sediciosos.* Flores Magón's defense of the rebels offered encouragement. He called the revolt "a movement of legitimate defense of the oppressed against the oppressor."[18]

Homeland politics thus produced mixed results. It introduced and reinforced divisions. It also cultivated a nationalist Mexican identity and communitarian ideals on both sides of the border. These influences were direct when mutual aid societies secretly or openly endorsed a particular exiled group in the area. On other occasions, mutualista organizations rejected an outright affiliation because of differences of opinion among the membership. This may explain why many mutual aid societies adopted rules that prohibited discussions of a political nature and assigned committees to first review issues before the membership discussed them during meetings. Members were left with the option of expressing their views independently or through other more partisan organizations. On the other hand, the revolution indirectly influenced political life in the Mexican community by increasing the numbers of immigrants who joined mutual aid societies or established new ones. Immigrants joined other more permanent residents who assisted them in adjusting to their new surroundings.

The unifying influences of the revolution notwithstanding, the most important force that contributed to mutualism orginated in the experiences that Mexicans shared in Texas. These included a condition of poverty that required the sharing of resources and efforts for survival and advancement, and the problem of discrimination and inequality that called for collective actions of defense and protest. Moheno as well as Idar, de la Luz Saenz, and the editors of *La Prensa* understood this well when they observed that Mexicans, regardless of nativity, skills, or prior job experience, suffered the same fate as exploited workers. They gave their Mexicanist views special force with moralistic arguments that defined what was proper and good and with nationalistic allusions that made the proposed cause just. The spirit of mutualism engendered mutual aid societies in Texas in the first decades of the twentieth century.

Las Sociedades

An imported artisan tradition associated with guilds and mutual aid societies in Mexico during the late 1800s had combined with a similar, yet smaller-scale artisan past along the border, giving rise to some of the first such organizations in Texas. Industrialization in Mexico had caused the decline of handicraft trades, forcing artisans to seek self-organization in order to defend their social status and to protect their economic interests. Mutual aid societies soon proliferated. The formality and ritualism of these alliances as well as the upstanding and self-respecting behavior of its members also must have contributed to organizational life in Texas. Local needs and grievances, however, were the most important and immediate determinants in the establishment of mutualista organizations. While the subordinated position and status of Mexicans in the socio-economy created the need to give institutional expression to overarching historical and contemporary grievances, the most pressing need was for mutual support.[19]

Mutual aid societies met the material needs of their members with emergency loans and other forms of financial assistance, job-seeking services, and death and illness insurance. They also offered their members leadership experiences in civic affairs, sponsored other institutions like newspapers and private schools, provided their communities with popular community events for entertainment and socializing, and offered public forums that addressed the important issues of the day. Mutualista organizations thus gave their members and communities a sense of belonging and refuge from an often alien and inhospitable environment. The community, in turn, accorded the members and especially the officers the highly respected status of responsible, civic-minded individuals. A lesser-known characteristic of mutualistas is that they served as a major point of organizational unity that spawned local and regional political struggles.[20]

Mutualista leaders promoted a Mexicanist identity and sense of unity in their communities with organizing appeals that were directed at both immigrant and U.S.-born Mexicans. Recinos noted this when he observed that Mexican nationals usually joined local organizations once they obtained a job and decided to stay for an extended period of time. He was so impressed with the prevailing spirit of cooperation evident among Mexican nationals and U.S.-born Mexicans that he remarked: "It is rare to find a city with fifty or more Mexicans that does not have a Mexican society. In cities where the Mexican population is large such as in San Antonio, Houston, Dallas, Laredo, etc., Mexican nationals become members of the numerous Texas Mexican organizations. The Texas Mexicans, in turn, join the Mexican nationals in their organizations."[21]

Mexicanist organizing appeals and critiques thus drew a popular response, primarily because workers sought material support and cooperation to meet the economic uncertainties of the day. Widespread concern and discontent over the issues of inequality and discrimination also served as a common frame of reference in the formation and development of mutual aid societies. This thinking was not limited to U.S.-born Mexicans and older immigrants. Discontent was an important motivation among the immigrants. According to a report commissioned by the Mexican Consul from San Antonio, there were

> hundreds, we might say thousands of complaints of Mexican citizens against both private individuals and corporations as

well as against public officials. These complaints have covered a wide range, from a single alleged infraction of a verbal contract relating to wages, up to claims for personal injuries, and for alleged gross miscarriage of justice when Mexicans were accused of a crime or were the accusers of others who were charged with committing a crime on their persons or property.[22]

Journalists played an important role in encouraging a Mexicanist identity and collective political action to combat discrimination and inequality. The editors of *La Prensa,* for example, always urged their readers to join mutual aid societies and contribute to the resolution of problems in their communities. In 1915 when a reader from Marquez complained that public school officials denied his son admission, *La Prensa* recommended that he join with other Mexican parents and organize mutual aid societies. *La Prensa* predicted that "From this redeeming movement will come unions of workers from the rural areas and from the cities, also Mexican schools for Mexicans, where the children will be able to learn to speak and write their mother tongue."[23]

The allusion to a "redeeming movement" denoted a moralistic sense of determined and committed purpose to public service befitting the circumstances that Mexicans faced. The leadership of the numerous mutual aid and Masonic organizations also demonstrated a righteous sense of responsibility and commitment to an all-encompassing cause for change, improvement, and protest. The popular Laredo Mason and educator Simón G. Domínguez, for instance, described the organization Logia, Benito Juárez, in a letter to a journalist friend as an organization working for "the general improvement of our people in this state of the American Union."[24] Domínguez may have been speaking for the entire Masonic network in the state. He ended his letter with the following exhortation: "Struggle, brother, and let us continue struggling, for among us we have hearts that though we have not worked for the Cause in the press, we have struggled in the temple, and we are prepared to struggle wherever the opportunity presents itself, joined in the goodness of our cause and confident that our name has never been undeserving of the virtue that we proclaim."[25]

Organizations that under other circumstances would have confined their attention to offering insurance coverage to their members were also compelled to embrace a higher purpose in service to the entire population. In Kingsville, an officer for the all-women Woodmen of the World, No. 1003, Ignacio A. de la Peña, for instance, made it a point to describe her organization in terms of a lofty principle: "In our circle we not only work for group insurance, but for the uplifting of our people until we are able to reach the greatest heights possible."[26]

The pressing problems facing the community no doubt compelled Mexicans to seek change and improvements collectively. The need for mutual support, and discontent over the effects of discrimination and inequality alone, however, do not explain the spirit with which they gave themselves to a high-sounding cause of redemption. Additional motivations originated in the indignation that Mexicans felt against a racism that denied them their humanity and sense of self-worth. A conversation between an immigrant named Carlos Ruiz and John Murray, the editor of the San Antonio AFL paper *Pan American Labor Press,* illustrates the bitterness with which some Mexicans responded to racism.[27]

The reported conversation began on the border, probably in El Paso, as Ruiz was undergoing the dehumanizing experience of fumigation. After pointing out that Mexicans did not treat their visitors in such a discourteous manner, he took Murray to a store where he bought him a then-popular postcard showing Texas Rangers on horseback with lariats tied to three dead Mexicans reportedly killed during the San Diego revolt. His point was that Anglo racists did not value the life of a Mexican. Clearly bitter about his reception and the racial violence that occurred in 1915, Ruiz then took Murray to a bookstore in the Mexican community, where he pointed out with a sense of injured pride books by leading writers including Poe, Spencer, Darwin, Kropotkin, and Marx which were sold at affordable prices. He added, "It is the Mexican in blue overalls, the labor leader, as you call him, that supports these libraries of world-wide knowledge and passes all that he learns to his brothers who may not be able to read. And more, those are the books read not only by Mexicans but by organized labor throughout Latin America."[28]

In obvious reference to the popular belief among Anglo labor that Mexicans were unorganizable, Ruiz ended the conversation with the observation that though Mexico had fewer industrialized cities than the United States, its workers organized at a higher rate.

Murray clearly sought to promote a more positive image of the Mexican worker in support of the alliance that the AFL was seeking with labor in Mexico. He could have embellished his conversation with Ruiz to demonstrate the AFL's interest in Mexicans and to encourage Anglo unionists to adopt a more favorable view of Mexicans. The basic ingredients of the story, however, reappear in other instances, suggesting that Mexicans were often responding to the dehumanizing implications of racism when they organized and spoke about a "redeeming movement."

Aftermath of an armed battle at Norias: Mexican bodies and
a captured flag (barely visible, held by center rider), 1915.
Courtesy Hidalgo County Historical Museum, Edinburg

Ruiz's insistence on demonstrating the true worth and importance
of Mexicans as a response to Anglo racism parallels the story of the
folk hero Gregorio Cortez. Cortez achieved widespread popularity as
a folk symbol of resistance when he shot a Karnes City deputy sheriff
in self-defense and successfully evaded a manhunt until he was appre-
hended near the Mexican border. The Cortez campaign attracted more
than the usual support given to the numerous statewide efforts on behalf of Mexicans suspected of being convicted unfairly. Cortez became
a celebrated hero in part because he captured the prideful imagination
and sense of indignation among large numbers of Mexicans when he
stood up to defend his honor and his rights, "with his pistol in his
hand," and to demonstrate his skill as a horseman during the well-
publicized chase. The story of Cortez was told and retold in South
Texas in the form of a popular ballad of "resistance against outside en-
croachment."[29]

The campaign to gain Cortez's release drew significant popular support, most of which was channeled through local mutualista organizations. Pablo Cruz, editor of *El Regidor* and spokesman for the campaign, initially called upon the entire Mexican population to join in

the effort as a demonstration of national unity against the indignities and abuses associated with racial discrimination and inequality. He followed by carrying in his newspaper a serial history of Cortez that depicted him as a national hero. *El Regidor* also published a running account of contributions by individuals and organizations from throughout the state. Fund-raising activities, including public rallies, meetings, and door-to-door visits by local groups of supporters, provided Cortez the legal representation that eventually won his release. More importantly, the Cortez campaign revealed a regional sense of identity that responded to appeals for unity around the politically charged and symbolically important issues of group honor and pride.[30]

Among the many organizing calls made through *La Crónica,* the one made by Clemente Idar in preparation for El Congreso Mexicanista underscored the salient issues in the community and revealed the prevailing Mexicanist sense of unity and purpose that guided regional organizing efforts. Prior to the conference, Idar gave his attention to such issues as lynchings, unity, and discrimination in the schools and in the work place. Among his most consistently expressed concerns was the exploitation of Mexican workers, an issue that chafed nationalist sensibilities because the land that they worked at one time belonged to their ancestors: "Texas-Mexicans have produced with the sweat of their brow the bountiful agricultural wealth known throughout the country, and in recompense for this they have been put to work as peones on the land of their forefathers."[31]

Idar affirmed a Mexicanist identity. Mexican nationals also suffered exploitation despite the guarantees of the Treaty of Guadalupe Hidalgo, while U.S.-born Mexicans were denied the protection and guarantees of the Constitution. He concluded that "we are in the same situation," as he urged his readers to assist the more recent arrivals adjust to their new life in Texas. After the conference he continued to encourage immigrant and U.S.-born alike to join as brothers in the redemptive cause against discrimination. He took special care to assure Mexican nationals that the U.S.-born would not abandon them: "We that have been born in this country understand our responsibilities as citizens, but we also feel a profound love for and the most exalted interest in our mother race because we are by destiny her progeny. This nationality and this deep love for the Mexican race runs like blood through our veins."[32]

Clemente Idar based his case for political unity primarily on the ensuing racial conflict and popular feelings of resentment: "The barbarous acts of cruelty and savagery committed against Mexicans, burning them alive, lynching them without just cause, excluding them from the public schools, robbing them infamously of their work, insulting them in a thousand ways, gives rise to feelings of compassion for the Mexican people and hatred and aversion for the American people."[33]

Clemente's father, Nicasio Idar, was the first to instill the Mexicanist call for unity with a moralistic tone when he welcomed the delegates. He paid special tribute to their on-going community activism as the natural fulfillment of a basic moral imperative: "You are the apostles of goodness, the propagandists of unity, the workers of culture, the soldiers of progress, the defenders of the right and justice of our people."[34]

The delegates who attended the conference also imbued their Mexicanist appeals for unity with a sense of moral righteousness and responsibility. The speakers argued passionately in an oratorical style, recounting the continuing loss of land, the violated rights of Mexican workers, school discrimination and exclusion, the violence against Mexican youth in legal custody, and the need for class and national unification. These were the same issues that Clemente Idar had enumerated when he made his call for the conference, indicating a general consensus among the delegates and the memberships that they represented.[35]

F. E. Rendón, Grand Chancellor of the Mexican Masonic network, paid special tribute to the patriotism, altruism, and "sense of humanity and nobility," that guided the work of El Congreso Mexicanista. They were fulfilling a high and noble purpose in seeking the moral emancipation and material improvement of Mexican people. Masonic organizations, Rendón noted, shared the delegates' concerns especially for the immigrant who was drawn by false promises and subjected to extreme forms of exploitation. Inspired by a sense of ethical purpose, Rendón ended his talk with a call for unity, under "the precious flag of Justice and Reason," and as "one grand family of high repute, before which the machinations and offenses of our enemies will fall."[36]

Youth and women also participated in the conference as official speakers. A young woman named Hortencia Moncayo, who came before the assembly representing a private school, Escuela "La Purisima," called for young people to follow the lead of the true mentors of youth, the civic-minded Mexicans who were participating in El Congreso Mexicanista. Like Rendón, Moncayo underscored the exploitation of Mexican workers as a critical concern among the delegates. She also expressed a sense of indignation juxtaposed with feelings of pride and patriotism: "I wish that everyone who has the blood of Cuauhtémoc running through their veins will unite as one and be respected by any foreigner who wishes to treat them like beasts of burden. Mexicans have always been free and sovereign and have shed their blood for liberty and for the beloved motherland that has given us birth."[37]

Señora Soledad Flores de Peña offered a women's perspective to the goals of unity and improvement. She first commended the delegates for their work as the "honest gladiators of Texas-Mexican rights," who had won the hearts of the people and had encouraged many to join their ranks. Many more were ready to second their initiatives. However, it was necessary to pause and reflect on the responsibilities of everyone concerned. "I, like you," Flores de Peña told the delegates, "think that the best means to achieve it [unity and progress] is to educate women, to instruct her, encourage her at the same time that you respect her."[38] The delegates apparently agreed with the idea of supporting the educational and economic advancement of women. They provided for the establishment of a separate organization for women, La Liga Femenil.

Lisandro Peña, local teacher, journalist, and secretary of La Gran Liga Mexicanista, presented a literary piece that made special note of the conference's historical significance. He recounted the history of the Mexican nation through the unselfish and responsible acts of its known and anonymous national heroes. Peña encouraged the delegates to see that their efforts on behalf of their communities fulfilled the most sublime nationalist responsibility in history: "Remember, they died like all brave men die, with their arms around their rifles and holding their flag high. They died for us, for the children of their tomorrow, so that they could have peace and good fortune everywhere, even in foreign lands."[39]

The high-sounding principles and statements of political resolve heard at El Congreso Mexicanista and in numerous public programs that voluntary organizations sponsored throughout the state suggests an enthusiastic and committed leadership. The impressive number of voluntary organizations that appeared throughout the state further indicates that Mexicans responded favorably to organizing appeals. What was the content of these nationalist appeals and how did the organizations manifest and reinforce the unifying ethic of mutuality in their communities and among their members? To answer this important question it is necessary to examine the internal workings of such organizations.

Inside Las Sociedades

Mutual aid societies gave concrete and conscious manifestation to a Mexicanist identity and the unifying ethic of mutuality through highly responsible and civic-minded activities. Their code of morality and mutual support owed much to the membership's genuine devotion to such cultural values as fraternalism, reciprocity, and altruism. Guiding statements of purpose regarding proper moral behavior and mutualism reflected this devotion. Mutualista members also adhered to strict rules that disciplined them into "examples of true moral values" and that cemented a Mexicanist identity. These statements of purpose and rules

Lisandro Peña (sixth from left, with hand on hip) and Jovita
Idar (second from right) among the staff of *El Progreso*,
1914. *Courtesy Institute of Texan Cultures, The University of
Texas at San Antonio*

were contained in nine surviving constitutions and by-laws, which are
representative sources of information because founding members normally made few modifications to copies that originated in Mexico and
circulated among associated organizations in Texas. The eight organizations that generated these documents represented five South Texas towns
and cities: San Antonio, Alice, Brownsville, San Benito, and Laredo.[40]

Members of mutual aid organizations clearly saw themselves as important members of their communities. They viewed their decision to
contribute to the moral uplift and material advancement of fellow Mexicans as the most responsible and honorable responsibility that anyone
could assume. These twin goals began with their membership. They
believed that by pooling their resources and establishing a death and
illness insurance fund, for instance, they not only helped each other but
instilled the unifying values of mutualism, which they saw as moral im-
peratives in their communities. They also spoke about extending their
spirit of mutualism beyond the confines of the organization. La Sociedad Mutualista Protectora, Benito Juárez, of San Benito, for instance,
declared that it sought "progress and unity among the entire Mexican

Detail from a panoramic photograph of a meeting in Houston between Houston's El Campo Laurel, Woodmen of the World, and Pasadena's Sociedad Mutualista Mexicana Miguel Hidalgo, 1926. *Courtesy Mary Beltrán Collection, Houston Metropolitan Research Center, Houston Public Library*

working class in this country, as well as of the U.S.-born." The Alice mutual aid society named Hidalgo y Juárez explained that "philanthropy and humanitarian sentiments" would guide their efforts to build unity among "all social classes."

Members adopted a number of specific objectives to promote mutualism within and outside the organization. All of them established an insurance fund which made disability payments to ill members for up to thirty days and paid funeral costs in case of death. They also contributed to an ad hoc widow's fund that provided a lump sum to the family of the deceased member. Other sources of mutual and community assistance included informal job-seeking services for their members, charity funds to help needy families in the community, and savings funds which extended emergency loans to members. In some cases, the organizations established libraries, newspapers, and private schools for children and adults in the community. In all cases, they sponsored celebrations during Mexico's national holidays and the organizations' anniversaries. All of these activities were central to their commitment to the concepts of moral uplift and material advancement.

The material benefits that insurance coverage, emergency loans, and job placement assistance brought to the members were obvious. Most of them were poor and often without a stable source of employment. Schools, libraries, and newspapers were also important contributions to the educational advancement of the membership and the community. These activities, however, also contributed to the moral regeneration of the members and the community that they served. The insurance and savings funds reinforced a measure of trust among members who contributed their meager resources with the expectation that their money would be handled honestly and that they would receive their due benefits. The regular and timely payment of the required monthly fees and contributions also fostered frugality and a sense of family responsibility.

The charity funds, schools, newspapers, and public celebrations broadened the organizations' sphere of influence as examples of disinterested and morally rejuvenating public service. In Laredo La Sociedad Unión de Jornaleros saw in the patriotic celebrations an opportunity to demonstrate their adherence to a Mexicanist identity. The organization agreed that it needed to sponsor the celebration of "national holidays with the necessary solemnity to insure that our members and our children do not lose the precepts of our nationality." The Sociedad Hijos de Juárez added that its members should seek to promote through the press or their own organ "ideas in support of the moral and material development of the social masses." In San Benito mutualistas made one of the most impressive gestures of community support when they decided to admit into their school children from families who could not afford to pay the required fees.

The strict internal rules that mutual aid societies adopted to define the responsibilities and proper "moral comportment" of their members contributed the most to the practice of the ethic of mutuality. First of all, persons who applied for admission had to be of sound moral character. The organization confirmed this by requiring recommendations from at least one member who acted as a sponsor; a committee formally investigated their local reputation as responsible family persons and law-abiding citizens. The membership was required to vote unanimously in favor of positive recommendations by the sponsor and the committee. Otherwise, the applicants were rejected.

Rules also prohibited behavior that, according to La Sociedad Hidalgo y Juárez, of Alice, was "unbecoming to honest men." Vagrancy, giving oneself to vices, irresponsible family behavior, slander, and defamation of the organization or their brethren were causes for depriving members of their rights, and in some cases for suspending them from the organization. Members were discouraged from informally accusing others of these failings. Instead, organizations instituted a formal grievance process that allowed the membership to render a judgement on the basis of a recommendation by a jury of between five and ten members who heard opposing arguments.

Mutual aid societies also observed strict rules during discussions and debates, in order to avoid unnecessary conflicts and to foster a sense of propriety and mutual respect. They placed time limits on the arguments or presentations that each member made before the body. They also strictly prohibited offensive language. The membership could suspend anyone who left a meeting in the middle of a dispute or who threatened to quit the organization because of a heated discussion. Moreover, they avoided conflicts by appointing a committee to review issues of a sensitive nature before the membership was given an opportunity to discuss the matter.

These efforts to control the nature of the internal discussions reflected a concern for maintaining fraternal relations among the members and for projecting an image of sobriety and mutual consideration. It did not necessarily mean, however, that they shunned controversial issues. For instance, although most of them declared a ban on discussions of a religious or political nature, they all endorsed the idea of political unity and, as other sections in this chapter indicate, the members participated in important political events in their communities. Their decided reluctance to treat controversial issues underscored the importance of unity on the basis of mutual respect over any particular belief or idea that anyone wished to advocate.

Mutualistas also promoted fraternalism by maintaining friendly relations with sister organizations. Members in good standing of sister organizations who visited or moved into the area were always welcomed and sometimes seated in a position of honor with the executive committee. Mutualistas encouraged members who moved to other areas to join sister organizations. They usually gave departing members letters of recommendation and other documents to facilitate their admission. Mutual aid societies also agreed to assume the responsibility of assisting groups in their areas to establish other organizations and to cooperate with them in civic affairs. La Sociedad Benito Juárez, of Laredo, for instance, proposed to "help in all ways possible in the development of other societies by establishing relations of reciprocity within and outside the country."

The internal discipline of the mutualistas and their attendant reputation as responsible and civic-minded Mexicanist institutions gave importance and ideal meaning to the ethic of mutuality as a source of unity, identity, and civic pride. This ethic, however, generally remained tied to mutual aid societies until intellectuals defined and translated key cultural values into specific political objectives or strategies.

Defining and Translating the Ethic of Mutuality

One of the best sources for examining the manner in which intellectuals conducted these translations were the formal presentations that they made during public meetings sponsored by mutual aid societies. In some important instances, they utilized moralistic and nationalistic precepts in support of workers' unity. Intellectuals demonstrated that collectivist values could be used to justify specific strategies such as unionism alongside efforts of a purely mutualist character. Like the presenters at El Congreso Mexicanista they often spoke about the need for moral rejuvenation and civic participation. Many of them, however, sought to promote the values of mutualism, fraternalism, and reciprocity within larger political struggles that sought to effectuate change in both Mexico and the United States. One of the most sought-after speakers in Laredo, one who contributed to this discourse on culture and politics, was Sara Estela Ramírez.[41]

Ramírez, a teacher, poet, journalist, and early supporter of the P L M, came to Laredo around 1895 from Saltillo, Coahuila, where she attended a teachers' school named Ateneo Fuentes. Like many other Mexicana teachers that arrived in South Texas during the turn of the century, she may have been recruited by one of the many mutual aid societies and

Commemorating historical events, figures, and themes at a
Brownsville private school — Benito Juárez — directed by Luz
Guillén, 1917. *Courtesy Harry Lund Collection, Archives
Division, Texas State Library, Austin*

groups of parents that established private schools, or *escuelitas,* in
response to the experience of exclusion and segregation in the public
schools. As a teacher, she joined numerous other young, usually single,
women who, by virtue of their roles as educators, assumed highly
respected roles as intellectuals and community leaders. During the twelve
years that she lived in Laredo, Ramírez was especially notable for her
literary activity in local Spanish-language newspapers, including poems
and articles in two of her own, *La Corregidora* and *La Aurora,* and
for her political association with the P L M.[42]

Ramírez's writings and speeches clearly place her within the liberal
political tradition that produced some of the more radical critiques of
the economy, the society, and the state in Mexico prior to the revolution. As one of the earliest supporters of the anti-Díaz P L M movement,
Ramírez exhibited a positivist style of thought and political nationalism that was popular in Mexico at the time. Underlying her critiques
was a view of change as inevitable in its evolutionary thrust towards
a more egalitarian society in a Mexico properly governed by just laws
and guided by morally responsible behavior among the country's citi-

zenry and leadership. Ramírez added an impressive ethical outlook that condemned exploitation and oppression and that justified cooperative ideals as the foundation for struggles in Mexico as well as in the United States. She gave a full exposition of her views in a talk during the twenty-fourth anniversary celebration of La Sociedad de Obreros, Igualdad y Progreso.[43]

Ramírez proposed the ideals of altruism and mutualism practiced by La Sociedad as moral guideposts for solidarity among workers seeking to build effective working-class unity throughout the world. She gave rhetorical force and ethical meaning to this view with a thematic allusion to the good and humane nature of people within a framework of determinism and free will. Ramírez's talk was in three parts. First, she complimented the organization for waging a "noble struggle" against such evil forces as egoism and avarice within its ranks. The organization's membership was bound together by a "law of humanity, by a sense of spiritually innate altruism." She used both altruism and mutualism synonymously to mean a sense of fraternal respect, and spiritual and material assistance, values that were within the reach of everyone by the very nature of being humans. This, according to Ramírez, was made evident by the exemplary behavior of the members of La Sociedad.

In the second part of her talk, she recounted the converse state of affairs among workers in general. They were alienated, divided, disorganized, and subject to failure as workers in struggle. They lacked both a spiritual sense of fraternity, reciprocity, and the knowledge that "their arms maintain the wealth and growth of industry." Sometimes even unions lacked a sense of common interest and purpose. Ramírez concluded by exhorting Mexican workers in the audience to unite and to draw from within, "something grand, something divine, that will make us sociable, that will ennoble us as human beings."

Ramírez reasoned that nature equipped humans with the spiritual capacity to practice fraternity. Humans, however, had created conditions that bound them to violate this universal law. Often, these violations were conscious products of the free will. A return to the natural order meant an acceptance of the dictates of nature. Only in total harmony among themselves could workers be complete human beings. As moral statements, their logic legitimated communitarian values as cornerstones in a workers' struggle and justified its continuance until an inevitable reconstructed end was achieved.

The writings of José María Mora, a socialist orator and labor leader from Laredo, also demonstrate support for the ethic of mutuality as the basis for local and international workers' struggles. History records little about Mora. He was actively involved in mutualista and unionist activities and may have been a member of Federal Labor Union, No. 11953, an AFL affiliate. He also published extensively in local newspapers on the need for political unity by Mexicans as workers. Mora delivered a speech before El Congreso Mexicanista as a member and official delegate of La Sociedad. In 1918, he once again achieved local prominence when he was elected president of a typographical union affiliated with the AFL.[44]

Like Ramírez, Mora propagated political ideas with an explicit moral thrust that he associated with the work of mutual aid societies. He also used nature to justify equality, fraternity, and reciprocity and to describe the objective conflict between workers and the bourgeoisie. Mora also urged the moral revitalization of workers' consciousness within mutual aid societies and labor unions. Moreover, he argued that it was especially important for Mexican workers to establish a natural order of equality and fraternity.

Mora believed that nature embodied reason in its most pure form and applied this reason without regard to alleged differences among humans and plants. It was as if nature prescribed moral behavior, treating everyone equally: "That is why we say that nature manifests EQUALITY; thus, in this sense we are all equal."[45] However, social forces and the political machinations of the bourgeoisie undermined this equality. The bourgeoisie justified the class structure and its privileged position in society through alliances with the state and its military apparatus and by claiming a special redeeming relationship with God. More importantly, the bourgeoisie reinforced its position with repressive actions against organized workers. This was the case with the textile workers in Orizaba, Mexico, and the railway workers in Laredo, Texas.[46] Mora suggested that the privileged classes were morally corrupt and beyond hope of true redemption. Thus, it fell on the actual producers in society, the workers, to redirect the course of humanity towards equality and fraternity.

Mora believed that divisions among workers were human creations and unnatural. The deliberate political actions of the bourgeoisie and its defenders often maintained these divisions. It was necessary for workers to understand that they had common material interests. They also had a moral obligation to practice equality and fraternity. Once in harmony among themselves, within the organizations that practiced the basic laws of humanity, workers were further obligated to extend principles of cooperation and support beyond their organizational confines. This meant that workers should treat other poor people with equal respect. Mora reasoned: "If we are happy when we unite as brothers, inspired by a principle of mutual protection, with common rights, without causing each other harm, without offending or even mildly hurting our fellow workers, we will be happier when everyone refrains from abusing the weak and defenseless."[47] Unity was sequential and directional. It began with workers in struggle. It involved mobilization and sought moral salvation. In Texas, Mexican workers were to fulfill the historical imperative of effective working class unity.

Mora's call for working class unity and struggle at El Congreso Mexicanista suggested popular support for the ethic of mutuality as an essential organizing element among Mexican workers. He reminded the delegates that "The issue that we are concerned with at this moment directs us to work for the unification of the Mexican worker and that united as one complete family we will be guided by the principle of fraternity."[48] Fraternity, according to Mora, was an inherent predisposition among humans, who often denied it by contributing to the oppression of others. This was the reason why in the mutual aid and fraternal societies, "it is said 'one for all and all for one,' and the avaricious ones say everything for us and damn the people."[49]

Conclusion

Feelings of indignation and concern over the effects of discrimination, inequality, and violence gave special importance to the working class ethic of mutuality as a source of Mexicanist unity and identity. In the face of divisions and difficult living and working conditions, Mexicans looked inward and reinforced an outlook that not only gave them a sense of importance, but also a meaningful recourse to address their myriad problems. Mutual aid societies reflected the popular ethic of mutuality and reinforced it when they assumed political responsibility for promoting its values of fraternalism, reciprocity, and altruism through self-discipline, internal services of mutual support, and civic involvement.

The leadership gave added meaning to collectivist and egalitarian ideals with a language of Mexicanist struggle and righteous cause. The members offered concrete examples of the proper moral behavior expected of truly responsible Mexicans in their communities. Intellectuals, in turn, provided refined philosophical formulations that translated moral precepts into specific political strategies and goals. The allusions to a God-like Nature by intellectuals like Ramírez and Mora suggests an added frame of reference, a Christian belief system that was popular among the largely Catholic Mexican population.

Although other political groups like the PLM also made organizing appeals on the basis of a collective Mexican identity and unifying cultural values, Ramírez and Mora demonstrated that calls for Mexican workers' struggles also drew inspiration and meaning from the values of mutualism. These values may have originated in a working class culture, but they acquired a Mexicanist political meaning in a world that often was defined in racial and nationalist terms. The result was the elaboration of a moralistic and nationalistic political culture that served as a basis for promoting several kinds of labor organizations.

Chapter Five

Unionism on the Border: Federal Labor Union No. 11953, 1905–1907

The familiar resolve for self-organization evident among mutualistas provided an early and impressive case of union organizing in the work of Federal Labor Union (FLU) No. 11953 of Laredo. The FLU began its singular history in 1905 as an independent workers' organization composed mainly of Mexican laborers employed at the local shops of Los Ferrocarriles Nacionales de México, or the Mexican National. It quickly obtained an AFL charter and assumed a central role in a campaign to promote unionism in the city and the surrounding area during an approximately two-year period from 1905 through 1907. Although the union had a short life, it left a memory as one of the most active and successful workers' organizations in the South Texas area. Two of its most lasting impressions were a devoted adherence to the popular unifying value of mutualism and a socialist ideology with an internationalist character.

The FLU represented two important traditions within the AFL. First of all, it typified a mode of entry often reserved for minority workers and immigrants in the United States. The AFL normally utilized the federal labor union, an industrial form of organization that disregarded job classification or occupational standing, to incorporate workers who lacked skills or who were isolated from the rest of the labor movement. The FLU served this important function among largely Mexican skilled and unskilled workers who were excluded from the labor movement by virtue of their geographical isolation and by the craft and racial exclusivity of the few Anglo unions in Laredo. Although the FLU continued to organize on an inclusive industrial or Mexicanist basis, it also endorsed craft unionism to accommodate the wishes of skilled groupings within the FLU and to build a family of independent unions under one federated roof in the city.[1]

The FLU represented still another trend within the trade union movement. As an industrial union professing socialism, the Laredo group ostensibly belonged to a political camp that challenged the exclusive craft orientation of the AFL. Such socialists were said to be "boring from

110

within" in an effort to gain control of the labor movement while inside the national federation. A key element in the leftists' internal challenge was support for the strategy of organizing workers according to industries as a necessary response to management's consolidated strength and influence. The F L U reflected the accompanying ideology that called for the communalization of property and the effective unity of the entire working class.

Although the F L U's alliance with the A F L is significant, the great distance that separated the Texas group from its parent organization suggests that the Laredo union developed in a relatively independent manner from the U.S. labor movement. This means that the decisions made by F L U leaders regarding their industrial form of organization and ideological outlook coincided with A F L policies and with the socialist strategy of "boring from within" but did not involve close collaboration. F L U leaders never claimed to be part of a minority community or a dissident group within the A F L. The union leadership adopted an all-inclusive form of organization in response to the initiatives of workers and in concert with their ideological commitment to build effective working-class unity on both sides of the border. Moreover, F L U leaders normally referred to their industrial organizing strategy in Mexicanist terms rather than in terms of policy defined and determined by the parent organization.

The F L U was one of the earliest unions that Mexicans organized in the Southwest. Historians have pointed out that the F L U was part of an incipient response by Mexican workers to survive and challenge their deteriorating condition during the beginning stages of industrialization. Scholars have also underscored the themes of self-organization and discrimination in the work place and in the union hall as a common regional experience. Historians, however, have taken less notice of two interrelated factors that explain the emergence of the F L U—interactions with political movements in Mexico and the politically charged atmosphere of Laredo. Geographically isolated from the U.S. labor movement, Mexican unionists built on local political traditions. Industrial developments of the late 1800s, however, set the stage for the appearance of the F L U.

The Industrial Context

Two railroad lines, the Texas-Mexican and the International and Great Northern, reached Laredo in 1881. They joined with the Mexican National, which was building its line south from Laredo to Monterrey. This important connection bypassed the Brownsville-Matamoros crossing and effectively linked Laredo with commercial interests from Mexico, the Texas coast, St. Louis, the Midwest, and the Mississippi Valley.[2] When other railroads later reached the area, the Laredo-Nuevo Laredo crossing became the chief point of international trade between Mexico and the United States on the Rio Grande below El Paso.[3]

In the first decade of this century, Laredo acquired the accoutrements of a growing urban center as it entered a more modern industrial period. Its population grew, new industries flourished, and a locationally stable and industrialized work force increased noticeably. About thirteen thousand inhabitants, or 75 percent of the total 1907 population, were Mexican. One of the principal population sources was the large Mexican immigrant flow through the area.[4]

The Mexican National employed between four hundred and five hundred workers from this newly developing work force. They shared occupational and ethnic interests, worked in the same site, and were numerically crucial to normal shop operations. This afforded Mexican wage earners the opportunity to develop a workers' consciousness and to collectively express common interests as Mexican workers. The company assigned the majority of them the lesser-skilled positions, usually as assistants to Anglo workers who were given classifications as skilled workers.[5] Although they were generally classified as laborers, the FLU eventually insisted on recognizing the skills of some Mexican workers by seeking to establish separate craft organizations for such groupings as carpenters, blacksmiths, boilermakers, painters, tin makers, moulders, masons, and coach makers.[6]

The Mexican National was no stranger to racially organized work forces. Although the Mexican government owned a controlling interest in the line, the company had traditionally given occupational and wage preference to Anglo workers in Mexico, an issue that assumed great importance in the development of nationalism during the revolution. It was not surprising, therefore, that the Mexican National adopted racial job classification and wage policies at the Laredo shops. Mexicans were concentrated in the lesser-skilled occupations and, regardless of job classification, received seventy-five cents for a ten-hour work day while Anglo machinists earned thirty-five cents an hour or $3.50 for a ten-hour work day in 1905. The organizing response to discriminatory pay practices initially involved the formation of an industrial union for all the Mexicans employed at the railroad shops.[7]

In early 1905, approximately two hundred workers, all of whom pledged to accept no less than an agreed-upon wage at the Laredo shops of the Mexican National, organized the union as an independent workers' organization. This effort was short lived, primarily because the organization took strike actions without first generating the necessary funds to support the strikers.[8] The workers then established a second organization, which subsequently applied for an AFL charter on September 30, 1905.

For a time, the FLU assumed a central role in local political circles as the fastest growing and most combative union in the region. One of its most unique characteristics was that its leadership embraced a socialist ideology as a guide for building effective working-class unity among Mexicans in Texas and Mexico. Underlying this ideology was a moralistic and nationalistic frame of reference that the FLU shared with other community organizations. As such, the FLU represented an outgrowth of local concerns for survival that achieved formal unionist definition and that continued to embrace a sense of organizing responsibility for the entire Mexican working class.

Common origins and work experience prompted Mexican railroad workers to establish an industrial union. The clear possibility of obtaining a strong bargaining position as a large pressure group also encouraged them to organize. They obviously understood that they could not bargain effectively any other way, since the role of any single craft-oriented group of Mexicans was not deemed vital to operations. They thus opted for one large union of Mexican workers. Union organizers sought out prospective members according to one single criterion— wage-earning status. This broader organizing policy quickly led the union to include other types of workers such as miners, butchers, store clerks, water carriers, cooks, and female dancers. By the latter part of 1906, the union claimed close to a thousand members and began to form separate craft organizations for some of its workers. However, it never concluded this process. Thus, the FLU maintained its industrial character until it expired in 1907.[9]

Laredo: The Secure Environment

Economic and industrial factors reveal the organization's particular historical course. In other words, the industrialization of the local economy not only shaped work experiences but also prompted Mexican workers to adopt industrial unionism as a means to safeguard their interests. Laredo's socio-political milieu, which was tied to political developments in Mexico, however, represented a more immediate and culturally persistent influence on Mexican self-organization. This atmosphere had a determining influence on the union's success in organizing and propagandizing.

The FLU emerged against a backdrop of prior and ongoing labor organizing in northern Mexico that strongly suggests formative binational interactions. Railroad workers on the lines in the border states of Tamaulipas, Nuevo León, and Coahuila were the first to establish a regional network of workers' organizations. Workers' federations developed rapidly beginning in 1887 with the formation of the first national railroad union, La Sociedad de Ferrocarril Mexicano, across from Laredo, in Nuevo Laredo, Tamaulipas. The growth of the railroads, combined with the facility of communications and travel that the industry naturally afforded its workers, allowed unionism to flourish among them as well as among miners and agricultural workers. As a result, the FLU joined an already established family of unions and exercised close fraternal relations with workers' organizations in Nuevo Laredo as well as in other major cities in the northern region and in the interior of Mexico.[10]

The formative environment that favored Laredo unionist activity during the early 1900s was also evident when the city hosted the PLM in 1904. When the PLM established its headquarters in Laredo, it strengthened the ties of local sympathizers with other groups in Mexico and the Southwest.[11] Although the PLM eventually moved to San Antonio to escape the harassment of Mexican and U.S. authorities, Magonistas like Ramírez, Juana B. Gutiérrez de Mendoza, and Elisa Acuña y Rosete continued to reinforce the border city's reputation as an international center of PLM activity. Internal divisions at San Antonio later led them to return to Laredo, where they reestablished *La Corregidora* and *Vésper* with circulation in Texas and in Mexico. When the post office denied them mailing privileges, they began writing *La Protesta Nacional,* another PLM paper which claimed Saltillo as its place of publication although it was published in Laredo. The women subsequently moved to Mexico City, where they continued publishing *Vésper.* Ramírez returned to Laredo, whle the other two women maintained close relations with her and with the FLU as officers of La Agrupación de Gremios Trabajadores, a Mexico City federation that sought to promote "Mexican socialism" through yet another newspaper, *Anáhuac.*[12]

Aside from the previously noted instances of binational interaction involving workers and PLM sympathizers in the Laredo area, the official organ of the FLU, *El Defensor del Obrero,* placed the union within Mexico's labor orbit with its constant sharing of news, information, and opinion with newspapers and workers' organizations south of the international line. The weekly socialist newspaper gave continuous and extensive coverage to railroad workers' grievances and strikes. The paper first appeared in July, 1906, ten months after the railroad workers formed the union. It issued its last number during the union's waning days, in March, 1907. The union had firm control over the newspaper, with the president and secretary, Rafael E. Guevara and Luis G. Alvarado, serving as the paper's editor and administrator, respectively.[13]

The editors of *El Defensor* and the leadership of the FLU expressed a fully elaborated socialist ideology with an internationalist thrust that can only be explained by prior experience in Mexico's labor struggles that exhibited like-minded formulations. *El Defensor* also informed its readers about important U.S. labor organizations such as the Western Federation of Miners and a New York-based federation of Jewish unions. The paper, however, did not provide comparable coverage to such organizations nor did it enter into substantive collaborative relationships with groups outside northern Mexico and the border region. The most obvious exception involved the affiliated relationship with the AFL, a fact that spoke more to the need for practical help in advancing the unionist and socialist cause than to any prior organic tie with U.S. labor.[14]

Other Laredo newspapers that supported labor made the ground fertile for the development of unionism in the border region, especially in Laredo. Papers with binational circulations like *La Crónica, Evolución, El Demócrata Fronterizo, La Corregidora, La Protesta Nacional,* and *El Chinaco,* although at times disagreeing over the merits of socialism or the course of the Mexican revolution, professed strong adherence to the value of workers' unity. Moreover, such editors as Sara Estela Ramírez and Paulino Martínez, local PLM sympathizers, maintained close working relations with labor groups in Monterrey, Saltillo, Río Blanco, Mexico City, and other cities and urged unionization among workers on both sides of the international line.[15]

The editor of *El Demócrata Fronterizo,* one of the most visible supporters of unionism, affirmed his long-standing views on unions and workers' demands for better wages by stating that "We have publicly expressed our doctrine in favor of the working people, and we have on numerous occasions supported the worker in strikes."[16]

The newspaper pointed out that readers needed only to inspect its coverage during the first twenty years of publication to recognize its sympathy with unions and workers' demands for wage increases.[17] This support was evident when it publicly endorsed the newly founded FLU in 1906: "The 'Federal Labor Union' is one of the best Societies of workers established in Laredo. It has an increasingly large number of useful members, as was witnessed during the recent February 22 [George Washington Day] parade. In addition to being mutualist, in the full sense of the word, it is a cooperativist organization with savings and even insurance benefits."[18] The paper further affirmed its support by reprinting a leaflet that union members distributed during the parade. The leaflet was representative of fliers that the FLU used during its organizing campaigns in Laredo and Nuevo Laredo. *El Demócrata Fronterizo* joined in making the following appeal:

Are you satisfied with your present condition?

Do you wish to continue being a slave to the bourgeois?

Do you want to do something to assure your future well-being?

Do you want to ready the projectiles that you shall use tomorrow to assure victory in the formidable struggle for existence?

If you think accordingly, quickly join the Federal Labor Union
Number 11953 and you will find yourself happily among its
members.

Do not, for one instant, forget that in union there is strength.
"Labor Omnia Vincit."[19]

Newspaper coverage of Labor Day celebrations provides additional
evidence that unionism in Laredo enjoyed a climate of public approval
during the first decade of the twentieth century. *The Laredo Times,* for
example, described the September, 1906, Labor Day festivities as the
"Biggest Celebration in History of Laredo's Labor Unions." The paper
called the parade the "Longest Labor Procession Ever Seen Here."[20] It
included city officials, police officers, firemen, machinists, boilermakers, and the F L U.[21] The workers in the parade reflected confidence and
a distinct sense of group identity. Two groups of Anglo workers—the
boilermakers and the machinists—wore shirts, pants, ties, and belts in
two different black and white combinations. Their less aristocratically
inclined Mexican brethren, members of the F L U, constituted the largest
group. They dressed in overalls, as a demonstration of their working-
class status.[22]

The Labor Day celebration of 1907 was equally as impressive. All
the local businesses closed their doors to join in the festivities. The au-
diences heard "prominent local Spanish-speaking orators" and watched
a parade that included twelve local labor organizations with combined
numbers described in the thousands. According to *The Laredo Times,*
the participants included the Council of Trade Orders; Master Blacksmiths, Cuauhtémoc, No. 240; Tinners Union, No. 1883; Apprentice
Blacksmiths, No. 304; Boilermakers, Rio Grande Lodge, No. 234; Foun-
drymen, No. 36; Miners' Union No. 12340, of Minera; United Workmen, No. 11953; Caballeros de Honor, No. 14; Obreros Society; and
Hijos de Juárez Society.[23] Favorable press coverage and the F L U's recognized standing in the local family of labor signified support for its well-
known activities.

Links between the F L U and local alliances were evident on other occasions. At least three organizations sent representatives to demonstrate
support during the union's first annual anniversary celebration. These
were La Sociedad Mutualista, Hijos de Juárez; La Sociedad de Obreros,

Igualdad y Progreso; and La Sociedad de Señoras y Señoritas. The festive spirit surrounding the celebration also gave notice of the prominent role that it played in the community. Following the installation of officers, the union sponsored an evening of festivities that included music by the popular Amado Ayala Orchestra, poetry readings by local youth, and presentations by well-known orators serving as the official representatives of local organizations.[24]

The planners of El Congreso Mexicanista also demonstrated the leading role that Laredo played in the larger political arena. The editors of *La Crónica* described Laredo as a home front, one of the last lines of defense against forces that threatened the well-being and future of Mexicans.[25] Mexicans from Texas "live in an environment poisoned by animal passions," noted Clemente Idar.[26] Laredo, on the other hand, provided a more secure environment:

> Here, we have not been trampled in such a manner. We have all the privileges and guarantees in private and public life, the same rights enjoyed by other citizens in this country, a large number of Mexicans in local positions with the city and federal government, banking and commerce, indeed, Mexican capital dominates. These conditions are the result of supreme efforts by our people, because we are in the majority and we remain united, ample reason for feeling happier than our countrymen in some places in the state, where they are constantly suffering numerous acts of oppression and abuses.[27]

The newspaper added a note of confidence regarding the political influence of Mexicans in Laredo: "Laredo, Texas, has demonstrated the value of consolidating Mexican interests for expressed purposes, and it is not difficult to see that the state of things in this community is solidly based, and that it will take many years to destroy the might of the local Mexican masses."[28]

The participants in El Congreso Mexicanista, especially Guevara, Alvarado, and José María Mora, a frequent contributor to *El Defensor,* no doubt agreed with the editors of *La Crónica.* Although the FLU had folded by then, it stood as an early reminder that Laredo granted workers enough latitude to develop unionism.[29]

Clearly, there were limits to unionist approval in Laredo. Debates over socialism and strike actions that pitted the FLU against the otherwise supportive *La Revista Mexicana* and *El Demócrata Fronterizo* underscored this fact. The exchange reached a dramatic peak during the early part of 1907, at a time when the union was involved in a bitter strike against the Mexican National. *El Demócrata Fronterizo* levelled serious criticism at union leaders for espousing radical political doctrines and for allegedly misrepresenting the views of the membership. *El Defensor* skillfully handled these charges by answering each with well-written and concise statements. One of the most convincing rebuttals made reference to the leadership's elected status, the union's rapid growth, and the paper's large circulation as ample proof of membership and readership approval.[30]

Although the debate between *El Defensor* and *El Demócrata Fronterizo* was spirited and at times even acrimonious, the newspapers never disagreed on the need for workers to form unions and to build working-class unity. The editors often disagreed on such matters as political philosophies, particular views on issues, and the general propriety of a given tactic employed by the union. There is no evidence, however, that *El Demócrata Fronterizo* ever criticized *El Defensor,* the union, or its leadership for promoting pure and simple unionism. The editors of *El Defensor* nevertheless took the critique seriously, concluding that support for union policies had waned as the union continued to strike. They suggested that middle-class journalists were abandoning the temporary alliance as the struggle instensified. Already a well-established union with a reputation as a defender of impoverished and exploited workers, the FLU continued to organize successfully and to hold steadfastly to its views as the morally justifiable and politically necessary response to Capital. These were accomplishments that few Mexican workers' organizations in other cities were able to claim.

The union's heyday period between 1905 and 1907 was short, but the group's dramatic organizing and strike activity denoted enthusiasm and discipline. By the middle of 1906, the FLU had fully organized Mexican workers in the local shops. It numbered seven hundred members in Laredo and approximately three hundred in three mining areas in the city's outskirts. The union's membership in Laredo constituted a significant part of the population, which was sixteen thousand in 1906. Assuming that each union member represented a household, conservatively estimated at five members, the aggregate family total was thirty-five hundred, or 21.8 percent of the total population. This suggests that a significant part of Laredo's population was directly associated with unionism and socialist thought.[31] The FLU thus demonstrated an impressive capacity to wage successful organizing and strike activity in Laredo during a two-year period.

After a series of highly successful organizing drives, in 1907 the FLU suffered a critical and insurmountable defeat at the hands of the Mexican National.[32] The strikes were occasioned by a salary dispute in Laredo in the autumn of 1906. During its protracted struggle with the FLU, the Mexican National twice moved its shops across the river to Nuevo Laredo, adding to striking grievances the issues of harassment of unionists and the hiring of strikebreakers.[33]

Strikes and Consequences

The union waged its first general strike on November 10, 1906, one year after its founding. The entire membership joined the strike, though only around three hundred members were railroad workers.[34] The union's secretary explained the unified action by noting that "the strike affects the entire membership no matter where they are employed."[35] The union demanded a better salary after noting the ease with which Anglo machinists had acquired a wage increase through the use of the strike against the Mexican National.[36]

The Anglo machinists had struck twice in 1906. In January twenty-eight members of the union walked off their jobs to protest the discharge of a fellow worker. Ten months later a wage dispute prompted the Anglo union to strike again. Management settled both conflicts promptly and amicably.[37] After the second strike the general superintendent of mine operations underscored the good relations that existed despite the strikes: "They have acted very gentlemanly and we do not think that there is any hard feeling existing on either side."[38] The company considered moving its shops to Nuevo Laredo but instead granted the union a three-cent hourly increase. As a consequence, the standard wage for machinists became thirty-eight cents an hour, or between \$110 and \$135 a month.[39]

The FLU reacted to the settlement with the Anglo union by demanding a twenty-five cent increase over the prevailing wage of seventy-five cents for a ten-hour work day. Union representatives met with company officials and submitted a formal request for a wage increase. The company publicly refused to comply, adding that only its board of directors could answer the demands at the next regularly scheduled meeting in April, 1907. Obviously incensed at differential treatment, FLU members convened in general session and decided formally to request permission to strike from the AFL executive committee. The federation agreed to the request, and the union struck on November 10, 1906.[40]

Fifteen days after the strike began, however, the union faced a runaway shop and a stubborn management. *El Defensor* boldly announced that none of the strikers had wavered. It added resolutely that "we promised when the strike began that it would be a fight to the death and that the Mexican National will have to leave the state of Texas or submit to Federal Labor Union No. 11953."[41] When the general manager of the railroad company arrived in town, the union refused to approach him. *El Defensor* exclaimed, "We are here to demand and not to request. If his excellency, the Manager, wishes a settlement he ought to call a meeting with the union's officers."[42]

A commission of six businessmen and prominent citizens in vain approached the company and offered to arbitrate the differences. During the third week of January, 1907, the general superintendent, Alvarado, and other union representatives met to discuss the strike. James Leonard, AFL representative from San Antonio, arranged the meeting, after which the company announced it would reopen the Laredo shops, rehire the strikers, and increase the wages to one dollar per day. The company, however, asserted its right to hire scab labor, unilaterally to determine employment policy, and to fix wage scales. This was tantamount to a refusal to recognize the union, because the company's position undermined the FLU's basis for bargaining in the future. The union found the company's offer unacceptable and announced that the strike would continue. *El Defensor* also noted that the central issue in the strike had become a racial one.[43] The general superintendent was quoted as saying that "he would have found the demands just and reasonable if they had been submitted by Anglo workers. But since they [Mexicans] were indios, the demands were unacceptable."[44]

The general superintendent became the focus of rancored attention. He had previously held the position of master machinist and, according to *El Defensor,* had once said he favored Mexicans in the shops because they were better workers than "gringos." Adding a touch of ridicule, the paper noted, "he even went as far as saying that he was Mexican."[45] The general superintendent reflected the company's uncompromising character. He, as well as other company representatives, introduced a highly volatile issue into the fray. The company was now vulnerable to charges of racism.

Additionally, management employed two familiar union-busting tactics, strikebreakers and court injunctions. Company officials contracted Laredo and out-of-town residents as strikebreakers. According to *El Defensor,* Laredo was so politically advanced that the company was unable to secure the scabs that it needed. It obtained strikebreakers by recruiting workers from outside Laredo and by moving more of its operations to Nuevo Laredo. During the peak of the strike, the company zealously guarded its workers by boarding them in the Laredo shops and by providing them protective escorts.[46]

The company obtained an injunction allegedly to restrain strikers from interfering with the strikebreakers. A local court tried at least twelve strikers for violating the injunction, and sentenced eight of them to serve forty-eight hours in the county jail. In two other instances the local police arrested sixteen union members.[47] According to *The Laredo Times,* strikebreakers "were attacked by a large mob of men and women," presumably strikers and sympathizers.[48] Meanwhile, the strikers maintained a daily vigil outside the shops to prevent the entrance of scabs. They also stopped railroad traffic but avoided interfering with the movement of cars carrying U.S. mail. Careful observance of government regulations allowed the union to continue its strike without federal intervention. However, city and county law officials intervened in the strike, presumably to prevent a violent confrontation between scabs and strikers.[49]

The union reached a favorable strike settlement on February 8, 1907, and the Mexican National decided to move its shops back to Laredo. It was a time for rejoicing. The union held a public dance, and the strikers thanked everyone that had lent support. The celebration continued the next day at a local park when the Amado Ayala Band gave a free public concert.[50] Not everyone shared the festive spirit. *The Laredo Times* expressed concern with the "acts of violence" that occurred during the strike. In obvious reference to the expressed disenchantment of *La Revista Mexicana* and *El Demócrata Fronterizo,* the paper also warned that "some articles that are appearing in the Spanish weekly styled the Defensor del Obrero and the organ of the federation of labor are causing some consideration on the part of some prominent citizens and are likely to cause some serious trouble."[51]

Trouble did occur. The company chose to retain some of its scab labor, and some strikers refused to return to work.[52] Also, one month after the strike settlement, the Mexican smelter workers walked off their jobs in protest of the recent hiring of a scab worker. The FLU threatened to call a general strike, but the company immediately conceded to the demands of the strikers.[53]

The union continued to negotiate for the removal of other scab workers. Labor leaders specifically protested the presence of a foreman who was identified as the company's principal scab-hiring agent during the November strike. The continued mistreatment of union workers and the company's refusal to answer grievances compelled union leaders to call a general meeting on March 18, 1907.[54] By unanimous approval the participants voted to stage a general strike if the Mexican National did not concede to the union's demands that same day. The company refused to comply, and the workers struck once again. Although the outcome of this strike cannot be determined conclusively, a favorable accord seems to have been tentatively established. The presumed victory was short-lived. Soon after the March strike the company once again transferred its shops to Nuevo Laredo and the union experienced a sharp decline in membership.[55] Unionization continued in the growing railroad work force of Nuevo Laredo, although the union now became affiliated with Mexican labor federations.[56]

A growing feeling of confidence may have hastened the union's decision to strike in March. During a four-month period the union had waged two successful strikes, increased its memberships significantly, officially installed a union at Minera, a nearby mining community, and organized new craft unions in Laredo. The union, however, failed to organize enough craft unions outside the railroad industry. Thus, the call for a general strike never became a viable means with which to force a concession from the company. Moreover, an inflexible economy and the impoverishment of its members added to the union's problems. Unemployed members, unable to secure employment, were forced to leave the city, thus weakening the organization.[57] Even when workers received financial support from the AFL's strike relief fund, large numbers were forced to seek employment outside Laredo.[58]

Organizing Workers

Despite the union's ultimate defeat, FLU leaders maintained an ambitious strategy that sought to organize the city's total work force. Beginning in July, 1906, the union's paper made broad-based appeals to its readership to join the FLU. By the start of 1907, however, divergent craft interests and tactical considerations forced the railroad workers to consider restructuring the union along craft lines. Some workers remained recalcitrant after the February, 1907, strike settlement and separately continued to strike in protest of the hiring of scabs.[59] Although the membership eventually voted to support this grievance, it may have felt that such strict interdependence among its occupational subgroups produced a constant taxing pressure.

Nine days after the strike settlement *El Defensor* carried the first official call for the creation of separate craft unions from among the numerous types of workers that the FLU had organized. The newspaper announced official plans to establish unions composed of miners, carpenters, blacksmiths, blacksmith assistants, boilerworker assistants, painters, printers, tin makers, moulders, machinist helpers, masons, teamsters, coach makers, butchers, store clerks, water carriers, cooks, common laborers, laundresses, and female dancers.[60] The paper later announced plans to form additional unions of barbers, electricians, brick makers, seamstresses, and cigar workers.

The last planned organizational phase included the formation of a central labor council with delegates from the newly installed unions as members. The union expired before it could effectively create separate craft organizations for all of its members. One of the newspaper's last issues told of three FLU-generated unions that had received letters of certification from the AFL. Three other organizations were awaiting formal AFL recognition.[61] Though the FLU leadership continued to urge all Mexican workers to join the union, it was understood that they were to eventually constitute separate craft unions. The industrial form of organization thus gave some way to a craft strategy based on skill scarcity as the basis for bargaining.

In order to form a citywide labor federation complete with a central labor council and its constituent craft organizations, it was necessary to first organize a substantial number of workers. The problem of formally assigning unionists to their respective craft union could be handled during a period of incubation or after a sufficient number of workers who shared a given craft joined the FLU. Thus, successful organizing was the union's lifeblood.

The union recruited new members by publicly addressing community organizations on the importance of workers' solidarity, by organizing workers in previously unorganized industries, and by using *El Defensor* to educate workers on the need for working class unity in the Americas. By November, 1906, the union was boasting 700 members in Laredo alone. The allied independent union at the nearby community of Minera had 175 members in October, 1906, approximately 200 in November, and around 285 in March, 1907. The Laredo union was growing at the rate of ten new members per week during March, 1907.[62]

The union's expressed democratic spirit also enhanced its organizing activity and contributed to growth. It integrated wage earners regardless of occupational, nativity, and gender differences. The FLU's most successful recruitment drive among nonrailroad workers involved the outlying mining communities of Minera, Cannel, and San José. Mexican miners from these localities had long been attempting to organize for higher wages and better working conditions. The FLU responded to their requests for help by sending delegations of speakers and organizers. Some of the miners joined the FLU and formed an affiliate organization. Further organizational assistance by Laredo's union facilitated the formation of an AFL miners' union. The union sent at least three official delegations. The last one, composed of delegates representing the Laredo union and mutual aid societies, installed Mine Workers' Union No. 12340.[63]

The union also organized women. Although the membership's makeup is difficult to determine, at least three occupational groupings within the union, laundresses, dancers, and seamstresses, were ostensibly female. Women also participated in the union's second strike of November, 1906, as part of a sympathy demonstration outside the shops.[64]

The editors of *El Defensor* continually addressed the need to incorporate women. They justified this on ideological grounds, pointing out that women were also workers and subject to similar forms of exploitation. On numerous occasions, however, they also described women in patronizing terms, as "the weaker sex" who required the special protection of unions and men from the morally degenerating and economically exploitative influence of Capital.

Philosophical Guideposts

The union's political philosophy had four major components: an ideology; a statement of goals and ideals; a designation of agencies of action; and a set of theories concerning workers, society, and history.[65] The union's ideology mirrored the ethic of mutuality professed by mutual aid societies and the philosophical treatises by Ramírez and Mora based on proper moral behavior. Union officials who participated in public programs alongside officers of mutual aid societies often paid tribute to mutualism as the prevailing ethic that all responsible community organizations shared. Union leaders, however, also professed the universal application of socialist principles through worldwide union organization, an outlook that gave greater emphasis to the taking of power through direct action rather than to initiatives that only sought the ameliorization of workers' conditions.

The massive concentration of wealth, they argued, had created forces that prescribed all forms of human behavior. The wide-ranging consequences of poverty and despair had led to serious social and moral problems among workers and their families. According to *El Defensor,* economic deprivation naturally led to moral degeneracy in social relations, especially within the family unit. The editors argued that since sole breadwinners were unable to adequately provide for their families, some youngsters were forced to leave their homes and enter the labor market. The disintegration of the family continued when young women were pressured to marry men they did not love, but who promised them economic security. Adultery and divorce were two of the most disruptive outcomes.

Union spokesmen foresaw a new society unhampered by class divisions and antagonisms. This new order, according to Guevara, was already being introduced by workers "who have become convinced that fraternity must not recognize borders, who know that in unity there is strength, and who firmly outstretch their hands to fellow workers from all nations without drawing distinctions based on caste, color, or national origin."[66] Guevara and other union representatives often served notice of an impending socialist millennium that would free workers of all oppression and guarantee their defense from all types of injustices.

Some of the more immediate and intermediate goals of the union included a shorter work week, higher wages, an end to usury, a well-informed and educated citizenry, the fraternal union of all workers, and the overthrow of capitalism. It was necessary to make people aware of class antagonisms and to build a movement for the establishment of a classless society. Thus, a desire to form a more humane society, one governed by secular humanist thought that called for workers' control over the state and the means of production, guided the union's development.

The union's principal agent for change was the worker, the only true producer in society who could redirect the course of humanity through effective political unity. Although Laredo socialists most often spoke about workers in universal terms, they occasionally particularized this axiom with references to the importance of Mexican workers in the development of wealth in Mexico and the United States. They gave wide publicity to this view in their newspaper, with a notable emphasis on the need for Mexicans to join other workers in claiming what was rightfully theirs. To this end, the union waged a persistent educational program through *El Defensor*. Aside from reporting on local, Mexican, and U.S. labor struggles, *El Defensor* expounded on the need to unionize and on the moral responsibility involved in defending the rights of the working class.

The union's world view, or theoretical formulation of society and nature, had the ring of Marxist thought. It held that the historically specific capitalist mode of production and the resultant social, political, and ideological configurations in the United States and in other parts of the world determined human existence. The union's leadership argued that the worker was the only element in the economy that was capable of placing value on a given product. The worker thus was morally entitled to share equitably from the existing power and wealth. In short, "Scientific socialism is an economic theory that holds that the means of production as well as the LAND should be owned by the COMMUNITY and not by individuals that constitute a distinct class; we, socialists, demand that all the riches that have been produced, be collectively distributed among the classes that have created those riches; and that such fortunes be taken from private associations to collectively distribute among that social entity that has created those fortunes; in order to accomplish these goals we demand the cooperation of the dominated and oppressed class."[67]

Such clearly formulated ideas that declared the centrality of the working class and that called for a basic transformation of society indicated intellectual maturity and political resolve difficult to find in the history of labor in the state of Texas. *El Defensor*'s propagandizing activities provide another dimension of the union's developed and determined commitment to the Mexican working class.

Propagandizing the Cause

The special role that the editors of *El Defensor* played in advancing the socialist and unionist cause was especially evident in their use of various literary approaches. Among the most entertaining pieces of propaganda were didactic dialogues involving a character named Panchita or Francis who regularly reached accords with male and female friends on the issue of unionism. The underlying message in these dialogues was that women should look beyond their romantic inclinations and recognize in themselves and prospective mates the responsibility to structure socially meaningful relationships. In one of the first such conversations, Panchita responded to an amorous proposition by stating that her decision depended "on you proving your devotion to the working class and joining Federal Labor Union No. 11953." On another occasion, Panchita informed her friend that she ended a relationship because her male friend had crossed the picket lines in the recent FLU strike. The editors of the paper later had Francis seeking to join and recruit for the unionist cause after attending a festive program sponsored by the FLU. She had been unable to experience care free enjoyment and, in answer to a query by a friend, the absence of her male friend had nothing to do with her pensive and seemingly sad state. The FLU's devotion to the community had impressed her deeply and transformed her profoundly. *El Defensor* obviously sought to indirectly contrast the union's public expression of fidelity with the wholly personal and at times frivolous romantic relationships and commitments. According to Francis, "Those people, though humble and poor, have captured the love of our entire community with their tenacity during the strike; their orderly and peaceful conduct has become a bright star in the annals of the history of our people."[68]

The paper also printed speeches delivered by unionists and union sympathizers in Laredo and Nuevo Laredo. Though union representatives organized workers on the job site, one of their most popular methods of organizing was through the use of oratory in public meetings. These public gatherings served as a source of entertainment, information, and cultural reinforcement for the local public. For unionists, they additionally represented a chance to formally participate in popular social events and to recruit new members. It was important for union organizers to demonstrate the necessary oratorical skills to inspire a following. These formal and dramatic performances were more than mere speeches. They were an art form which unionist speakers probably mastered during their previous association with mutual aid societies. The numerous private Mexican schools in Texas that included oratory in their curriculum, no doubt, also contributed to presentation skills among community leaders and to expressions of popular approval among the public.[69]

One of the most sought-after speakers in the city was A. C. Tamez, the official orator for the union. He delivered the major presentation during the FLU's first-year anniversary celebration. Guevara also represented the union on a number of alliance-building occasions like the installation of affiliated craft unions and the establishment of Concordia, a Nuevo Laredo mutual aid society that maintained fraternal relations with the FLU throughout the life of the union. Others who spoke during the important labor day festivities assumed equally distinct positions of honor. These events gave the union and its paper the opportunity to demonstrate experiential and ideological linkages with working-class struggles around the world. Mora and Julian Buitrón, also frequent contributors to *El Defensor,* had the distinction of seeing their eloquent orations featured by the paper as part of the union's first labor day celebration in 1906.

Mora obviously drew from a master text in his repertoire, a salient characteristic in oratorical presentations. As noted later in his speech before El Congreso Mexicanista, he spoke of the worker as a self-sacrificing and morally upstanding person who came to pay tribute to a God-like image of work. Moreover, he expressed an artisanal view of work as the main source of material as well as spiritual sustenance that imbued workers with the righteous means to regain their central and autonomous role in society. The worker, exhorted Mora, "at this moment does not remember his past, nor his pain, nor his current misery. He only knows that he is a worker, and that he is fulfilling his duty by participating in this festive event, demonstrating to his brothers that he is worthy of being called a worker, and that he has the right to demand what he is entitled to as a worker."[70]

Mora also addressed the popular theme of irresponsible behavior that included allusions to individualistically oriented workers who did not know the benefits of union, fraternity, and mutualism. Workers who worked towards the "common good," on the other hand, had faith that through union they could destroy society's "evil tendencies and passions."

Buitrón, an official representative of the apprentice blacksmith union, La Unión Fronteriza No. 304 de Ayudantes Herreros de Laredo (blacksmith assistants), also spoke about the unity of workers as the most important means for individual advancement and further social progress. In the artisanal tradition of giving divine qualities to work, he gave special attention to the inevitability of this exalted sense of "union," a feature of the modernizing sweep of a rapidly industrializing global economy. According to Buitrón, the "civilizing torrent" of change had opened new possibilities for the fulfillment of workers' aspirations in the United States. Developments included new and inspiring ideas as well as well-organized, disciplined, and powerful organizations intent on "marching forward and demanding justice, respect, and all the considerations that are due . . . us the workers." The demands were justified, noted Buitrón, since the worker was the most important element in building society and in giving it hope for further social progress.[71]

Like Mora, Buitrón spoke about the worker in universal terms and without any explicit reference to the Mexican identity of his audience or to the specific political programme of the FLU and its affiliates. They were clearly giving major emphasis to the need to join the larger working-class community. By placing local organizing within the context of a world-wide struggle, they were also legitimating the work of the FLU. Less clear, however, are the ideas and opinions that speakers and their audience shared and understood. The direct association that listeners and readers could make between the speakers and the local labor struggles minimally suggests that the audience witnessed the Labor Day oratory with clear understandings regarding the need and importance for Mexicans to continue promoting left-wing unionism in Laredo. The added publicity that *El Defensor* gave these presentations clearly heightened public awareness and acceptance of the FLU-directed struggle as a legitimate expression of larger movements.

The labor weekly used still another literary approach to proselytizing. It offered its readers an opportunity to submit poems that spoke about workers and the class struggle. *El Defensor* thus marshalled the use of local poetic sensitivities and visions to give an added dimension to the call for working-class unity. Although little is known about the poets, their work varied in quality and content, a clear indication that they were both experienced as well as momentarily inspired writers. In any case, the poems represent a further illustration of the prevailing ideas and concerns shared by union leaders, members, and sympathizers.

One of the earliest poems to appear in the paper addressed the evils of alcohol, an issue that often drew the moralistic attention of mutualistas and unionists alike. The paper urged workers to resist temptation, because drinking placed them under the corrupting influence of individuals and businesses that robbed them of their hard-earned money. Echoing the admonitions of mutualistas, writers in *El Defensor* called on workers to be responsible family members and workers, and to stay away from drinking, card-playing, and even the "morally reprehensible" spectacle of the bullfight. The poet Rodolfo Menéndez gave added play to this tradition of social criticism by warning that the tavern was both "the prison and the crime" worthy of the following ominous inscription at its entrance:

> There is no hope nor comfort
> For whoever enters here,
> He will only discover in me
> Dishonor, misery, mourning,
> His body and soul will be lost
> When he enters this door.[72]

A number of poets, including one named Juan G. Holguín, opted for instilling among workers a sense of importance and purpose as the real producers in society. He went further than most in the way that he attributed divine qualities to work. God, he reasoned, "also sought to be a worker" when he opted for constructing the universe instead of creating it in an instant. Workers, moreover, fulfilled God's purpose on earth because they made Nature reach fruition as they converted the lowly piece of coal into beautiful and radiant light. In doing God's work, they were themselves transformed. The poet explicitly used coal as the metaphorical equivalent of workers who became part of the celestial plan as enlightened or politically conscious persons. Under these circumstances, workers were no less than God's priests, obeying and interpreting the sacred law. They had sufficient reason to feel meaningful and necessary.[73]

A poet named J. M. Borrego also utilized allusions to God as he urged workers to trust that work and struggle would inevitably reward them. Being poor left workers with no other alternative but to venerate work as if it were God. The worldly challenge lay in the workers' ability to recognize their true high worth so completely that they could even find pride in the sweat on their brows,

> Because nothing in this world is more beautiful
> Than to feel it roll, each and every drop.[74]

In a clear attempt to draw the public's sympathy for the FLU members who were striking at the time, Ruperto J. Aldán presented a moving story in the life of a destitute striker. The striker was forced to beg on the streets and to suffer humiliating experiences at the hands of the local constabulary and members of the upper class. He felt his greatest and constant pain, however, in not being able to feed his starving family. In one of the poem's most moving scenes, he almost ate a discarded piece of food in the street but suddenly remembered his hungry family. He rushed home and fed his desperately ill boy. The striker was momentarily relieved until things turned tragic. The child experienced convulsions and died. The father, blinded by a desperate parental concern for his child, had brought home poisoned food intended for a dog. The father immediately succumbed to grief, and the mother hopelessly directed her lament to the heavens:

> The worker fell dead.
> The mother lost her faith
> And lifting her eyes to the heavens,
> She clamored: Justice-loving God!
> Why, dear Lord, Why?[75]

A poet that signed his work anonymously as "a worker" contributed several works that consistently touched on various aspects of the workers' struggle. In a poem entitled "Poder del siglo XX," he condemned the oppressor for daring to call himself human. Like the violent beast in the jungle, the oppressor wields power against the weak and considers himself sovereign. The worker, however, has begun to accumulate power as "he kills and captures frightening beasts."[76] Additional reason for hope lay in the thought that "sooner or later justice will prevail."[77] Many of the poems as well as the printed orations that appeared in *El Defensor* expressed this hopeful view to encourage workers to join the local struggle. The cause was just, according to "the worker," because it held the promise of a reconstructed future that was free of want and oppression and that accorded them due respect.[78]

Poets also conveyed a defiant tone in their treatment of the class struggle. Joaquín Dicenta may have issued one of the most rebellious views when he used the voice of a politicized worker to issue the ultimate threat against the propertied class.

> From this lowly work bench I defy you
> See me well; your building is mine;
> Mine from the very top to the foundation,
> Mine because my arms have built it.
> And these arms, the arms that build
> Are also the ones that can destroy.[79]

Dicenta's poem appeared in the union's weekly at the same time that the FLU was waging its first major strike against the Mexican National and leading the initial organizing drive among mine workers in the area. Such complementarity was repeated often during the life of the paper, suggesting ongoing support for the union. Literary production that favored unionism also represented part of the FLU's strategy to win over converts and to encourage its members in the class struggle.

Conclusion

The FLU was the first known independent Mexican workers' organization from deep South Texas to formally align with the AFL. This underscores further the themes of isolation and self-reliance evident among the independent workers' organizations. The proximity to Mexico, along with the arrival of increasing numbers of workers and political exiles from Mexico, contributed to the close relations that the FLU maintained with Mexico. This may explain the union's socialist programme, which expressed ethical concerns similar to the ones expressed by Ramírez and Mora and also exhibited a theoretical focus on workers that was evident in the anarcho-syndicalist formulations of the San Diego insurgents.

The FLU was first organized among a large and concentrated work force employed by an industry that was important in both local and international economies. Moreover, the shared work experiences of the large core membership gave the FLU a sound organizational base. The Mexican National and the advanced stage of capitalist development that it represented provided the FLU with a natural and immediate target for its socialist critiques.

One of the most obvious strategies of the FLU was to lead an effort to unionize a large number of workers in the city. In other words, it did not simply seek an improvement in the working conditions of its members. Reflective of the regional organizing strategy popular among other community organizations, the FLU sought the unification of local workers both in order to improve general social and economic conditions in Laredo and to contribute to a workers' struggle throughout the Americas. Its leadership openly and formally described the local struggle within a broader context of workers versus management. As a consequence of this organizing strategy, the FLU formed alliances with other workers' organizations from the Laredo area and Mexico, and headed general organizing activities during public gatherings, at work sites, and through its newspaper. An added characteristic was the union's attention to the organization of women. Although it partly justified this on paternalistic grounds, the union leadership also promoted the incorporation of women as part of its general political programme in favor of unifying the entire working class.

The FLU's organizing strategy, however, did not involve a well-defined political position on racial discrimination and inequality, both problems seriously affecting its broad potential constituency in South Texas. Admittedly, Laredo did not exhibit the same degree of anti-Mexican sentiments nor the racial organization of work evident in the upper part of South Texas. However, racial discrimination and inequality was evident in Mexico and at Laredo, especially in the railroad shops. This was made dramatically clear when management refused on racial grounds to negotiate with union representatives. This case, as well as ongoing wage and occupational discrimination against Mexican railroad workers in both Mexico and Texas, stirred national feelings and passions. Yet the FLU's leadership rarely made explicit appeals for national unity, nor did it ever elaborate a formal, guiding treatise on the question of race in the socio-economy for the labor movement that it wished to build among Mexican workers from South Texas.

Despite the somewhat rigid class outlook, the FLU made important contributions to Mexican labor activity. It organized a large number of workers and led a collaborative effort with other workers' organizations from Laredo to build a local labor movement. Also, the FLU provided refined critiques of the socio-economic order that served as ideological guideposts for its membership and for the Mexican society at large. To its added credit, the FLU demonstrated that Mexican workers from South Texas would participate in the U.S. labor movement despite the minimal support by the AFL leadership and the aloofness of the local Anglo railroad brotherhoods and unions.

Chapter Six

Socialists and Magonistas
in the Cotton Belt, 1912–16

Five years after the Mexican National had moved its shops to Nuevo
Laredo and the FLU had expired, another group of Mexican workers
in the southwestern tip of the cotton belt area embraced the cause of
labor and socialism under the banners of the Texas Socialist Party and
the Partido Liberal Mexicano (PLM). Mexican socialists from the cotton belt belonged to approximately twenty industrial unions of farm
renters, farm laborers, and urban workers affiliated with the Texas Socialist Party's economic organizations, the Renters' Union of America
and its successor, the Land League of America. A substantial number
of these unionists maintained a close relationship with the PLM, an affiliation that began during the first decade when they participated in
the initial organizing campaigns and armed uprisings of the revolution
in northern Mexico.[1]

The combined membership of the Mexican socialist unions was approximately one thousand in 1915, the peak year for Mexican participation in the Land League. The New Braunfels and Seguín locals, the
largest unions, boasted a combined membership of 215 workers.[2] F. A.
Hernández, one of the leading organizers in the Land League, reported
in 1914 that he was corresponding with twenty Mexican locals throughout the region.[3] The socialist union network included locals at Fentress,
New Braunfels, Marion, Clear Springs, Seguín, Devine, Whitsett, Camp-
bellton, Mathis, Tilden, Rockdale, Nordheim, Runge, Helena, York-
town, Charco, Cuero, Thomaston, Belmont, Hunter, and "in Travis
County and adjoining counties."[4] Organizing activity continued until
the early part of 1916 and may have increased the number of locals and
total membership figures.

The influence of the PLM among Mexican socialists clearly preceded
the arrival of the Texas Socialist Party. Many socialist locals originated
as PLM clubs during the first decade and subsequently operated as dual
organizations affiliated with the Texas Socialist Party and La Agrupación Protectora Mexicana, one of the most active federations of Mexican community organizations of the 1910s. These early alliances dem-

onstrated that the community was intimately tied to political developments in Mexico and consequently reflected prominent trends in that country. The association with the P L M imbued the Mexican socialist cause in Texas with an energized sense of political purpose expressed in highly impressive organizing drives and a brand of socialism that was more radical than the Socialist Party's agrarian unionism and parliamentary politics.

The Socialist Party

The predominantly Anglo Texas Socialist Party was formed in 1903 as part of a growing leftist challenge against management and against A F L conservatism that swept the country during the first two decades of the twentieth century. In 1911 the party adopted the I W W model of industrial unionism to form the Renters' Union of America in its fight against the evils of "landlordism." The labor federation sought to organize the growing number of displaced farmers and exploited farm laborers in order to build an agrarian contingent within the party and thus strengthen the cause for the election of socialist candidates and the communalization of land. The party broadened its operations in 1914 when it replaced the Renters' Union with the Land League of America and began to welcome urban workers into its ranks.[5]

The founding convention of the Renters' Union adopted a plank which argued that use and occupancy conferred the only genuine title to the land. Party leadership also held that a confiscatory tax should be levied on land withheld from cultivation for speculative purposes. Texas socialists additionally agitated for a state governmental policy of rent regulation to ensure that farm renters were not defrauded. Socialist campaigns in favor of land taxation and more equitable land rental practices led Gov. James E. Ferguson to support the passage of a new land rental law in 1915. In a more conservative vein, socialists rejected the orthodoxy of national leaders who believed that the rural petite bourgeoisie, or small farm owners and tenants, should be excluded from the organization.

The Renters' Union also exhibited a narrow class consciousness when it excluded blacks and expressed strong antipathies toward Mexicans. The federation removed this barrier in 1912 and adopted a policy of incorporating minority workers through parallel unions. Despite this policy change, the rank and file, as well as some of the leadership of the Land League, continued to express racial concerns about Mexican tenants as job competitors and laborers as low-wage workers. The decision to admit Mexicans and blacks thus constituted a significant demonstration of interracial solidarity in an otherwise racially divided political landscape.

Professing solidarity was one thing. Incorporating Mexicans was another, especially since their disenfranchised status did not promise an attractive return at the polls. The politics of unity presented yet another test of the declared principle of solidarity. Mexico's revolution, particularly its more radical precursory activity represented in Texas by the PLM, offered Texas socialists the opportunity to practice international solidarity with like-minded groups seeking revolutionary change in Mexico. Party leadership often spoke about the Mexican Revolution as a harbinger of possible world-wide convulsions and endorsed the political and military campaigns headed by figures like Ricardo Flores Magón, Francisco Villa, and Emiliano Zapata. On a few occasions party spokespersons adopted the revolutionary rhetoric of these leaders and hinted at armed struggle in Texas. Support for the revolution, however, rarely went beyond borrowed language, poorly informed journalistic activity, and support for jailed Magonistas or PLM activists. At one point Texas socialists even discredited the revolutionary fervor in Mexico in an attempt to present their ideas as rational and non-threatening alternatives to change. According to a Renters' Union petition with fifty thousand signatures that was delivered to Gov. Oscar B. Colquitt in support of a new land tax law, "our people have enough education and enlightenment to prevent bloodshed on this side of the Rio Grande."[6] Possibly because they feared political repercussions, Texas socialists did not build a formal, lasting alliance with the PLM or maintain a relationship of active support for any revolutionary group in Mexico. A possible drawback could have been an Anglo rank and file whose idea of international working-class unity was limited by widespread anti-Mexican feelings. The leadership often shared these antipathies in the party's official newspaper, *The Rebel*. They also described Mexican immigrants as possible job competitors rather than as likely allies in the socialist cause.

The self-serving manipulation of public fears concerning immigration and the revolution was not new to Anglo socialist circles in Texas. For example, the Political Refugee Defense League, the socialist alliance that in 1909 brought to Texas a campaign for the release of jailed PLM leaders, secured the support of TSFL allies from San Antonio by warning them that the continuing repression of the PLM would introduce a race war and by depicting the policies of the Díaz regime as the principal cause of immigration. The League gave wide publicity to protestations by San Antonio unions representing carpenters, painters, and paperhangers as expressions of international solidarity and progressive ideals.

The San Antonio protest, however, reflected and reinforced a perception of the Mexican national as a potential agitator, competitor, and strikebreaker when it pointed out that "the cheap peon-labor of Mexico is the greatest menace which the American working people face today."[7]

The socialists' public stance in support of revolutionary groups in Mexico and the official pronouncements in favor of the unity of all workers nevertheless were the most important early inducements for Mexicans to join. Previously organized groups composed of Mexican renters and laborers thus began to seek affiliation when the Land League adopted a deliberate plan to incorporate them in 1915.[8] When the party began to welcome Mexicans, it drew a significant number of PLM sympathizers from the cotton belt. Their prior experience with the PLM explains why they joined so suddenly in large numbers.

Although Mexicans initially joined the socialist cause without benefit of an official policy to incorporate them, Anglo leadership eventually welcomed and even encouraged them to join. The new policy to incorporate Mexicans, though lacking in adequate logistical and financial support, stood in bold contrast to the indifference and the exclusionary practices of the AFL and TSFL-affiliated unions in the state. This interethnic alliance within the Texas Socialist Party structure represented a form of ideological dissent from the prevailing anti-Mexican and xenophobic attitudes and racial divisions in Texas. It was a tentative fulfillment of the socialist ideal of working-class unity, made possible in large measure by the initiatives of Mexican workers.

Organizers and Organized

Mexican socialist leadership included two of the most popular and effective backwoods organizers in the Land League, José Angel Hernández and F. A. Hernández. José Angel Hernández was a young married immigrant from Mexico. He first came to the notice of the Mexican Consul at Galveston, who kept a watchful eye on local Mexican political activity. According to the consul, Hernández was the president of a local PLM organization, established in 1911, which was showing signs of growing dissatisfaction with the Mexican government.

Hernández spent a few years working in Houston and Indianapolis. While at Houston, Hernández chaired a meeting of three hundred Mexican socialists protesting the imprisonment of one of *Los Mártires de Texas* and PLM leaders, Jesús María Rangel. In February, 1915, while raising campaign funds in San Antonio, Hernández was arrested and accused of attempting to incite an IWW-inspired revolution. He organized unions at Fentress and Marion and assisted F. A. Hernández in setting up another local at New Braunfels. His effectiveness as an organizer and orator aroused the ire of legal authorities and farmers from New Braunfels, Clear Springs, and Seguín. In each case he met threats of arrest and violence. His troubles followed him to San Antonio, where he was arrested a second time in August, 1915.[9]

F. A. Hernández was a sharecropper from Nordheim. He periodically traveled on horseback throughout South Texas in search of new recruits for the Renters' Union and the Land League. These trips usually took him away from his family and his crops for several days. His travels included numerous stops in hostile communities on his route to locations often more than one hundred miles distant. Organizing involved the use of contacts along the way and assistance from established organizations. In some instances, he formed new organizations among previously unorganized Mexican workers. Most of the time, however, he convinced existing organizations to affiliate with the Renters' Union and the Land League. He traveled as far as Corpus Christi and organized locals at Thomaston, Cuero, and Mathis. His earnings on the organizing trail were drawn from the initial membership dues paid by newly affiliated locals.[10]

F. A. Hernández became one of the most successful organizers for the Land League in 1915. W. S. Noble, secretary treasurer of the Land League, praised his work: "When Hernandez gets to work it is bad for land-lordism as he has organized more locals and accomplished more by his generalship than anyone organizer in the League."[11]

Until 1913 F. A. Hernández had confined his organizing to the area surrounding his home. The positive response to his organizing overtures subsequently encouraged him to request permission to expand his work among Mexicans throughout the state and into other southwestern states. The Land League leadership was obviously equally encouraged, particularly as it was then expressing support for the Mexican Revolution and espousing an internationalist brand of working-class solidarity. Soon after Hernández obtained the right to organize in the state, he reported four new locals with a combined membership of 118 workers. Only one other organizer, one who claimed ten locals and 129 members, exceeded his work. In 1915 Hernández attended the party's annual convention as an official delegate representing Mexican locals. In that same year, Hernández was reelected to serve a third term on the Land League's executive committee as an assistant state organizer with the responsibility for organizing Mexican workers.[12]

Despite these official designations and formal affiliations, Mexicans were generally left on their own in their organizing efforts. Mexican organizers like José Angel and F. A. Hernández were usually the only Socialist Party representatives that reported organizing Mexican workers. An inability to speak Spanish and a general unfamiliarity with the Mexican community no doubt discouraged Anglo organizers. As a result, a separate Mexican organizational network of unions developed and collaborated with other Mexican community associations in initiating recruiting campaigns that were relatively independent of their Anglo counterparts.

Self-organization involved translating socialist literature for use by Mexican organizers. F. A. Hernández, for instance, arranged to translate the Renters' Union constitution for use in his campaigns. Mexicans also established separate sets of activities that involved other Mexican groups, rather than Anglo socialist locals. This was the case with the public meetings and rallies organized by José Angel Hernández, larger regional meetings held at places such as Gurley and Uhland, and revival-like encampments that F. A. Hernández and S. C. Cárdenas, a teacher-organizer from Helena, organized in 1913. Hernández reported that he and other organizers also worked on letter-writing campaigns that presented union members and the Mexican public with socialist literature and information concerning forthcoming meetings and other activities.[13]

Impressive organizing results indicated that Mexican workers welcomed the opportunity to embrace the unionist struggle within the socialist camp when given the opportunity. They participated in the formative organizing stages of the Texas Socialist Party and its labor federations. The aforementioned work by Father Hagerty in organizing Mexican railroad workers in 1903 may have been associated with the early history of the Socialist Party. Mexican miners from Bridgeport and fishermen from Matagorda Bay also formed large locals that affiliated with the Socialist Party before the formation of the Renters' Union and prior to the official declaration of intention to build interracial and parallel unions of Mexican and black agricultural workers. J. C. Samora, of Yoakum, began selling subscriptions for *The Rebel* the same week that the paper was established, while J. F. Botello, of Devine, organized the first and also the largest Land League local in Texas. In 1913 F. A. Hernández recruited the most workers and established in 1915 the largest number of Land League locals in the state. In 1912 Mexicans participated in the party's effort to build one big industrial union of railway workers. The founder and leading organizer of the Texas Trackmen's Union, George Andrew, discovered, as had Father Hagerty earlier, that "Mexican workers were often more class conscious than the whites."[14]

By 1915 Land League officials were reporting in *The Rebel* that an impressive number of Mexicans were entering the socialist ranks. They were particularly impressed that Mexicans were joining the Land League despite overwhelming odds. The descriptions of Mexican socialist organizing activity in *The Rebel* often expressed a tone of amazement that the Land League utilized to challenge the seemingly faltering will of Anglo workers. *The Rebel* pointed out that Mexicans were "furnishing an inspiration to the American renters and actual farmers who have less difficulties to overcome but have until lately done less for the freedom of their wives and children than have those strangers in a strange land, that certainly are of a better metal than the poor fools that call them 'greasers.'"[15] W. S. Noble added that "the Mexican renters will live on boiled corn to win a just contract but the average American is so afraid of his boss he fears to join the league."[16]

Despite the early participation by Mexicans, some Texas socialists did not seriously believe that Mexicans would react favorably to organizing overtures. The doubters thought that Mexicans, along with blacks, could pose a political problem as strikebreakers. Serious doubts, however, made way for a welcomed surprise: "When the Renters' Union was started there were many that said: 'It won't succeed because the landlords will import Mexicans and Negroes to break the union.' But lo and behold the Mexican renters are flocking to our standard faster than the Americans, while the Negro shows every sign of being ready for organization."[17]

The Rebel praised the impressive advances by Mexican organizers, especially beginning in 1915. On several occasions the editors indicated that Mexicans were the backbone of the labor federations since they set the most aggressive example despite severe exploitation and repression. This lesson was especially important in 1915, the year the Land League increased its total membership by only 5 percent.[18]

Anglo socialists may have feigned surprise when they began to see growing numbers of determined Mexicans join the Land League and the party. They were particularly aware of P L M organizing in the area. The P L M had been active in the state since at least 1904, and its leaders had begun publicly to urge P L M adherents to join the socialist cause in the United States by 1911. Although Anglo socialists never acknowledged the P L M's proposed plan for working-class unity, it became increasingly clear during the 1910s that Mexicans were coming into the socialist camp by way of the P L M.

The Partido Liberal Mexicano

The P L M had emerged in 1901 as part of Mexico's nationalist reform movement that made the overthrow of the Porfirio Díaz regime one of its principal points of unity. Ricardo Flores Magón, the publisher of

Regeneración and co-founder of the P L M, had originally embraced liberal reforms within existing Mexican institutions. Díaz's repressive measures, however, forced Flores Magón and other dissidents to begin entertaining more radical views regarding Mexican society and the state. The P L M and its leadership eventually sought the security of the United States border to agitate for armed action, the ouster of Díaz, and the creation of a just society characterized by representative democracy and constitutional guarantees. Flores Magón and the more radical wing of the party privately embraced an anarchist ideology at the turn of the century. They did not publicly endorse positions such as the worldwide unity of workers or direct action to abolish institutional authority and private ownership of the means of production until they had established an impressive number of affiliate organizations and initiated the first rebellions along the border.[19]

Beginning with the publication of *Regeneración* at Los Angeles in September, 1910, the P L M began to issue increasingly radical critiques. The publication of the P L M's 1911 manifesto finally made anarchism an explicit set of guiding ideas. The decision to openly espouse a more radical perspective resulted from a need to counter the ascendancy of reform-oriented leadership in the revolution. The P L M also hoped to lead the popular discontent that leaders believed would naturally emerge as Mexicans realized that political change had failed to produce a thorough social and economic transformation. Publicly embracing anarchism, however, precipitated the organization's decline. Serious problems emerged, one engendered by the decision to permit the participation of Anglos in the abortive takeover of Baja California in 1911. Political figures in Mexico stigmatized Magonistas as traitors, while U.S. officials initiated the most serious legal actions against P L M leaders for violating neutrality laws.[20]

In some important instances historians have focused on the P L M's growing interest in the Mexican community of the Southwest. Scholars conclude that the P L M movement initially provided a patriotic issue, the overthrow of Díaz, that helped unify segments of the Mexican community. This sense of patriotic unity encouraged Mexicans to establish organizations with a dual character, that is, organizations that joined a concern for Mexico's future with a focus on the Mexican community's welfare in the United States. P L M influence eventually encouraged its supporters to apply anarchist ideas to their own experience as workers in the United States. The P L M's influence on the resident Mexican community was initially unintentional and perhaps even unforeseen by a leadership that was divided and tentative on the kind of Mexican support that they wished to obtain in the United States.

As early as 1901 the volume of correspondence received by the P L M from Texas sympathizers demonstrated that their opposition to the Díaz regime was well received. Support was further evinced by their success in Laredo in 1904. Encouraged, Flores Magón and the more radical wing of the party insisted that the P L M go beyond using places like Texas for safe havens and seriously consider them as fields for propagandizing and recruiting. More cautious members rejected the idea because they felt that the exiled group in Texas was not sufficiently prepared to wage such an organizing campaign. Other differences occurred that split the leadership, leaving Flores Magón and his more radical supporters in control of the P L M by 1905. In the process of defining a course of action, the tactical decision was made to recruit Mexicans in the United States, regardless of nativity.[21]

With time, other concerns surfaced. For instance, P L M leaders feared that authorities would point to the recruitment of local Mexicans for armed actions in Mexico as a violation of neutrality laws. A related concern that surfaced during the second decade was that the P L M would be accused of violating Mexico's sovereignty with the use of foreign-born troops. Another problem that became increasingly important was the public perception that the P L M was radicalizing local labor struggles, especially after it publicly embraced anarchism. This constituted one of the organization's most important ideological trials. Their public espousal of anarchism and international class struggle meant risking repression and the loss of exiled status. Nevertheless, beginning during the second decade they openly critiqued discrimination and inequality and supported organizing efforts among Mexican workers in Texas. However, they were also cautious. Flores Magón, for example, did not openly critique the Mexican condition in the United States with the same ideological determination and strength that he applied to Mexico.[22]

The P L M consistently but circumspectly applied its radical views on problems facing Mexicans in the United States. The leaders' dedication to ideological principles undoubtedly contributed to this consistency. The participation and radicalization of significant numbers of immigrants and U.S.-born Mexicans in such places as Texas made it inevitable. The call for democratic reform and for the ouster of Díaz attracted widespread support from Mexicans in the United States. The declared cause of an international class struggle with millenial visions, on the other hand, encouraged P L M sympathizers to expect the organization's support in their efforts to improve their condition.

The P L M's public ideological shift coincided with an upsurge of Magonista activity that increasingly addressed problems Mexicans faced in the United States. The P L M also called on its sympathizers to build alliances with U.S. socialist groups as part of its effort to build an internationalist movement. The PLM's declining fortunes may have further led Magonistas to seek solidarity with existing Mexican federations and socialist allies in the area.

Mexican Socialists from the Cotton Belt

An initial period of insurrectionist politics that produced the first armed revolts against Díaz's regime preceded the PLM's transition to a more overtly anarchist and internationalist organization. Most of the revolts staged in Coahuila were planned in San Antonio, a city that was often called the Mexican exiled capital of the United States because of the numerous Mexican political movements that were set afoot in the inland city. The PLM established its headquarters in San Antonio in 1905, and although the leadership was forced to leave the state within a few months, Magonistas continued to operate from the city throughout the first decade. Itinerant PLM organizers stationed in San Antonio, Waco, and Laredo usually traveled throughout the state recruiting new adherents. Local sympathizers who maintained correspondence with Flores Magón or with statewide leaders normally assisted organizers in planning rallies or secret meetings.

Indicative of the importance that the PLM gave the cotton belt, two of the PLM's principal military leaders, Coronel Encarnación Díaz Guerra and Coronel Jesús M. Rangel, were stationed at different times in Waco, Austin, and San Antonio during the first decade. Díaz Guerra was the PLM's first commander and Rangel the second commander of the third zone of the north which encompassed Coahuila, Nuevo León, and Tamaulipas. Díaz Guerra personally led recruits from the cotton belt and the border area around Del Rio in one of the first armed actions along the border, the Las Vacas fight of 1908. Rangel became an important functionary in the PLM's Los Angeles headquarters and served as an envoy to revolutionary forces led by Emiliano Zapata in southern Mexico. He returned to Texas where he became the principal organizer and leader of the cotton belt group of Mexican revolutionaries that was intercepted by authorities at Carrizo Springs, imprisoned and later celebrated by Magonistas as *Los Mártires de Texas*.[23]

Antonio de P. Araujo, coeditor of the Austin PLM newspaper *Reforma, Justicia y Libertad* and an important PLM operative in Arizona during the second decade, was one of the principal recruiters of Mexican land renters and laborers in Waco, Holmes, San Marcos, Runge, and Fentress for the Jiménez, Viesca, and Las Vacas fights. Araujo coordinated his work with other local activists like P. Dávila, a well-known PLM organizer who, according to a local newspaper, "lectures among the

A group of "filibusters" arrested in the Laredo area while attempting to cross the international line to join the Mexican Revolution, ca. 1914. *Courtesy Laredo Public Library*

Mexicans of San Antonio and gives his attention to the Spanish-speaking members of the local socialist organization." Another of Araujo's local organizers was Casimiro H. Regalado, a land renter from the Waco area, who operated between Waco and Houston. On one occasion, he personally assured Flores Magón that he could raise an army of several thousand troops in Texas and enter Mexico at various points in the state of Tamaulipas, an area that he knew well. Regalado worked closely with Rangel and a Waco organization affiliated with the PLM, El Club Melchor Ocampo.[24]

Araujo's 1906 organizing campaign made use of a network of Mexican organizations that corresponded regularly with Flores Magón and contributed financial support for the planned revolts. One of the men he recruited was Eulogio García, an officer of the Junta Unión Liberal de Agricultores Mexicanos, a PLM organization of farm workers from Holmes. García was commissioned captain of one of the guerilla contingents that fought at Las Vacas in 1908. Marcelino Ybarra, president of the San Antonio PLM group El Comité Liberal assisted Araujo in his recruitment efforts. He, as well as Espiridión Torres—president of the Fentress junta and kin to some members of a socialist workers' organization established in the town during the second decade—could not join the group that fought at Jiménez. Nonetheless, Araujo's and Torres's organizations donated money, purchased and supplied arms and horses, and recruited soldiers from among their fellow members.[25] Other explicitly PLM organizations such as the Liga Liberal Benito Juárez, of

San Antonio, and the clubs Liberal Benito Juárez and Liberal Mexicano, Sebastian Lerdo de Tejada, of Seguín, also participated in these organizing drives.[26] The response to the 1906 organizing drive was so successful that one adherent was led to ask suggestively, "In Texas, there is a great shortage of cotton pickers, I wonder why?"[27]

The organizing drives that occurred between 1906 and 1908 were part of larger statewide campaigns that lasted until the second decade. According to one of the many government informants that infiltrated the PLM in Texas, an organizer named Hermenegildo Garza arrived in San Antonio during the latter part of 1908 seeking recruits for a meeting that was to be held at an undisclosed location between Brownsville and Laredo. The plan was to bring together a fighting force of two thousand troops. Garza met with sympathizers in the area and promised to return with more definite information regarding the time and place of the proposed gathering. Twenty other recruiters were reported traveling throughout the state in preparation for this meeting, which no doubt was a prelude to the PLM's second major round of rebellions coinciding with the official start of the revolution in 1910. *Los Mártires de Texas* represented still another effort by the network of Mexican organizations from the cotton belt to send armed PLM filibustering expeditions into Mexico.[28]

In many instances, individuals and groups of workers, some of whom may have been in contact with PLM organizers, independently applied for membership and reported to Flores Magón on their local activities. J. López, for example, communicated in 1905 that he and three other Magonistas were distributing leaflets and doing general propaganda work for the PLM in Alvarado. Juan Ballí Rodríguez submitted dues for thirteen new members from New Berlin and reported support for PLM activities. Asencio Soto wrote frequently from somewhere in Gonzales County, transmitting organizing reports and ideas for the PLM's political programme including a recommendation that the Mexican government assist Mexicans who wished to emigrate. Narciso Ramón, of Smithville, announced the formation of a club and news that local African Americans wished to become Mexican citizens and PLM members. Although local chapters were mostly composed of men, some groups in the larger cities like San Antonio were made up entirely of women. The San Antonio organization El Club Liberal de Señoras y Señoritas, Leona Vicario y Antonia Nava, was formed in 1904 and assumed an important leadership position when many of the men were forced to go underground to escape arrest. Some of the women who played key roles in this organization included the sisters of Antonio Villarreal, Andrea and Teresa, as well as Sara Estela Ramírez, Juana Gutiérrez de Mendoza, and Elisa Acuña y Rosete during their short stay in San Antonio.[29]

Some of the strongest adherents to the revolutionary cause were women. An all-women group from Dallas, for instance, wrote to Flores Magón an unwavering statement of support that reflected ideological maturity: "[we are] workers who are emancipated from the bothersome preoccupations that have kept humanity enslaved. If men have not opened their eyes to see it all, we women will not allow corrupt politicians to deceive us. Comrade Magon: fight hard against the bourgeoisie who seeks to position himself to maintain the workers under the yoke we have suffered for centuries."[30]

Newspapers played as significant a role as the local organizations in promoting the P L M's cause throughout the state. Newspapers provided the primary means by which to disseminate party news and information to sympathizers and potential supporters. P L M journalists also participated in the continual debates concerning the merits of nationalism, anarchism, and the different political projects being advanced by other reformist and revolutionary groups in Mexico and the United States. Some of the most prominent P L M newspapers published consistently or intermittently in the area included: *Regeneración* (San Antonio, St. Louis, and Los Angeles, 1904–17); *El Eco del Obrero* (San Antonio, 1904); *Resurreción* (San Antonio, 1908); *Reforma, Justicia y Libertad* (Austin, 1908); *La Mujer Moderna* (San Antonio, 1909); *Lucha de Clases* (San Antonio, 1915) and *El Amigo del Pueblo* (San Antonio, 1908–16). Other P L M newspapers published elsewhere in the state were also distributed in the area.[31]

The P L M's official organ, *Regeneración,* had the widest circulation by the second decade, numbering approximately twenty-five thousand subscribers, many of whom lived in the cotton belt. The Austin newspaper *Reforma, Justicia y Libertad* devoted much of its circulation to that area with subscription stations in the same counties and towns that later registered socialist workers' organizations.[32] The readership was larger than subscription lists indicated, because local P L M organizations usually allotted time during their meetings for lectors to read to the members the entire content of the papers. Some of these organizations functioned as sponsors for the newspapers. P L M affiliates, for instance, sold and distributed subscriptions to *Reforma, Justicia y Libertad.* The Club Liberal "Constitución" from San Antonio functioned as the official sponsor of *Resurreción,* while Mexican organizations affiliated with the Socialist Party called *Lucha de Clases* their own.[33]

Like the widely circulated newspapers, P L M organizers served as important links between the Mexican Revolution and local struggles in the Southwest. Lázaro Gutiérrez de Lara, a well-known P L M sympathizer and labor organizer of the second decade, probably best exemplified such a connection. Gutiérrez de Lara was one of the principal P L M organizers in the famous Cananea, Sonora, strike of 1906 which helped spark the Mexican Revolution. After the strike, he traveled throughout the Southwest as a P L M organizer. Although he became estranged from the P L M by the second decade, Gutiérrez de Lara continued to identify himself a socialist seeking an international labor alliance and a radical transformation of Mexican society. He became well known among Anglo socialists in the United States as an orator and writer on the Mexican Revolution and drew their support for the campaign to gain the release of jailed P L M leaders in such places as Texas.[34] He was also instrumental in drawing popular attention to prerevolutionary Mexico with the publication of a devastating critique of conditions under Díaz, *Barbarous Mexico,* ostensibly authored by John Kenneth Turner although credited to Gutiérrez de Lara by people who knew him well.[35]

When the revolution broke out Gutiérrez de Lara joined Francisco Madero's forces and subsequently toured Mexico to promote the socialist cause. He next appeared in the northern Coahuila area, where he helped to organize the first national union of Mexican miners, La Unión Minera Mexicana, among P L M sympathizers in the area across from Eagle Pass. He was forced to leave the country in 1915 when he opposed the alliance between Venustiano Carranza and organized labor that resulted in the formation of the military phalanx of workers called *los batallones rojos.* Gutiérrez de Lara subsequently moved to San Antonio in 1915 and became one of the most popular bilingual and pro-Carrancista orators for the socialist and unionist cause among Mexicans.[36] From San Antonio he traveled to Arizona, where he became the leading organizer during a wave of strike activity by Mexican miners from Globe, Miami, Clifton, and Morenci. In 1917 he returned to Sonora once again to organize miners. He died that same year at the hands of his political enemies.[37]

While in San Antonio Gutiérrez de Lara worked in concert with the Mexican unions affiliated with the Land League and the P L M. He spent several months lecturing on socialism in 1915. He and his wife devoted all of their time to the lecture circuit in San Antonio and in the area south and southeast of the city.[38] Gutiérrez de Lara explained his motivation in a report of his organizing activities to an officer of the Texas Socialist Party. He spoke on behalf of Mexicans in Texas because of the violence and exploitation that he witnessed, including "the most brutal peonage to which the Mexicans are subjected by the feudal exploiters of Caldwell [County], . . . and how the Mexicans are shot and sent to prison or to the penitentiary under trumped-up charges for refusing to be peonized."[39]

Partly as a result of the work of such organizers as Gutiérrez de Lara, PLM organizations during the second decade reflected the ideological shift of their parent organization and its focus on the resident Mexican community during the numerous organizing meetings that they held. This was apparent in meetings held at Uhland and Gurley in 1912 and 1914, respectively. Organized by Mexican PLM and Land League members, the revival-like meeting at Uhland brought together tenants, sharecroppers, laborers, and their families for a full day of speeches and entertainment. At least one thousand delegates came from Fentress, Prairie Lea, New Braunfels, Seguín, Gonzales, Hutto, Cedar Creek, Garfield, Kyle, Maxwell, Reedville, Lockhart, Martindale, San Marcos, Buda, Creedmoor, Mendoza, and Austin. Some of the participants represented official delegations from PLM organizations. They first heard Roberto Barba, a fellow worker and PLM organizer, deliver a blasting critique of the "bourgeois" press represented by the conservative weeklies of San Antonio, *El Regidor* and *El Imparcial*. He spoke well, on the other hand, of the "honorable press" composed of the radical papers *Regeneración* (Los Angeles), *La Cultura Obrera* (New York), *Tierra* (Habana), *Tierra y Libertad* (Barcelona) and *Renovación* (San José, Costa Rica). Barba ended his speech with the following exhortation: "Let us boycott the infamous press and protect the press that is honorable, the libertarian, the communist, the anarchist!"[40]

Antonio Valdez, representing an Austin-based Land League organization which had adopted the PLM's new anarchist motto, "Tierra y Libertad," next addressed the assembly with a talk on the problems of the landless Mexican in Texas, though his allusions to land appropriations may also have had Mexico in mind. He noted that Mexican laborers had made the land valuable, yet they had none of their own. The only option was to take the land, for it properly belonged to those who worked it. Taking the land, however, required that the workers commit themselves to the idea of revolutionary change: "The Social Revolution is before us. Let us embrace it and let us join its columns. She will save us from the misery of hard and infamous work and from all our tragedies."[41]

An unidentified speaker ended the meeting with a stirring appeal for the unity of Mexicans with workers' struggles throughout the world:

> We don't have bosses here. All of us are equal. The "señor" and the "señora" are the bourgeoisie. This is a celebration of work.

> We come to commemorate it like the workers from France, Spain, and Germany celebrate it on the first of May, like the North American workers that celebrate it on the first of September, and like the workers from Austria, Hungary, Great Britain, Belgium, and Holland celebrate it at other times. The Mexican proletariat comes together today and it sings the hymns of liberty under the unfurling waves of that Red Flag that at this moment maintains the principle of expropriation on Mexican lands.[42]

The smaller Gurley meeting was held at the home of Teodoro Velázquez to celebrate the anniversary of the 1911 PLM Manifesto.[43] Velázquez opened the meeting with a reading from the manifesto to representatives of PLM and non-PLM organizations from Gurley, Guda, Houston, Lorena, Rosebud, and Waco. José Angel Hernández, the PLM and Socialist Party organizer, spoke on the "wealth of Texas, its workers and the results of their work." Luisa Guajardo Soto, of Lorena, followed him with a talk on the rights of women. Eustolio García gave an anticlerical speech, while Gumersinda Miranda Soto addressed the dismal future awaiting women under the current circumstances. Velázquez read from the Manifesto Mundial issued by the Grupo Regeneración Humana from Havana, Cuba. A young boy named Merced Velázquez recited a poem, and the Miranda Soto women sang "a revolutionary duet." Hernández ended the meeting by asking the participants to join the PLM, "the only one in the area of ideas and action that fights for the complete emancipation of the working class."

Relations with La Agrupación

The influence of the PLM and the radicalization of its adherents in the cotton belt became increasingly apparent as the exiled movement began to introduced divisions within established Mexican organizations such as La Agrupación. This involved successful recruitment efforts by the PLM that often dipped into the memberships of other Mexican organizations. Organizations that belonged to federations like La Agrupación also may have sought an alliance with the Socialist Party as the PLM discarded its purely nationalist principles of unity and advised its locals and sympathetic groups to seek alliances with the left in the United States. The conflict between the leadership of La Agrupación and the PLM, involving ideological debate and accusations of a personal nature, represented more than the radicalization of Magonistas. It also revealed a political-ideological division in the Mexican community that directly stemmed from the PLM's increasing influence.

La Agrupación was established in June, 1911. By August, 1911, it claimed over twenty chapters in Texas, with the number of chapters increasing to thirty-five by 1914. Most of the member organizations appeared in the area south and east of San Antonio, though affiliates were also created in Brownsville and Waco, in Louisiana, and in Roswell, New Mexico. Membership was open to all Mexicans, regardless of nativity and gender, and it included mostly farm renters and laborers.[44] The organization's general purpose, according to its secretary, Emilio Flores, "is to come out for its members in the courts, where outrages are committed with them, such as cold-blooded murders, lynchings, and so forth, or the taking of their homes or crops in direct violation of the law."[45] Flores added that La Agrupación was a decentralized confederation of semi-autonomous local organizations, or mutual aid organizations. Their organizing campaign literature announced that local chapters could adopt separate sets of constitutions and by-laws as long as these did not contradict or negate the governing principles of the central body.[46]

La Agrupación often employed its Mexicanist identity and conflicting racial relationships as reference points to organize Mexican workers. Its leaders promoted a mutualist tradition by urging the Mexican community to nurture national bonds with fraternity and *compañerismo*. La Agrupación had a "noble" and "patriotic" mission that struck an obvious collective chord, as evidenced by its popularity and growth.[47]

Although La Agrupación experienced sudden growth in 1911, internal divisions between 1912 and 1914 brought it close to extinction. By the early part of 1915 renewed interest among farm workers in the San Antonio area revived the group. During a reorganizing campaign Flores announced in *La Prensa* a broad program of action reaffirming the organization's goals and interests. La Agrupación was to organize male and female workers for the purpose of protecting the general political and economic interests of the Mexican community. Public educational conferences were held, a public library was established, a recreation hall was opened, and attorneys were contracted to offer legal advice primarily to land renters in the area.[48]

According to testimony that Flores presented before the 1915 Committee on Industrial Relations, three interrelated factors accounted for the internal divisions and near extinction of La Agrupación. First, unfavorable court rulings caused members to lose faith in the organization's legal services. Most of these cases involved contractual disputes between Mexican renters or laborers and Anglo landowners. Flores noted that the organization was unable to convince its dejected members that appeals to higher courts could produce better results. Racial discrimination in the probate courts discouraged them from seeking redress in the state or federal courts. Consequently, the enthusiasm evident in the recruiting campaigns and in the statewide conferences waned. Obviously demoralized by major setbacks, Flores concluded that beyond its initial organizing success La Agrupación had accomplished little "in the way of betterment in the conditions of the workingman, the tenant, or the renter for money or on shares of crops."[49]

Flores also attributed the demise of the organization to economic factors. A drop in the price of cotton in 1914, coupled with the already exploited condition of Mexican workers, forced many members to drop out. It is possible that the scarcity of money placed the payment of dues beyond the ability of the Mexican worker. Flores's description of the Mexican agricultural work force, the population from which La Agrupación drew its members, leaves no doubt that the organization was directly susceptible to slumps in the cotton economy. Also according to Flores, foreclosures, violence, contractual deceptions and violations, low wages, high company store prices, and racist landowners who refused to sell land to enterprising Mexican renters and sharecroppers were the general rule in the area.[50]

The third and most important factor that debilitated La Agrupación involved political-ideological differences among the rank and file and between the membership and the leadership. These differences coincided with a political division between the leadership of La Agrupación and the PLM. Some members of La Agrupación supported the political programme of the PLM that called for world wide working-class unity and revolutionary change in Mexico. The actual number of members that actively sustained the PLM is unknown. However, this support was substantial enough to produce serious divisions within La Agrupación.[51]

The internal divisions of La Agrupación became a public issue by 1914 and brought the organization's leadership into open conflict with the PLM. One of the most publicized conflicts involved the resignation of eighty PLM sympathizers from the Martindale chapter. The PLM newspaper *Regeneración* reported that the Martindale members bolted the organization because they were dissatisfied with the "bourgeois interests" of La Agrupación and the corruption of its officials. The PLM kept up its attacks on the federation's leadership by granting a position of honor to the leader of the disaffected members, Miguel Pavia, during the Uhland meeting.[52]

Ricardo Flores Magón accused the officers of La Agrupación of squandering the organization's funds and of refusing to assume public leadership positions in the face of continued violence against the Mexican community. He described Emilio Flores as "a bourgeoisie through and through that calls us the libertarians, conspirators against order and society. The old man is not far from the truth. We conspire against the bourgeois order and the capitalist society."[53]

Since Flores Magón believed that the central problem in La Agrupación was its leadership, he openly called on workers to assume control of the organization and drive out the politically conservative leaders. He used this opportunity to underscore an important socialist principle: "Mexican workers, kick out from the locals of La Agrupación all the bourgeoisie so that only the proletariat remains. It is impossible to have a union between the bourgeoisie and workers. There ought to be only hatred between the two social classes."[54]

Flores answered this criticism with some of his own when he testified before the Committee on Industrial Relations. In an attempt to discredit the PLM before government officials who were investigating, among other things, sources of unrest in the Southwest, Flores associated the group's radical politics with the large numbers of immigrants that were entering the state. The more recent immigrants, according to Flores, "are almost generally revolutionarily inclined at all times and have great influence with their countrymen already here prior to them." Moreover, various dailies and weeklies from Texas, including *Regeneración,* were responsible for the increasing radical political activity among Mexicans. Flores called the PLM newspaper "filthy," "obscene," and "disgraceful." He credited the paper and the PLM with provoking racial violence and with instilling revolutionary thought. Flores added suggestively, "how the United States has ever consented to such a publication as that to go through our mails is something we cannot understand."[55]

When Flores returned to San Antonio, he published a report on his testimony in *La Prensa.*[56] The report, however, excluded his lengthy discussion on immigration. He had stated that immigration posed an economic as well as a political threat, since it introduced radical thought and increased competition among Mexican workers. This competition, in turn, created serious divisions that could only be resolved with effective restrictions on immigration. He had described these divisions in terms of older versus newer immigrants and U.S.-born versus immigrant workers. Flores's manner of expression left little doubt that although he was concerned with the plight of immigrants, he preferred to identify with the U.S.-born: "They have their own ways of living in their own country, and it is absolutely different from ours. We people who were born in this country feel for them because they are our own race, although we were born and educated here in this country; we feel for these poor unfortunates, and we would not like to see them come here any more unless conditions are changed a great deal."[57]

The public report also excluded Flores's critique of the PLM. He may have deleted the two most important sections of his testimony for fear of antagonizing the membership and the workers he hoped to recruit in the 1915 organizing campaign. Also, his reluctance to publicly admit his ethnic orientation suggests that he was out of step with the prevailing Mexicanist identity as well as with the ascendant politics of working-class solidarity.

Emilio Flores's views on immigration and left-wing politics stood in bold contrast to the PLM's advocacy of revolutionary change and socialism. The internal conflict lasted almost the entire lifetime of the organization. It reached public proportions soon after La Agrupación was established and contributed to the organization's near demise in 1914. The bad fortune of La Agrupación demonstrates that although Mexican workers continued to demonstrate a preference for the mutual aid form of organization and an inclusive Mexicanist political orientation, they kept a critical eye on political currents sweeping through their communities and joined or rejected organizations accordingly. Moreover, it is clear that the internal divisions of La Agrupación signalled the emergence of radical thought associated with the PLM and that some dissidents rejected nationalism as a preferred source of unity. Of particular importance was the active role that Ricardo Flores Magón played in the conflict, a clear example of the PLM's internationalist concern for working-class unity. Lastly, the red-baiting tactics employed by Flores revealed a serious point of vulnerability among the Magonistas. At the same time, Flores' private anti-immigrant, nativist, and conservative views registered another distinct yet still unpopular political orientation in the Mexican community.

The Reaction

The political repression that eventually undermined the work of the Mexican socialists evolved out of the fear that the Mexican Revolution was threatening to spill over into Texas. According to this view, as expressed by Flores, the PLM was the principal cause of the diffusion of revolutionary thought, and the 1915 San Diego revolt represented prima facie evidence that Mexicans in Texas already subscribed to the idea of a race war. It did not matter that Flores Magón disavowed any connections with the San Diego Plan. In the public's mind, three sets of facts suggested otherwise: the PLM association with Mexican socialists in Texas, Flores Magón's denunciation of discrimination and violence against Mexicans as the cause of the revolt, and his public calls for social revolution. Government officials were particularly convinced of a causal link. They were privy to intercepted correspondence between Flores Magón and numerous PLM sympathizers from throughout the state, including Aniceto Pizaña, one of the leaders of the revolt. The suppression of the PLM, therefore, was an attempt to forestall the spread of radicalism among Mexicans in Texas as well as an effort to counter its influence in Mexico.[58]

Flores's anti-immigrant stance could not easily find fertile ground; but voices within the Mexican community did raise warnings that the PLM's increasing popularity among poor workers would cause a reaction against the community, particularly its recent immigrants. The editors of *La Prensa*, for example, often expressed concern that the PLM and socialist thought jeopardized the safety and welfare of immigrants, or "visitors," to the United States. In 1913, for instance, they warned that Flores Magón was "extending socialism among Mexicans residing in the United States with his continuous preaching and the wide circulation of socialist literature with a touch of anarchism."[59]

Two years later, when the San Diego revolt began in South Texas, *La Prensa* announced that the socialism preached by the PLM had engendered the uprising. The San Antonio paper followed with reports of activists arrested for allegedly seeking to overthrow the government, thus suggesting that PLM influence was beginning to produce similar results in the area. One of these reports involved a man who was arrested in the *corrales,* or the west side of San Antonio, for allegedly seeking to incite a rebellion against the U.S. government. He had attempted to organize Mexican railroad workers in the city.[60] There is no evidence that *La Prensa* ever suggested that these arrests might rather be examples of the clearly overzealous reactions by local authorities. Aside from expressing a clear ideological distaste for the PLM, the editors of the San Antonio paper were fearful that the ongoing Anglo reaction to radical politics would reinforce popular anti-immigrant feelings. Their warnings rang true as the cause of socialist labor and PLM organizing became increasingly intertwined with the Mexican Revolution.

One of the most publicized cases of PLM influence prior to the 1915 San Diego revolt involved *Los Mártires de Texas.* The PLM and the Comité de Defensa that handled the 1912–13 campaign in support of *Los Mártires de Texas* gave wide publicity to the arrest and conviction of the fourteen survivors. The persons heading the Comité de Defensa were Elisa Alemán, Eustolio García, and José Angel Hernández. All three were PLM organizers, while García and Hernández organized for both the PLM and the Land League. Although the case of *Los Mártires de Texas* may have reinforced the popular negative image of the PLM, it also served as an issue around which Magonistas in the PLM and in the Texas Socialist Party boldly organized.[61]

Flores Magón's appeal for *Los Mártires de Texas* left no doubt that he viewed their arrest as an example of repression being directed against all Mexican radicals in the United States. He urged support as a matter of revolutionary principle: "Are we, who consider ourselves conscious of our responsibilities, to remain quiet while our compatriots [*Los Mártires de Texas*] are treated as they are? If that is what we are going to do, it is best that REGENERACIÓN cease operations, that we stop calling ourselves revolutionaries."[62]

The campaign energized local political activity and escalated conflict further. This was evident in 1913 when one hundred twenty-eight Mexican land renters and laborers that sympathized with the PLM wrote a letter to Governor Colquitt protesting the jailing of *Los Mártires de Texas* with the declaration that the state had always committed violence against "men loyal to the human race and to the liberation of oppressed people." The group, headed by José Angel Hernández, stated that if authorities continued to jail and execute Mexican activists, "Texas would have to answer before the entire Mexican people for these crimes without precedent in legal history." The governor responded by warning them that if harm came to any American citizens they would be held responsible, adding that he was ready to call out the National Guard to put down a suspected armed movement by Mexicans.[63]

Mexican organizers associated with the Renters' Union and the Land League reported numerous incidents of threats, unlawful arrests, office break-ins, and mob action that were prompted by fears that the Mexican Revolution was overflowing into the state. In 1912, for instance, Antonio Valdez reported that Anglo farm owners and renters south of Austin were harassing Mexican workers and Land League organizers. Anglos were alarmed by the political stirrings among Mexican farm workers, and they threatened to fire and deport anyone who spoke or hinted of "revolution or socialism." Landlords from Hays, Travis, and Caldwell counties also discouraged Mexicans from organizing by accusing them of fomenting revolution in Mexico.[64] Public officials contributed to a mood of hysteria with highly questionable stories of near doom. Governor Colquitt's reaction to the previously mentioned letter from disgruntled supporters of *Los Mártires de Texas,* for example, suggested that Mexican socialists were preparing for a revolt in Texas.[65]

The ever-present editors of *La Prensa* employed rumors and circumstantial evidence to substantiate the governor's allegations. Moreover, in 1915 when José Angel Hernández and Eustolio García were arrested while raising funds in San Antonio for *Los Mártires de Texas,* the paper charged that the PLM and the IWW were masterminding a rescue of their imprisoned brethren. The paper noted that many of the persons involved in the alleged San Antonio conspiracy were "old time agitators" and signers of the previously cited letter to Colquitt. According to *La Prensa,* Flores Magón was once again implicated because "he is in large part responsible for the spread of Socialism among Mexicans in the United States."[66] Ideological and organizational links existed between the PLM and such socialist groups as the Mexican Land League locals. Additionally, some persons and groups may have entertained the thought of organized violent reprisals against the state. However, Colquitt's charge and *La Prensa's* reporting were overly suggestive and inflammatory.

Other papers carried similar apparent fabrications that implicated Mexican socialists in plotting violent uprisings. In 1915 one such story resulted in a false alarm of a Mexican revolt in the Taft and Beeville area. It began when an intoxicated Mexican in nearby Sodville allegedly made racist statements against Anglos. Some people rumored that the now imprisoned Mexican had said that a Mexican uprising was pending. When the story reached Taft, it included the warning that Mexicans had in fact revolted at Sodville and that three hundred armed Mexican rebels were on their way. Women and children were rushed to a hotel, while armed men were stationed around the building. Morning came without a Mexican in sight, and the embarrassed would-be combatants returned to their homes.[67]

Newspapers from Nixon and Karnes City contributed to the growing state of hysteria when they reported that authorities had barely prevented the wholesale massacre of Anglos in the area. The editors of *The Rebel* noted with some concern that "considerable excitement prevailed in the city of Nixon last Friday when the rumor was noised abroad of an unsuccessful attempt of Mexicans to instigate a reign of terror by destroying the town, massacring people and if possible restore Texas to the republic of Mexico."[68]

The alleged uprising was to have also included the towns of Pandora, Smiley, Stockdale, Leesville, and Floresville. The leader of the plan, G. L. Medellín, was reportedly arrested and the revolt averted. The story on the near-revolt ended on a note that encouraged further fear and reaction. According to *The Rebel,* the excited journalists from Nixon and Karnes City warned that "the American people will not tolerate longer this continual jeopardy and imposition."[69]

F. A. Hernández branded the story a lie intended to undermine the work of Mexican socialists. He described the Mexican informant cited by the papers as "one of the several Mexican stool-pigeons that are being used to discredit any movement to organize the Mexican worker of the Southwest into the Land League or Socialist Party."[70] Hernández added that Medellín had spent the entire time that the uprising was to have occurred among friends during a Mexican patriotic celebration at

Runge. To further demonstrate that the charges were groundless, he cited the fact that Medellín was never arrested.

Another incident attracted public attention in 1915. In August, 1915, State Sen. F. C. Weinert warned that Mexicans from Guadalupe, Gonzales, and Hays counties were holding secret meetings for the purpose of waging an armed revolt. Radical Mexican organizers from San Antonio were said to have been visiting these counties and telling Mexican workers that "this is our land and we should reconquer it." Weinert supported his allegations with questionable evidence. He reported that Mexicans had committed acts of violence and that some farmers had received threatening letters. A group of Mexican workers from Seguín refuted the charges in a letter to *La Prensa*. They attributed Weinert's accusations to the hysterical antics of landlords who opposed a new state rental law that organizers sought to publicize and promote among Mexican renters. The new law required farmers to limit their rental fee to one-fourth of the tenant's annual harvest. Farmers had apparently reacted to the aggressive informational campaign by Mexican socialists. According to *La Prensa,* Mexican organizers reportedly threatened renters from Seguín to keep them from entering into contractual agreements on the basis of the old one-third arrangement. The campaign involved a Knights of Columbus lodge, an unnamed mutual aid society, and a Land League local with an aggregate membership of approximately 250 Mexicans.[71]

According to Clarence Nugent, an attorney affiliated with the Socialist Party, rampant hysteria granted public officials the necessary latitude to repress Mexican socialist labor activity. He offered the case of José Angel Hernández as an example.[72] Hernández was arrested in August, 1915, while organizing socialist locals in San Antonio. Nugent noted that his arrest occurred at a time "when the excitement over bandit raids on the border was at its height, and when public sentiment was believed to be such that a legal frame-up on a Mexican would pass unnoticed."[73]

Hernández was arrested for allegedly "planning to incite a rebellion" while speaking to an audience of a thousand Mexicans at the Market Place, a popular center of community activity. Two other persons were arrested with him for distributing his newspaper, *Lucha de Clases*. At least twenty-five spectators were rounded up the next day, charged with vagrancy, and held without bond for a few days. Hernández's two companions were fined one hundred dollars and two hundred dollars; the rest paid ten dollars and were released on the condition that they "not participate in the future in meetings similar to those held on Market Plaza Sunday." Local officials insisted that the speakers were part of a PLM and IWW-inspired plot to instigate racial violence. Swift action in conducting the San Antonio arrests and in confiscating *Lucha de Clases* as well as other locally distributed newspapers published in Mexico allegedly nipped the revolt in the bud. The chief of police ended his report to the local papers with a note of assurance, "they have been taught a good lesson. From now on the Plan of San Diego will have little success here."[74]

Hernández, however, indicated that he had only urged his audience to establish schools modeled after the positivist experiment by the Spanish educator, Francisco Ferrer, and to organize Land League locals. In an interview with the editor of *The Rebel,* Hernández pointed out that "it was this speech that was purposely misinterpreted to mean that I had advised the Mexicans to organize and get guns and kill everybody in sight. It was on false testimony of this sort that I was arrested by the city police and then turned into the Federal authorities."[75]

Hernández's explanation to the socialist readers of *The Rebel* seemed a reasonable exposition of the case against him. San Antonio authorities, however, operated with a different frame of mind, one that feared any form of militant expression by Mexicans. Although the socialist leader may not have urged racial violence, his speech and newspaper were considered sufficiently inflammatory to warrant an arrest and a public campaign to discredit Mexican militancy. An article translated and reprinted from *Lucha de Clases* in a local newspaper, for instance, was enough to excite public fears, particularly since it intimated the possibility of armed struggle:

> Working people hear: Ye producing host of all the useful and beautiful that exists, abandon your brutal task and hear my words.
>
> Ye, who build palaces, avenues of flower gardens, and who pave the streets of our thoroughfares, ye, who install an excellent lighting system, ye, who extract from the bowels of the earth its precious minerals and pile up its treasures in the coffers of the influential rich, ye, who manufacture beautiful fabrics and who every day increase the amount of foodstuffs in the warehouses; what do you get for all this?
>
> In return for the palaces and gardens inhabited by wealthy drones, you have filthy and pestilential garrets where the impure air which you breathe increases your diseases and causes your children to grow up feeble, pale, and sickly.
>
> And to destroy this state of things, what should you do?
>
> Rebel against those who sustain this injustice, exterminate the causes of this bad social organization, but let not your rebellion be without knowledge. Do not throw yourself against a

man (whom you believe to be guilty of evil conditions) in order
to establish another. Study the causes of those things. If the
tempest comes, rebel not only with word or pen, but carry a
gun in your hands (for only thus can you recover your rights),
throw yourself into the social revolution with the shout of,
"Long Live Anarchy."[76]

Texas Socialist Party officials understood that they were witnessing
a major reaction against Mexican socialists and consequently decided
to wage a vigorous campaign to free Hernández. The campaign became
a central issue around which the plight of the Mexican worker was fully
exposed by the *The Rebel*. During the campaign Hernández's lawyers
placed special emphasis on the fact that he had merely attempted to
enlist Mexican workers into a large Land League local, an act any Anglo
socialist would have been allowed to perform. The leader eventually won
an acquittal and presented a hero's speech at the Texas Socialist Party
and Land League conventions of 1915.[77]

The acknowledgements that Hernández received from Anglo socialists accompanied a decision by the party and the Land League to more
actively organize Mexican workers. This was a welcomed development
primarily because repression had left Mexican socialists with a critical
need for support that the party and the Land League could give them.
Harassment, threats, violence, and arrests clearly discouraged Mexicans
from joining the socialist ranks and impaired the work of Mexican organizers.[78] Such reactions, however, also drew Mexican socialists together and advanced the idea of solidarity among some of their Anglo
counterparts. An added factor that may have driven the Mexican socialist leadership to seek fuller integration into the party and the Land League
was the demise of their other parent organization, the PLM.

An Ambivalent Reception

The year 1915 was a benchmark for Mexicans in the party and in the
Land League. The campaign in defense of J. A. Hernández gave the
party and the Land League an important organizing issue that directly
involved Mexicans. Texas socialists gave the Hernández case full publicity in their paper and used the occasion to launch one of their last
important organizing drives before the First World War. Also, the party
and Land League gave Hernández a position of honor at the 1915 conventions. He, as well as F. A. Hernández and J. F. Botello, participated
in the deliberations of the Land League convention.[79]

The 1915 Land League convention delegates adopted an official plan to organize Mexican workers and also established a legal defense fund to assist jailed Mexican socialists. Equally as important was the decision by the Party's Committee on Literature and Propaganda to translate socialist literature into Spanish and to establish a Spanish-language paper. The Committee decided that materials would "be translated, edited and published for the benefit of the Spanish-speaking citizens of Texas whom we must arrange to supply with propaganda in their native tongue, and if necessary to cooperate with other states to this end."[80] Six months later, *The Rebel* announced that the "Mexican comrades" had translated the party's platform and that "those desiring to help in this work may send a small contribution to F. A. Hernández."[81] There is no evidence that the newspaper venture succeeded.

Notwithstanding the 1915 convention resolutions, the party and Land League support of Mexican socialist activity was often ambiguous and inconsistent. *The Rebel* always spoke in glowing terms about the effectiveness of Mexican organizers. Yet, with the exception of the campaign to free J. A. Hernández and the election of F. A. Hernández as an organizer, there is no record that the party or the labor federation took significant organizing initiatives among Mexican workers. During the 1915 conventions party and Land League officials decided to make a major concerted organizing effort that promised to strengthen the prior and ongoing work by Mexican organizers. However, Texas socialists usually delegated this responsibility to Mexicans themselves.

Additionally, although many Anglo socialists professed class solidarity, there were others who took exception when dealing with Mexican workers. The refusal by numerous Anglo socialists from San Antonio to support the campaign for the release of Hernández is a case in point. Other instances of indifference and even hostility were evident among Anglo socialists. For example, *The Rebel* printed letters which expressed anti-Mexican ideas and attitudes. Also, on one occasion the Anglo socialist leadership refused to lend support to Mexican Land League members involved in a wage dispute. The circumstances surrounding this case are unknown; however, the incident left deep impressions. A unionist representing C R O M participated in the dispute and announced at the 1918 Pan American Federation of Labor conference that Anglo labor leaders in the United States, regardless of ideological orientation, were anti-Mexican.[82]

Little is known about the Mexican socialist labor unions after 1916. The party and Land League conventions did not register Mexican participation. Moreover, both organizations disintegrated at the start of the First World War, primarily because of wartime hysteria and government suppression.[83] Given the more intense reaction against Mexican socialists, one can speculate that they were among the hardest hit by repression.

Conclusion

Mexican participation in the socialist labor federations appeared in the upper part of South Texas during a relatively short period of time. The rapid increase in the numbers of Mexican workers and organizations in the Renters' Union and the Land League followed and accompanied PLM activity. Mexican socialists openly endorsed the PLM during the first decade and organized socialist unions under both the PLM and party banners. The association with the PLM provided Mexican socialists with more than just a formative influence. It made them subject to a general state of hysteria that evolved around the idea of a Mexican uprising, the possibility of which was made real by the Mexican Revolution and the San Diego revolt. Repressive actions against Mexican socialist organizers presaged the later effects of the wartime hysteria that destroyed the party and the Land League. This repressive environment effectively eliminated for Mexican socialist unions their two sources of formal political association.

Political-ideological divisions in the Mexican community accompanied the wave of Mexican socialist activity. At one level, one can say that class consciousness competed with a purely nationalist outlook and an incipient ethnic identity. Underlying the opposition to the PLM and socialism was a fear that radical politics would result in violence and repression directed indiscriminately against all Mexican organizations. Repression in the end eclipsed the development of Mexican socialism, but not before the PLM and Mexican socialists had demonstrated an impressive ability to build a following among some of the more exploited workers in the state, Mexican agricultural renters and laborers.

Though Mexican socialist unions were part of the socialist labor federations, they maintained a separate political life which involved their own encampments, organizing drives, propagandizing campaigns, and Spanish-language newspapers. Also, some of these Mexican socialist unions collaborated with other organizations in local Mexican politics. Ideologically, the Mexican socialist leadership reflected the influence of both the Texas Socialist Party and the PLM. They endorsed the idea of an alliance between laborers and renters within industrially based unions. Also, they adopted PLM planks for a socialist reconstruction of Mexican society.

The association which Mexican socialist unions had with the Texas Socialist Party and its labor federations sheds additional light on the process by which Mexicans gained entry into the U.S. labor movement. The process of incorporation involved a radical parent organization professing a form of workers' solidarity that went beyond the exclusiveness of its conservative counterparts, the AFL and the TSFL. The open declaration to organize Mexicans, the Hernández campaign, and participation of some Mexicans in an official capacity shows that the Socialist Party was not issuing mere rhetoric on the question of solidarity. However, the practice of solidarity also revealed inconsistencies. The Texas Socialist Party and the Land League did not make a deliberate attempt to incorporate Mexicans until the success of Mexican organizers encouraged them to do so. Also, the socialist leadership often remained aloof from the actual work independently initiated by Mexican organizers. Consequently, the alliance was at best ambivalent and did not allow for the full incorporation of Mexican workers and the building of effective working-class unity.

Chapter Seven

The AFL Opens a Door

The story of Mexican labor would be incomplete without examining the more traditional and conservative labor federations, the AFL and its state affiliate, the Texas State Federation of Labor (TSFL). Mexican participation was almost negligible from 1900 to 1920, in part because occupational discrimination generally denied them the skilled occupations represented by craft-oriented federations and locals. An added problem was the racism of Anglo labor. Organized labor supported occupational segregation, and locals by and large excluded all but Anglos. The anti-immigration and anti-Mexican reaction of the second decade reinforced the view of Mexicans as an economic threat and justified their continued exclusion from the world of Anglo labor. The threat from below, however, also upset traditional understandings about exclusion.

Continued immigration and increasing competition by Mexican workers led Anglo unions to reexamine the two options before them. Should they continue to exclude Mexicans and preserve union jobs for Anglos, or organize and include them? The AFL officially adopted the latter strategy beginning in 1918 as part of an effort to regain control of the labor market and to extend its influence into Latin America. The implementation of this strategy in Texas, however, had to overcome the attitudes of Anglos who were accustomed to excluding Mexicans or to segregating them into separate locals. A compromise evolved that limited participation to U.S.-born and naturalized citizens.

Mexicans responded to this opportunity with an impressive organizing impulse observed among independent workers' organizations, the FLU, the PLM, and the socialist union network from the cotton belt. The result was a dramatic increase in participation. Most of the new unions had a prior history as independent workers' organizations. Clemente Idar, the Laredoan of El Congreso Mexicanista fame, played an important role as an AFL organizer. Samuel Gompers appointed Idar in 1918 as part of his commitment to organize Mexicans in the United States. Idar worked diligently in Texas and contributed significantly to the organizing and chartering of Mexican unions. He was also respon-

Clemente Idar, Galveston, 1928. *Courtesy Institute of Texan Cultures, The University of Texas at San Antonio.*

sible for both improving racial relations within Texas labor and further-
ing the influence of the AFL and trade unionism in Mexico. He was
most impressive in his ability to accommodate the fears of Anglo labor
at the same time that he implemented their idea of conditional solidarity.[1]

The Federations

The story of organized labor in Texas is normally associated with the
AFL and the TSFL, the two major federations that have dominated despite important challenges from the left during the 1910s and during
the period between 1937 and 1955. These challenges from within and
without ostensibly focused on organizing on a broad industrial basis,
that is, according to industries and regardless of skill, race, or gender.
The challenge failed during the early 1900s when the Texas Socialist
Party and the IWW, the two major proponents of industrial unionism,
succumbed to internal divisions and political repression.[2]

Craft unionism made a major advance in 1900 when delegates representing locals and city labor councils from Galveston, Houston, Fort
Worth, Waco, Dallas, Cleburne, and San Antonio met to form the TSFL.
Until the AFL granted the TSFL a charter in 1903, local unions maintained their affiliation with the national federation through such parent
national organizations as the United Mine Workers and the railroad
brotherhoods. The more complete incorporation of Texas labor, however, did not result in immediate growth. The poor showing was due
to a relatively low and uneven rate of industrialization, strong antiunion
campaigns usually known as open-shop movements, and a tight labor
market especially evident in the border region. Additionally, the AFL
provided little organizing support. Despite constant appeals, the AFL
did not send a paid organizer to Texas until the second decade. In the
meantime, mostly volunteer organizers associated with local unions,
city labor councils, and the national unions assumed responsibility for
bringing new locals into the AFL.[3]

Organized labor in Texas registered its most significant growth beginning in the 1910s among workers in the state's leading industries—
manufacturing, transportation, and mining. The unionization of the
building trades also kept apace as construction activity quickened. Although state federation membership records did not include all the AFL-
affiliated locals in the state, they provide a reliable barometer of change.
By 1915 the federation claimed six hundred AFL-affiliated locals with
a combined membership of between fifty thousand and ninety thousand members. Twenty percent, or between ten thousand and eighteen
thousand workers, belonged to the railway brotherhoods. The wartime
economy provided full employment and encouraged further growth. The

government's unprecedented interest in guaranteeing labor the right to unionize and bargain collectively also contributed to labor organization. The 1920s, however, witnessed a major membership decline, primarily due to open-shop campaigns and slumps in the economy. The total number of unionists dipped to a low of twenty-five thousand in 1927.[4]

The federations primarily emphasized achieving "pure and simple" goals of higher wages, shorter hours, and improved working conditions. Although their leaders professed the principle of workers' solidarity, they favored the higher-skilled Anglo workers in urban areas outside South Texas. Moreover, Anglo unionists normally expressed a job-scarcity consciousness, primarily because they feared competition from Mexican immigrants. As a consequence, the great majority of trade unionists during the early 1900s were Anglo skilled workers who often expected their unions to be more than instruments to challenge employers. They also counted on unions to safeguard their jobs. They defended their positions on racial grounds, although their logic of entitlement rested on arguments that pointed to sacrifices and hard-won gains.

Mexican Participation and Representation

The significant improvement in the participation of Mexicans in organized labor beginning in 1918 can be best appreciated by examining the poor record of the previous two decades. Mexicans normally participated in separate unions organized in large urban areas with sizable Mexican populations. These organizations were usually industrial unions and included both skilled and semiskilled workers of scarce financial means. Their numbers were markedly small throughout the first decade and most of the second.

Laredo registered the largest number of separate Mexican unions. The earliest ones appeared as direct by-products of the organizing activity led by Federal Labor Union No. 11953. With the exception of the failed effort to reorganize the FLU in 1910, there is no other evidence to indicate that Laredo unionists attempted another concerted organizing drive until Clemente Idar began organizing AFL locals in 1918. Independent workers' organizations, however, continued operating in the city and kept the union spirit alive in collaboration with labor organizations from Mexico. These organizations do not seem to have opted for an AFL charter, thereby remaining isolated from the world of Anglo labor.

San Antonio Mexicans also reflected a low rate of union participation at the same time that they registered a significant number of independent workers' organizations with a working-class focus and orientation. La Sociedad Artes Gráficas, an oganization of typographical workers, for instance, adopted as its guiding purpose "the unity of the craft within a mutualist program." Its motto was *Labor omnia vincit,* and its nationalist emblem was the bust figure of Fray Servando Teresa de Mier, the Spanish missionary who brought to Mexico and the Americas the first printing press.[5] Bakery workers, on the other hand, formed La Sociedad Morelos, Mutua de Panaderos and in 1917 led a successful strike primarily against local Mexican bakers. The workers reached an agreement that called for a reduction of hours and increases in pay and subsequently presented it to their employers. The strike against the bakers who refused to accept the demands lasted for about a year until a Department of Labor mediator settled the dispute in favor of the workers.[6] Other independent workers' organizations that maintained cooperative relations in the city included El Gran Círculo de Obreros, La Sociedad de Albañiles (masons) Mexicanos, La Sociedad Mutualista Mexicana de Sastres (tailors), La Sociedad Ignacio Zaragosa (railroad workers), and La Sociedad Porfirio Díaz, Mutua de Zapateros (shoeworkers).[7]

A small number of organizations obtained A F L charters as separate Mexican unions and collaborated with their sister organizations to advance the cause of unionism much like the F L U had done in Laredo. Their efforts, however, produced few results, in part because the poverty of their members and isolation from Anglo labor often limited them to simply keeping their unions alive. The International Hod Carriers and Building Laborers' Union of America, No. 93, the longest-surviving A F L-affiliated Mexican union in Texas, typifies the experiences of other Mexican organizations that left a more scant record of information.

A group of sixteen Mexican workers, some of whom were employed by the city, organized the union in 1900. Three years later they obtained a charter from the international union of hod carriers. The union originated during the period of intense exiled political activity in the area, thus indicating the continuing importance of political interactions with Mexico. The P L M may have played an influential role in the local's early history since some of its leaders were aligned with the exiled organization. Cenobio Andrade, one of the union's officers, was a P L M member and organizer.[8]

Local 93 was organized for the expressed purpose of combatting job and wage discrimination. While Anglo carpenters and masons were guaranteed an eight-hour work day and a regular salary by the city, Mexicans were assigned jobs as laborers with a work schedule of between nine and ten hours a day for wages that did not exceed $1.25. In obvious response to the racial hiring policy, one of the founders insisted the group should approach the mayor "as a people demanding our rights." They eventually adopted what they considered a more cautious approach. The group selected a delegation and officially instructed it to visit the city's head administrator as a class of workers.[9] The outcome of this meeting is not known.

The members were skilled and semiskilled workers. Many of them were laborers who periodically traveled to the outlying agricultural areas to supplement their meager earnings in the city. The most striking characteristic of the union was its unstable membership history. The union's average monthly membership ranged between a low of twenty-eight in 1909 to a high of two hundred and forty-seven in 1919 (see Table 8). Average monthly figures remained relatively stable between 1910 and 1918. The high influx of Mexicans who arrived in San Antonio in 1910 contributed to the first noticeable increase. The wartime demand on the local economy and the occupational benefits that the workers received as a result probably caused the second increase. Recruiting efforts by Idar and by other organizations that joined the A F L organizing campaigns in the city also may have contributed to the membership increase in 1919.

Reminiscent of El Congreso Mexicanista, the F L U, and the Socialist Party unions, the local's leadership intended to create one large umbrella union of Mexican workers in San Antonio. In June, 1915, they claimed that the Central Labor Council from San Antonio had granted them permission to expand their organizing activities among all Mexican workers in the city. Local 93 may have decided to seek this official dispensation because of the relative absence of Mexican A F L locals. This one attempt to bring Mexican workers under one big union does not appear to have succeeded since the union's membership and financial records did not reflect an accompanying increase.[10]

The union's inability to collect dues from the entire membership made for a financially unstable situation. This was evident in the obvious discrepancy between membership figures reported to local papers and the numbers that the union registered in its financial records. For instance, in October, 1919, *El Unionista* cited a "more than 300" membership figure, while the local itself reported 217 dues-paying members to its parent organization.[11] Instability was also evident in the union's high rate of attrition (see Table 9). The union's initiation figures between 1911 and 1920 show that on any given year the great majority of the members had joined within the previous twenty-four months. Although the union continually replenished its ranks with an increasing number of recruits, a high attrition rate prevented it from maintaining stable growth.

At Austin Mexican workers belonged to a maintenance-of-way union and Federal Labor Union No. 16493. The unions may have been made up totally of Mexicans in 1920. Local unionists openly declared Mexicans ineligible in fourteen of the city's thirty-six locals.[12] Similar divisions among Galveston unionists in 1917 may account for the installation of a separate laborers' union for Mexicans. On May 28 an organizer named J. W. Young reported to the council that the AFL had granted the Mexican federal labor union a charter. However, on June 11, the council reported that a hod carriers' union had submitted a formal grievance, "against the organizing of a Mexican Common laborers' union."[13] Mexicans were similarly encouraged to practice solidarity among themselves at Kingsville where La Unión de Ayudantes Ferrocarrileros No. 2832 and La Unión Local de Trabajadores No. 14722 demonstrated a preference to join with other Mexican groups in separate public celebrations and community-wide meetings during the second decade.[14]

Mexicans also participated in the AFL as members of locals with a mixed ethnic membership, usually in urban-based unions that represented local industries with a sizable Mexican work force. The numerical extent of this type of participation is difficult to ascertain, although cases in which Mexicans served in important leadership positions indicate their presence among the rank and file. This indicator, however, as well as actual references to Mexican participation in mixed unions, rarely appeared in statements by labor officials, in union meeting records, or in the TSFL annual convention proceedings.

The earliest convention delegate representation recorded for Mexicans from San Antonio was in 1909. N. Guerra represented the Flour Mill Workers' Union, while M. A. Domínguez represented one of the largest mixed unions in the city, the United Brotherhood of Carpenters and Joiners of America, No. 14.[15] The probable peak year for Mexican carpenters was 1912 when M. A. Domínguez was elected delegate to the city's Central Labor Council. Although another delegate replaced him that same year, he reemerged as a "trustee" in 1919. The city's Typographical Union No. 172 included L. A. Bravo in its Executive Committee in 1915. The following year only one Mexican, Pascual M. Díaz, was a member of the union.[16] Mexican membership in the union increased immediately after the First World War, principally as a result of the AFL's shift in organizing policy. Other mixed unions like the Boot and Shoe Workers' Union No. 195 and the Brotherhood of Maintenance of Way Laborers and Railroad Workers No. 1588 also registered increases in the late 1910s.[17]

The minute books of the Austin Trades Council listed one single Mexican entry between 1904 and 1910. In January, 1910, the central body received union credentials from Rudolph Luna, representing the Cigar Makers Local. The Galveston delegation to the 1906 TSFL convention included one Mexican, A. Gómez. Gómez represented a dock workers union, the Screwmen's Local No. 217.[18] The minutes of the Galveston Labor Council for the period 1914–20 also indicate low Mexican participation in mixed unions. Of 267 delegates to the Labor Council between 1914 and 1917, three were Mexicans. Their representation decreased between 1917 and 1920 to one delegate, Frank P. Rodríguez, of the Boiler Makers and Ship Builders Union No. 132. Rodríguez was continuously elected as a delegate beginning in 1914.[19]

A more impressive record of Mexican participation was evident in the United Mine Workers' Union locals. The large Mexican work force in the Bridgeport area coal mines, the site of a previously mentioned socialist local, contributed a significant number of members to Local No. 787. Their participation resulted in the emergence of some leaders, including Marcos Galindo, who attended the 1906 TSFL annual convention.[20] Mexican participation was even more impressive at Thurber during the period between 1903 and 1926. Their numbers may have increased significantly after 1903, when the national union assigned a Mexican organizer to the area. Mexican representation in the Thurber union dwindled as a result of the 1926 deportation.[21]

The modest numerical incorporation of Mexicans coincided with their low representation in such important labor events as the TSFL annual conventions. The conventions between 1904 and 1920 listed few Spanish-surnamed delegates (see Table 10). Admittedly, the Spanish-surname method of determining representation is not very reliable, especially in the case of the Thurber unions that included a considerable number of Italian members with Spanish-sounding surnames. Also, delegate records do not list the total number of separate Mexican unions. The FLU from Laredo was not recorded, and the Hod Carriers Union No. 93 was only listed once. Financial and language difficulties may have kept these unions as well as others from sending representatives. On the other hand, Central Labor Council delegates may have indirectly represented them as member organizations in the city federations. Nevertheless, the fact that some unions either did not send Mexican delegates at all or sent them irregularly indicates underrepresentation in separate and mixed unions.

Thurber unions had the best Mexican representation, counting a total of fourteen delegates in seventeen conventions. Again, the highly questionable Thurber data may have inflated the real figures for Mexican representation. Delegate distribution was uneven, except in the case of the highly unionized city of San Antonio where representation was fairly consistent between 1916 and 1920. The area south of San Antonio did not register a single Mexican union delegate. It is difficult to identify a chronological trend, although the year 1920 recorded the highest number of possible Mexican delegates.[22]

Causes of Low Participation and Representation

The federations' organizing policies accounted in large measure for low Mexican participation and representation. The federations as well as the railroad brotherhoods restricted their organizing attention to the crafts in the belief that skill scarcity afforded them the necessary leverage to maintain job control and to bargain improvements. By disregarding the lesser-skilled ranks that included the vast majority of Mexican as well as African-American workers, labor reflected and reinforced racial divisions in the work place. The federations also paid little attention to the agricultural industry, the most important single employer of Mexican labor, and none to South Texas, the region where Mexicans predominated. The industrial and geographical bias also reflected a tactical decision in favor of higher industrialized settings that granted craft workers a theoretical advantage by virtue of their concentrated numbers and highly specialized skills. As previously stated, the TSFL was also in an embryonic stage of development during the first decade and was limited financially in its ability to support organizing campaigns.

Another explanation underscores the importance of political forces in inhibiting unionization. Paul Taylor and Manuel Gamio observed that farmers introduced large numbers of workers from Mexico into an increasingly tight labor market to discourage unionization and to maintain low wages.[23] The practice of occupational discrimination in the urban areas compounded the problem by keeping Mexicans beyond the reach of the federations. Also, the perception by Anglo labor that urban employers were dipping into the bulging sector of low-wage labor led to a reaction that further reinforced occupational discrimination and bolstered barriers to union participation.

Anglo workers excluded Mexicans from some unions even while the federations sought to selectively incorporate them during the 1920s to relieve the perceived threat. This apparent anomaly in fact represented two aspects of an attempt to regain control of the labor market. Antialien and antileft campaigns, in other words, excluded potential competitors, while labor organizing checked the growing power of employers. Overall, however, the anti-Mexican atmosphere generally limited the effectiveness of the AFL's policy of incorporation.

Bars to union membership were especially pronounced against Mexican nationals during the second decade when Samuel Gompers began to openly urge their expulsion from AFL-affiliated unions unless they became citizens. Most Mexican nationals, on the other hand, refused to join precisely because they were required to become citizens. The decision to seek naturalization and forego their Mexican citizenship was tantamount to rejecting their loyalty to the motherland. When their place of employment became unionized, Anglos and naturalized Europeans insisted that Mexicans become naturalized and threatened to kick them out of the unions and their jobs if they refused to do so. In the majority of cases, they refused.[24]

Racial antipathies contributed to labor's more obvious failing, its inability to acknowledge the strategic need to more fully incorporate the Mexican skilled workers already organized within independent workers' organizations in the larger urban areas outside South Texas. The benign reason for this state of affairs was general indifference by organized labor, according to Clemente Idar and Antonio I. Villarreal, a member of the PLM during the first decade, and cabinet member of the Carranza administration and governor of Nuevo León during the second. In 1918 Idar noted, "it is absolutely certain that heretofore, no complete effort has ever been made to unionize Mexican and Mexican-American workingmen."[25] Villarreal added that "up to the present time no serious, hard and decided effort has been made to assimilate, within the organized labor movement of the United States" the Mexican worker.[26]

Other critics were more blunt with their indictments. Juan Rico, official delegate from Mexico to the Pan American Federation of Labor (PAFL) conference, reported widespread discrimination by AFL locals on the basis of a fact-finding tour throughout Texas in 1914. According to one of his informants, Pascual M. Díaz, it was almost impossible to gain admission into AFL locals.[27] Idar's brother Eduardo also pointed out that Mexicans who managed to gain entry encountered discrimination within ethnically mixed locals. He claimed that the Anglo leadership usually granted the first and choice work assignments to their Anglo members and refused to use Spanish during their meetings.[28]

An added factor that inhibited the incorporation of Mexicans throughout the early 1900s was the persistent isolation and second-class status that they usually inherited as members of federal labor unions. Mexicans who wished to participate often had the limited option of joining as a federal labor union, an industrial form of organization that was never fully integrated into the federations as a partner of equal status. Despite the fact that a federal labor union allowed Mexican workers to retain their culturally familiar environment as all-Mexican organizations, it separated them from the rest of the labor movement. One of the major problems was that federal labor unions were directly affiliated with the AFL and were never sufficiently incorporated into the state federation. This isolation became an especially serious problem when the TSFL refused them assistance on the grounds that it was not responsible for them.

The problem became evident in at least two cases involving Federal Labor Union No. 12858 from Galveston and Federal Labor Union No. 14365 from Big Spring. The unions did not specify the kind of assistance that they sought, preferring instead to make a general appeal for any type of help that the federation could extend. The officers of the Galveston local, J. Guerra Díaz and Benjamín Herrera, described the condition of their membership in 1910 as "critical." They worked as laborers for the street railway company ten hours a day at very low wages. There is no evidence that the federation or the Galveston Labor Council answered their plea. The Big Spring local made a similar request for assistance in 1914. The all-Mexican union of railroad laborers complained that management paid unionists lower wages and had recently released seven of them. The delegates to the 1914 state convention referred the matter to the AFL with the recommendation that the national federation assist the Big Spring local in affiliating with the appropriate railroad union so that it could be serviced properly.[29]

The cases of the Galveston and Big Spring locals underscored the fact that sheer poverty made it difficult for Mexican workers to sustain organizations during difficult times. The payment of membership dues and fees for strike and relief funds also discouraged members from continuing in the unions or from sending delegates to the annual conventions, especially when the federations did not, or could not, extend assistance in the form of paid organizers and financial help. The published proceedings of the TSFL annual conventions and the numerous cases reported by such labor papers as *El Defensor del Obrero, Pan American Labor Press,* and *El Unionista* provide examples of Mexican unions that were hampered by the lack of resources.

In some cases workers freely opted to remain outside organized labor. Some of these workers, according to the editor of the Austin weekly *La Vanguardia,* simply did not accept or fully understand the merits of unionization.[30] They may have preferred to pursue a wage-cutting or strike-breaking route as the best option given the uncertainties of the labor market and their lack of faith in concerted workers' actions. Others chose alternative forms of organization for ideological or practical reasons. These included unionists affiliated with the Texas Socialist Party and the PLM. Still others selected to remain in the organizations that were closest to their communities—the independent workers' organizations. The declaration of a policy to incorporate Mexican workers, however, encouraged many of them to join the AFL.

A Door Is Opened

In order to appreciate the role that the AFL played in shaping labor relations in Texas, it is necessary to step back and examine its larger sphere of interest and activity. Long opposed to European immigration, the AFL held that newcomers posed an economic and political threat to U.S.-born workers. AFL leaders believed that foreign-born workers threatened job security and political stability with their added numbers and radical ideas. The rise in Mexican immigration during the first decade, along with the claims of imported radicalism and intensifying competition, drew the AFL's attention to the Mexican border. National union leaders responded to Mexican immigration with a vigorous lobbying effort in favor of restrictions. Failing at this, they established an alliance with labor from Mexico that resulted in the adoption of a plan to regulate the immigrant flow and to organize Mexican workers in the United States.[31]

AFL leaders began entertaining a collaborative strategy to deal with Mexican immigration as early as 1911 in response to pleas for help from the TSFL and other southwestern state federations. A delegate to the annual TSFL convention reported that "the work of organizing these people [Mexicans] will receive more attention from the A.F. of L." The AFL was then directing its state and local affiliates to implement an Americanization scheme among European immigrants. In Samuel Gompers's eyes it was not enough to lobby for immigration restrictions; the AFL had to extend its own brand of conservative unionism. Despite the union's organizing promises and expressed concern regarding the Americanization of immigrants, there is no evidence that it expanded its plan of incorporation to include Mexicans. However, it is significant that the labor federations had finally begun to direct their attention towards the Mexican community.[32]

The idea of organizing Mexican workers resurfaced in 1914 when the AFL proposed a Mexican American labor alliance to the Confederación del Obrero Mundial (COM), the leading national labor federation at the time. According to the AFL, the proposed alliance was intended to discourage Mexican immigration and to court millions of Mexican workers in the United States who were thought to be difficult to organize and who were perceived as an economic threat to American labor. The more militant COM welcomed the opportunity to extend the international struggle and to cooperate with the AFL in averting a war between

Mexico and the United States. The alleged raid by Francisco Villa at Columbus, New Mexico, and the Pershing expedition that crossed the international border ostensibly in pursuit of Villa heightened tensions to dangerous levels. COM, however, fell out of favor with the Carranza administration, and the idea of a labor alliance was shelved. But the AFL continued to entertain the idea as Gompers increasingly intervened in Mexico-U.S. diplomatic circles and proclaimed himself a key intermediary seeking peace between both nations and better protection for labor in Mexico.[33]

Mexican miners' unions representing the Arizona State Federation of Labor revived the proposal for an international alliance at the 1917 AFL convention. The successful organizing campaigns among Mexican miners encouraged the view that Mexican workers were organizable. According to the resolution submitted by Canuto Vargas, one of the leading spokespersons for the Arizona delegation, "the Mexican is as quick to organize and maintain the solidarity of the labor movement as the American worker." The federation endorsed the resolution and instructed its leaders to initiate plans for a PAFL conference in cooperation with La Confederación Regional Obrera Mexicana (CROM), the new national labor federation that had recently achieved prominence in Mexico.[34]

During the PAFL conference held at Laredo in 1918, Gompers declared the policy to organize Mexican workers as part of a plan for an international labor alliance. The AFL announced that it sought, in conjunction with labor representatives from Latin America, to establish the PAFL, organize permanent and temporary Mexican residents in the United States, restrict immigration, and cultivate friendly relations between the labor movements, the peoples, and the republics of Mexico and the United States. Mexican labor, represented primarily by CROM, gave primary importance to the concept of organizing Mexicans in the United States and to the practice of exchanging union cards during the planning of the first conference and during all the PAFL conferences held during the 1920s. Organizing Mexican workers represented a key commitment, but it was by no means Gompers's central motivation in building a labor alliance. He also sought to recruit the assistance of Mexican labor to win Carranza to the Allied cause. The war ended a few days before the PAFL convened, allowing Gompers to devote his full attention to his other key concern, immigration.[35]

Although the AFL and CROM entered into formal agreements regarding immigration and Mexican workers in the United States, the overarching understanding remained undefined until 1925. William Green, the president of the AFL after Gompers's death in 1924, called a jointly sponsored conference at El Paso to seek an agreement "upon immigration policies which might be recommended to our governments." The delegates to this meeting formulated the principle of voluntary self-restraint as the basis for continued understanding and cooperation. According to this principle workers had the right to travel freely, although each country had a responsibility to restrain its people from migrating, if their actions threatened the rights and welfare of its neighbors. A corollary of this principle granted each group the right and obligation to safeguard their interests in their own country.

Both parties thus agreed to cooperate on restricting immigration from Mexico and on advancing the unionist cause. The AFL responded to pressures by CROM representatives by promising to accept the exchange of union cards and to continue incorporating Mexicans into its locals. Green, in turn, assured the AFL Executive Council that voluntary restraint instead of restrictive legislation would control Mexican immigration. The AFL thus remained committed to the idea of an alliance which made it subject to CROM pressures to incorporate Mexicans.[36]

The decision by the AFL to court Mexican workers in Texas was associated with another set of concerns. Gompers was interested in promoting craft unionism in Mexico and along the border as a response to the growing influence of the left. By this means the AFL hoped to counter the growing influence of anarcho-syndicalism in the Southwest and in the northern region of Mexico. Labor militancy and industrial strife had also shaken the foundations of the national socio-economy. The wartime demand on the U.S. economy added to the political crisis and produced an alliance between Pres. Woodrow Wilson, corporate leaders, and social reformers like Gompers. This alliance implemented readiness and wartime programs that promised economic efficiency and political stability on the home front.

Gompers played a key part in this plan. He assumed a collaborative role in 1916 when Wilson appointed him labor representative to the Advisory Board of the National Council on Defense and named him president of the American Alliance for Labor and Democracy. Part of his political reward included money that was used to finance the PAFL and its bilingual organ, the *Pan American Labor Press* (San Antonio, 1919–21). Months before the PAFL conference, Wilson authorized twenty-five thousand dollars to establish a "labor loyalty press" after Gompers advised him that the German influence was especially threatening in Mexico and along the international border. The president also authorized an additional twenty-five thousand dollars for the labor leader's use.[37]

Upon his election President Wilson had inherited pressing security concerns associated with the Texas-Mexico border. Increased revolutionary activity on the Mexican side and claims that the revolution was inspiring German intrigue and Mexican depredations on the Texas side alarmed the president. The San Diego revolt and the celebrated Zimmerman note of 1917 confirmed local fears and justified further militarization of the border. Wilson's support for Gompers thus represented a strategic move to counter the political influence of the left and to use C R O M to win Carranza to the Allied cause. Gompers kept Wilson informed of developments in Texas. Clemente Idar wrote to the president, perhaps at Gompers's behest, stating an A F L position that played on Wilson's concern over political stability in Mexico and Texas. The continuing armed conflict in Mexico had reached dangerous levels, he said, and the situation "looks very unpleasant in reference to the safety of our southern border line at a time when we need the services of our large armed forces for internal safety and for cooperation with our allies in the European Continent."[38]

Inattentiveness, according to Idar, imperiled the Carranza administration and placed the southern border under the influence of German agents. More importantly, elements within the Mexican community in Texas, namely the daily *La Prensa* and the weekly *La Revista Mexicana,* of San Antonio, were "carrying a seditious movement against the present Government of Mexico." Idar concluded with a note of warning that "any propaganda carried on in this country calculated to disturb conditions in Mexico, can bring about most disastrous results against our own welfare if permitted to continue, for it can be readily seen that in the present crisis we must maintain peace in Mexico, so that our common enemies may not harass us by instigating trouble and uprisings in Mexico, which would be tremendously vexing."[39]

German propaganda, the catch-all cause of dissent attributed to Mexicans along the border, achieved public notoriety during the San Diego revolt and in subsequent military conflicts along the entire Mexico-U.S. border. When the German conspiracy theory resurfaced to explain the almost sudden exodus of Mexican laborers who feared the military draft, Idar was leading the advance team sent by the A F L to prepare for the P A F L conference in Laredo. He joined the statewide pro-immigration campaign that included chambers of commerce, civic organizations, and public officials from South Texas who feared that the outmigration placed the agricultural economy in jeopardy. The A F L thus quickly began to play an important role in local as well as international politics.[40]

Although labor representatives from various countries participated in the P A F L conference, the main actors were the A F L and C R O M. The discussions over such issues as Mexico's neutrality and the A F L's opposition to the labor left in the United States resembled a confrontation between surrogates representing Mexico City and Washington, D.C., however, in the end the issue of Mexican workers in the United States became the major point of apparent conciliation.[41]

It was clear from the beginning that issues related to Mexican workers in the United States would assume a central position in the conference's deliberations. The AFL's advance team, which included Idar, an AFL official, and an organizer of the International Confectionery Workers' Union, gave wide publicity to the upcoming meeting. They met privately with independent workers' organizations from both sides of the border and organized a public rally that was attended by approximately three hundred workers. Idar convinced several presidents of organizations to request AFL charters and act as hosts of the PAFL conference. The effusive welcome by the unions of carpenters, painters, blacksmiths, retail clerks, and other Mexican unions impressed AFL officials "with an enthusiasm never given before to any public assemblage on the boundary line."[42]

Luis Morones, head of CROM and the Mexican delegation, also took notice of the large number of local Mexican unionists and attempted to strengthen his negotiating hand with the AFL by winning them over. During the opening ceremonies at a local park, he departed from the standard formalities to address in Spanish the large crowd that had gathered. He assured them that the Mexican delegation had not come "to render vassalage" to the AFL, but to challenge its record among Mexicans in the United States. Morones added that his delegation had come to meet with them and

> to get first hand information as to the position in which you find yourselves, and to learn if the Mexican worker is really respected in this country and if he is treated in a just manner. If, as we hope, the results of this Conference will correct many errors and dispel the misunderstanding which, unfortunately, has guided the acts of certain elements that do not understand nor recognize the value of the Mexican people who work in this country, then you will be among the first to gather the fruits of our labors.[43]

Morones asked them to step forward and submit their grievances to the Mexican unionists. He, no doubt, anticipated a confrontation with AFL leaders on the issue of discrimination within the federation and wished to obtain supportive evidence.

Among the Mexican delegates representing the United States were José Reyes Estrada, of the San Antonio-based Sociedad Artes Gráficas, and George Montijo, of the Dallas Central Labor Council and United

Leather Workers' International Union, Local No. 28. Delegates representing the important Mine, Mill and Smelter Workers locals from Morenci, Metcalf, and Clifton, Arizona, included J. Ignacio García, Luis E. Soto, and Guillermo Quiroz. Vargas, who became the Spanish-language secretary of the PAFL and coeditor of the PAFL's official organ, the *Pan American Labor Press,* also attended as a representative of the Arizona State Federation of Labor. Clemente Idar, one of the key figures at the meeting, assisted in translating the speeches and in the overall coordination of the conference.[44]

Lively debates between AFL and CROM delegates threatened to undermine the possibility of establishing an alliance. The CROM delegates, under heavy criticism at home from leftist labor leaders for "selling out" to U.S. imperialism, tested the AFL's sincerity by accusing it of allowing its unions to exclude Mexican workers. Other Latin American labor delegates and Mexican unionists from the United States also charged the AFL with violating the principle of working-class unity by lobbying for immigration restrictions. CROM delegates, however, levelled the heaviest criticism against the AFL. They accused the organization of practicing racial discrimination and demanded substantive efforts to correct this problem. The Mexican delegates were adamant on this point and would have bolted the conference if the AFL had not acknowledged the problem of discrimination and demonstrated a willingness to organize Mexicans.[45]

Gompers and other labor leaders first responded defensively by pointing to the federation's standing practice against dictating policy to its subordinate organizations. Although claiming to be powerless to prohibit discriminatory practices, Gompers also announced what amounted to a commitment in favor of incorporating Mexicans. To demonstrate his support for the new AFL policy, he appointed Idar to work as an organizer. The AFL also promised to bear the major burden of protecting Mexican workers by urging its affiliates to accept Mexican union cards, by placing labor representatives along the border to "protect" immigrant workers, and by appointing additional organizers to work among Mexican workers.[46]

The issue of immigration became the major point of contention between the AFL and CROM during subsequent PAFL meetings. The AFL continued lobbying for immigration restrictions despite periodic criticism from CROM and Mexican unions from Arizona. The view expressed privately by an advisor to Wilson became increasingly clear to even the most casual observer: Gompers "had no interest in Mexican labor other than to keep them from coming here to compete with our labor after the war."[47] Gompers reminded his critics that he was first responsible to American workers and that immigration had introduced job competitors who were not only reluctant to join unions but were prone to become strikebreakers. He expected more serious problems during the postwar period because of an anticipated production decline, a drop in the demand for labor, and the need to rehire returning veterans. This position on immigration was accommodated by CROM largely because of its waning influence in Mexico and the organizing support that it obtained from the AFL.[48]

An AFL commitment to Mexican workers in the United States, however, had been won. The AFL pledged to promote labor solidarity through active union organizing among Mexican workers. Beginning in 1916, the federation made public pronouncements to this effect in every annual convention, during several PAFL conferences, and in the *Pan American Labor Press*. The national federation also influenced the TSFL to adopt the new policy through various communications involving official representatives like Idar. Idar's appointment, though limited by his broad jurisdiction and his added responsibility to discourage immigration, was one of the most important contributions to the implementation of the new policy.

Idar and the State Federation

Although Clemente Idar spent a great deal of time organizing in various parts of the Southwest and in Mexico, he devoted most of his attention to Texas. Gompers apparently saw Texas as a major linchpin in his attempt to build an alliance with CROM.[49] Also, Texas shared the longest border with Mexico and was the major point of destination for Mexican immigrants. Moreover, Texas had the distinct reputation of being torn by sharp ethnic conflict characterized by charges of unfair immigrant competition and countercharges of widespread discrimination. As a consequence, Gompers utilized Idar to implement a plan that would respond to Anglo labor's preoccupation with immigration as well as with CROM's concern over discrimination. This meant that Idar had to bring Mexican workers into the TSFL fold but at the same time prevent others from becoming threats to Anglo labor. He sought to accomplish this by chartering existing Mexican workers' organizations and by organizing repatriation campaigns among unemployed agricultural workers in urban areas. Idar's third overarching responsibility was to assist in improving relations between the TSFL and CROM and to communicate the AFL's new conciliatory approach towards Mexican workers.

Idar undertook two additional related responsibilities that underscored his role as one of Gompers's most trusted representatives in Texas. He coordinated various aspects of labor's nonpartisan political campaign in the state. This involved visits to central bodies and locals throughout Texas to raise funds for friendly local and statewide candidates seeking political office. Idar also participated in local campaigns to elect labor candidates. Although more research is needed to determine if Idar's involvement in labor politics represented yet another strategy to incorporate Mexicans as voters, he directed most of his attention to securing Mexican voters during the 1924 San Antonio elections.[50]

Idar also interceded on behalf of Gompers and his successor, Green, in the diplomatic arena. AFL and PAFL leaders had always feared U.S. intervention in Mexican political affairs, and Gompers was especially adept at assuming credit for averting war between Mexico and the United States. He continued to present the AFL as a useful ally, especially when CROM officials asked the federations to intervene in support of political leaders and groups that were friendly to labor. This allowed Gompers to accumulate bargaining chips with CROM on the issue of immigration. The 1923 revolt by Adolfo de la Huerta against president Alvaro Obregón gave the AFL leader his last major opportunity to intervene before his death. He ordered Idar to visit the ports of Galveston, Port Arthur, and Beaumont and report any arms smuggling by rebel forces to federal authorities. Although there is no evidence that the AFL prevented the de la Huerta forces from obtaining arms, it demonstrated to Obregón and CROM the usefulness of the labor alliance.[51]

Green also sought to maintain good relations with labor in Mexico by instructing Idar to negotiate with the Texas governor for the release of *Los Mártires de Texas*. When the men obtained their freedom, the Mexican Foreign Office requested that Idar accompany them back to Mexico. Although Green did not approve the request for fear of overstepping legal boundaries, Idar became known for his intimate association with the AFL and PAFL leadership, a fact that gave his work in Texas a great deal of credibility.[52]

Idar began organizing prior to his appointment. As stated previously, he prepared the ground for the PAFL by helping numerous Mexican organizations obtain AFL charters. This allowed the AFL to present Laredo as a showcase of its magnanimity, in anticipation of CROM's accusations of discrimination. At the same time Mexican unionists in Laredo demonstrated a capacity and willingness to embrace craft unionism, thus favorably impressing Anglo unionists, who were prone to see Mexican workers simply as threats. Idar, of course, was not alone in his work. Numerous Mexican community leaders in Laredo contributed to these outcomes by capitalizing on the opportunity to obtain affiliation. In addition, John Murray and Vargas, English-speaking and Spanish-speaking secretaries of the PAFL, respectively, gave wide publicity to the cause of unity and understanding as editors of the San Antonio–based *Pan American Labor Press.*[53]

One of Idar's first direct attempts to influence the TSFL leadership involved the Laredo Central Labor Union. The secretary of the city federation, Rafael García, had forwarded a resolution to the 1921 annual convention requesting a Spanish-speaking organizer to help "maintain the existence of the labor movement" in Laredo. Employers were hiring Mexican immigrants in the city's booming construction industry, thereby displacing U.S.-born workers and depleting the union ranks. Serious financial problems resulted, and the city federation could not even afford to send a delegate to personally request assistance from the assembly.[54]

Idar may have suggested that they submit the request for assistance to the TSFL, since he frequented Laredo and worked closely with local unionists. In 1921 TSFL President George H. Slater accompanied Idar to Laredo. During their twelve-day stay in the city, they visited all the locals, helped reorganize the Central Labor Union, and officiated in the affiliation ceremonies of two locals, the Boot and Shoe Workers' Union and the Painters' Union. Slater's subsequent description of Idar as "an earnest, sincere and untiring worker," in a speech to the 1922 TSFL annual convention, represented yet another important consequence of the Laredo visit.[55] Not only did Slater's commendation help establish Idar's reputation within the federation as an able and trusted organizer, but it advanced the idea of incorporating Mexican workers.

The 1922 convention also provided Anglo labor an opportunity to meet labor leaders from Mexico and broaden their racial views. Hosting the convention, the El Paso Labor Council decided to invite six leading unionists from Mexico to address the assembly. This move represented a major change from the usual speeches and resolutions that only spoke of the Mexican as a potential job competitor and strikebreaker. The federation, of course, sought to promote an alliance in keeping with the AFL's effort to regulate the flow of immigrants into Texas. The convention delegates received the Mexican speakers with great enthusiasm and loud applause, no doubt impressed with the advances that labor had made in Mexico and with their spirited calls for unity.[56] Slater, like many of his fellow unionists, had assumed that Mexicans were politically backward and that he was going to have to teach them a thing or two about labor politics. His change of heart reflected a major improvement in his view of Mexican labor: "I was under the impression that I was going to be able to be of some service to the representatives of the labor movement in Mexico, and after hours of conference I discovered I was being taught what the labor movement could do."[57]

Slater was making reference to a four-hour private meeting during which the Mexican labor leaders explained what they meant by unity and cooperation. They sought the exchange of international union cards. The negative response by the TSFL dampened whatever expectations the Mexican leaders had. It also made the issue of cooperatively addressing the problem of immigration a moot point. The next day Slater explained to the assembly that the federation agreed in principle with the proposition. He added, however, that the federation could not honor the request because it did not have the necessary jurisdictional power over the internationals. Slater's comments served as a reminder that the TSFL could declare improvements in understanding and promote official interactions, while at the same time seek to regulate the immigrant flow without observing the important principle of union card exchange. In other words, the TSFL was beginning to implement the AFL's patchwork understanding.

Circumstances within the TSFL similarly circumscribed whatever favorable impressions that Idar, Mexican workers' organizations, and labor leaders from Mexico made on Anglo labor. Affiliated locals were leading antialien campaigns in major cities outside South Texas and were refusing to admit Mexicans or to recognize union cards from Mexico. Moreover, delegates to the annual conventions were submitting numerous complaints alleging that Mexicans were depressing wages and threatening to cross picket lines. Contributing to a tendency to define the alleged Mexican threat in racial terms was the almost negligible representation of Mexican workers in local and statewide labor circles until the early 1920s.

As a result of conflicting views, the 1925 TSFL convention adopted a narrowly defined policy for incorporating Mexicans. The federation did this by passing a resolution acknowledging that immigration also undermined the condition of "bona fide" Mexicans, that is, U.S.-born and naturalized Mexican citizens, and suggesting that they, too, be included in the house of labor. The federation made a distinction defining the limits of incorporation that the AFL's policy ostensibly dictated. In an attempt to assuage prevailing fears over immigration, the resolution also recommended that the AFL call an international labor conference with representatives of the AFL, CROM, and the state federations of Texas, Arizona, New Mexico, California, and Colorado. The aforementioned conference, according to the TSFL delegates, was to discuss the issue of immigration with the hope that CROM would seek "the solution of these problems" in collaboration with the Mexican government.[58]

Idar played a key role in the deliberations that led to the federation's new interest in the U.S.-born and naturalized Mexicans. Although he did not challenge the idea of limited incorporation, Idar did express serious concern with the persistent racial allusions to Mexicans. In his estimation, wholesale racial depictions contradicted the new policy, disregarded the experiences of poverty and discrimination among Mexicans, and discredited the federation in the eyes of potential members and labor leaders from Mexico. The propensity to inject racism into matters that he considered purely economic also made for a highly volatile situation that benefitted no one. Moreover, it denied the common cause of workers. He expressed these concerns on at least two occasions, during the TSFL's 1924 and 1925 annual conventions.

The 1924 assembly held in Port Arthur heard from Idar through a letter read by Lucien Andler, a TSFL vice president from Port Arthur. No doubt conscious of possible racial distrust and suspicions among Anglo labor, Idar first validated his position of authority by noting that Gompers had assigned him the job of addressing the problem of immigration in Texas. He reminded the delegates that management was responsible for pitting large numbers of immigrants against organized labor.

The crisis, he noted, had also victimized the Mexican worker, underscoring the fact that the fundamental problem was an economic one. He had dealt with the issue of immigration in 1921 and 1922 when unemployment and continuing immigration had resulted in tensions and even violence against Mexican workers. For Idar, the anti-Mexican violence in such places as Thurber and Ranger had been "bread-and-butter riots—not riots based on racial antagonism." Although racism was clearly an overriding factor, Idar sought to structure the discussion over immigration in more manageable terms, that is, in ways that would emphasize the machinations of management and the victimization of the entire working class. Matters were not appreciably different in 1924, and as Idar observed, "Racial antagonism is not involved in this new crisis."[59]

Nor was the Mexican government responsible for the large number of Mexican immigrants in Texas, according to Idar. In fact, he noted, Mexico had intervened, presumably at the request of the AFL, restraining approximately thirty thousand Mexicans from crossing the border. The Mexican consular offices were similarly disposed, for humanitarian reasons, to discourage further immigration and to repatriate those that were already here. On the other hand, in Texas cities unemployed Mexicans, including both immigrants and U.S.-born, were barely surviving their difficult condition.

In an effort to emphasize the workers' common class interests, Idar told of the large number of unemployed Mexicans in Houston, Port Arthur, San Antonio, and "all border points" who were also victimized by management. Houston alone registered one thousand unemployed Mexicans, "with prospects of having a larger number within the next fifteen or twenty days." Without any visible means of subsistence, they were experiencing some of the more extreme forms of hardship, including the lack of food. Numerous unemployed Mexicans in Houston with whom he had spoken claimed that employment agencies had misled them into believing that jobs were available in Texas cities. Idar concluded his letter by proposing a resolution that astutely reaffirmed the federation's opposition to immigration by expressing concern for the welfare of Mexican workers in the United States. According to the resolution, the TSFL delegates asked Gompers to do everything in his power to stop immigration because of "the suffering it will cause to thousands of men, women and children who are being induced to come to the United States by agents, propaganda and literature operating in the Central States of Mexico, all of it financed by American industrial and agricultural interests."[60]

Idar's 1925 exposition before the TSFL convention meeting in Amarillo lacked the formal preparation of the first, yet it expressed personal feelings and ideas that explain his views on racism and on the federation's selective policy of incorporating Mexican workers. Idar was unexpectedly prompted to address the delegates when Ernest O. Thompson, mayor of Amarillo and later chairman of the Texas Railroad Commission and candidate for governor, welcomed the federation on behalf of the city and local commercial and industrial interests. Thompson drew Idar's ire when he ridiculed Mexicans with his off-handed description of Amarillo's population as "100 percent Americans": "What I mean by 100 percent Americans is native-born, none of those are Mexicans or negroes. All upstanding folks. Now down near San Antonio, when they say 100,000 population, 40,000 of them are Mexicans, red-blooded, some of them red-headed (Laughter—the speaker being red-headed). But that doesn't hurt any. (Laughter)."[61]

Idar immediately stood up to speak. He castigated Thompson for insulting Mexico, a friendly nation that claimed the first labor government in the western hemisphere and that answered the call by the recently departed Gompers to build an international labor alliance. Idar leveled his strongest personal criticism against Thompson for inserting race into the federation's deliberations. No intelligent labor man, Idar noted, should divide workers on the basis of race, religion, creed, or philosophical beliefs. Thompson's remarks were particularly offensive to Idar because they implied disloyalty among the U.S.-born Mexicans. Moreover, they cast doubts on the decision to incorporate Mexicans by encouraging delegates to view them as possible political subversives simply because of their ancestry. Idar's comments on the issue of loyalty were unequivocal, though suggestive of a defensive ethnic identity:

"Those of us who happen to be of Mexican ancestry, and thank God, by force of destiny, born in this country, are just as loyal to our American civilization, just as loyal to the American flag, just as loyal to the American government, just as loyal to the American historical traditions as any one, and just as fundamentally American as any of you in this audience or any of you in this section may feel that they are."[62] Idar added that Mexican nationals had shown their own form of loyalty by contributing "the strength of their hands and their arms to the growth of this nation; they have contributed with every possible effort to industry, to agriculture and to the peaceful pursuits of the land."[63]

Idar ended his impromptu speech with additional comments on the irrationality of racial thinking in the labor movement. What did solidarity mean, after all, in the labor movement? Did it not mean the unity of all workers? And what about alliances with other labor movements in the hemisphere? The delegates could only agree with Thompson at the risk of contradicting the principle of solidarity. Idar thus finally rested his arguments against racism on the declared purposes of organized labor. Though he conceded to the federation the right to restrict organizing among the U.S.-born and naturalized, he insisted that the federation's conditional form of solidarity retain a race-free outlook, lest it be accused of being exclusionary and divisive.[64]

The delegates responded to Idar's speech with frequent applause, indicating that he had articulated the new governing set of ideas in the federation regarding the Mexican worker. The federation, in other words, had the right to limit membership to its own citizens. Citizenship, not race, however, was to serve as the basis for admission. To do otherwise was truly to contradict the principle of solidarity. Moreover, it would invite trouble unnecessarily, particularly since the federation was participating in an effort to build an alliance with Mexican labor. According to this tenuous alliance, CROM was to assist in the regulation of immigration, with the expectation that American labor demonstrate some solidarity. If the TSFL could not guarantee this at the local level, it could at least disavow racial discrimination in its annual deliberations and officially sanctioned organizing activities. For Idar and the numerous Mexican organizations that obtained AFL charters, this represented a historic opportunity that they utilized to improve their condition. Making use of this opportunity, however, meant conforming to the understanding of conditional solidarity.

Chartering and Organizing

In keeping with the federations' concern over immigration, Idar devoted a great deal of his time to activities intended to regulate the immigrant labor supply. He traveled extensively, usually on orders from Gompers to intercede in situations where Mexican workers were said by local Anglo unionists to be posing a threat as job competitors and strikebreakers. Idar's 1921 Fort Worth assignment is a case in point. In March of that year, John Hart, president of the Amalgamated Meatcutters and Butchers of North America, wrote Gompers with a request for the temporary appointment of a Mexican organizer in Fort Worth to forestall an alleged Mexican threat. Local meatcutters were planning a strike and feared that recently arrived Mexicans would be used as strikebreakers. Gompers instructed Idar to "investigate the situation reported and extend all assistance you can in the interest of the Amalgamated and Butcher Workmen." Idar was to remain in Fort Worth for a few days and devote his exclusive attention to the expected trouble.[65] A 1922 El Paso assignment was similar. Idar was told to prevent possible interference by Mexican strikebreakers during a conflict involving miners and railway workers on the U.S. side. Idar crossed the international border and convinced Mexican unions in Juárez, as per Gompers's instructions, "that Mexican workers refrain from coming to the United States at this time in search of employment."[66]

Idar also helped engineer a program of repatriation among Mexican families from South Texas. He reported in a letter to a local paper that the repatriation idea had germinated in a series of public meetings held by Mexican workers during the latter part of 1920. Idar noted that a union of agricultural workers he organized requested his assistance in the local repatriation effort. Idar became one of the principal intermediaries between the Mexican government and the newly organized Mexican collective, the Unión Colonizadora Mexicana. By July, 1921, Idar reported that thirty-five thousand Mexicans, presumably from throughout the United States, had returned to Mexico and that the Mexican government had spent $250,000 in the repatriation campaign. Five months later, President Alvaro Obregón reported that his government had spent over one million dollars in Mexico and the United States to assist fifty thousand repatriates. Fort Worth alone had seen two thousand Mexicans leave. Nearby Dallas also registered a large number.[67]

In a talk before the Unión Colonizadora Mexicana, he resolved the apparent contradiction involved in repatriating Mexicans who were actual or potential members of organized labor in Texas. He was reported to have stated that "even though some of the unions that he had recently organized would probably lose members as a consequence, he did not entertain the notion that his work was disrupted by said movement; he felt obligated by the principles, interests, goals, and objectives of the organized labor movement in the United States to offer its deep and sincere support."[68] Four months later Gompers encouraged Idar to continue his work in order that "we should all cooperate to bring about the best results both as workers of the United States and of Mexico to aid each other in every other way in furtherance of the possible relation of the peoples and the governments of the two republics."[69]

Gompers believed that it was in the best interest of everyone concerned to reduce the Mexican work force to improve the strategic position of organized labor. Idar apparently agreed. One should not assume from this, however, that Idar was only interested in regulating the immigrant work force. Although the AFL leadership reneged on its promises to incorporate Mexican nationals, possibly dampening local organizing spirits, Idar continued to build on this key understanding in the AFL-CROM alliance. Idar and the editors of *El Unionista* urged the incorporation of Mexican nationals even after the numbers of Mexican unemployed rose dramatically during the middle of 1920. Idar pursued this strategy at the same time that he openly criticized immigration and helped Mexicans return to Mexico. In other words, he maintained a more open organizing policy in the Mexican community than in Anglo labor circles.[70]

His organizing efforts among Mexican nationals notwithstanding, Idar may have supported a selective policy of incorporation because it conformed with his own bias in favor of U.S.-born Mexicans. This reflected a change in Idar's earlier Mexicanist stance, expressed during the planning of El Congreso Mexicanista. He now endorsed an ethnic strategy that coincided with the AFL's selective approach for incorporating Mexicans. Idar's letters and reports to Gompers indicated a strong bias in favor of the U.S.-born, who by virtue of their citizenship could presumably make a more effective claim for equality. Although Idar may have embraced this view independent of the AFL, the federation's new policy no doubt encouraged his ethnic proclivities.

While in Texas, Idar was almost always the only organizer who brought Mexicans into the AFL. Anglo organizers normally submitted reports that spoke about Mexican workers as job competitors and strikebreakers. This means that Mexican workers who gained admission into the AFL as a result of the work by Anglo organizers did so as part of the rare ethnically mixed craft unions. Also, Idar was the most important organizer in the almost sudden incorporation of Mexicans into the AFL and the TSFL. He devoted most of his attention to Laredo, San Antonio, and Corpus Christi and expanded his work beyond these localities with the help of local labor leaders associated with Mexican workers' organizations. He generally directed campaigns that encouraged existing organizations obtain AFL charters. With time, he assisted in the formation of new unions of Mexican as well as Anglo and African-American workers.[71]

According to Eduardo Idar, Clemente's brother, the Mexican AFL organizer formed ten unions in Laredo prior to the PAFL conference. Although Eduardo credited Clemente with organizing the unions, some already existed as independent workers' organizations. Clemente himself stressed in a report to John Murray that he had helped two unions acquire AFL charters: "I believe that Laredo has the two largest locals of Mexican carpenters and bricklayers existing on this frontier and their affiliation was affected only a few months ago through my personal activity in having brought organizers to accomplish said affiliation."[72]

Idar's organizing work was done in preparation for the PAFL conference. Two AFL officials who arrived in Laredo in September advertised the meeting as an attempt to unite the workers of the Americas, and they urged existing workers' organizations to join in the effort as AFL unions. Idar, along with other local labor leaders, lost little time in responding. In most instances, they organized public meetings and attracted workers from different mutual aid societies. At other times organizations reconstituted themselves into unions. The result was the formation of unions of carpenters, bricklayers, typographical workers, barbers, clerks, painters, cooks, and waiters.[73] One of the first groups to coalesce was the decorative painters and upholsterers. The widely publicized affiliation ceremonies included speeches by some of the most respected labor leaders in the city, including Idar, Luis Dávila, secretary of the union, and Rafael Trujillo, long-time orator and journalist.[74]

The typographical union, an organization with a prior history as an independent workers' organization, was chartered on the eve of the PAFL conference. The affiliation ceremonies of the Unión de Impresores included as official guests the Mexican delegates to the PAFL conference, who had just arrived in the city. The guests from Mexico included such dignitaries as Luis N. Morones, Juan Rico, Ezequiel Salcedo, Cayetano Pérez Ruis, and Rafael Quintero. Also present were José Reyes Estrada and Emilio Flores, officer of the defunct La Agrupación Protectora Mexicana. José María Mora, the popular socialist orator and writer previously aligned with El Congreso Mexicanista, La Sociedad de Obreros, and the FLU, was elected president of the typographical union.[75]

The formation of the barbers' union around this same time period underscored the importance of chartering reconstituted or existing groupings. Laredo already had a barbers' union before the 1918 organizing drive. A new group emerged in 1918 and adopted as one of its first items of business the idea of seeking affiliation. The decision was postponed, however, until the older and independent union of barbers could be convinced to join them as one unified body.[76]

Another union, possibly one of railway workers chartered in 1918, demonstrated the ease with which some of these organizations could revert back to their independent mutual aid status once their ties with the AFL were severed. The union left the AFL seven months after obtaining a charter and resumed operations as a mutual aid society. On January 20, 1921, the organization merged with La Sociedad Mutualista, Gremio de Carreteros, an organization of cart drivers. Nine months later it merged with La Sociedad Mutualista Obreros Unidos and became La Sociedad Mutualista, Conductores y Obreros Unidos, the previously discussed mutual aid society.[77]

Idar compensated for these losses by continuing to focus attention on his hometown. First of all, he assisted in the formation of a sufficient number of Mexican unions to revitalize the local labor movement. Indicative was the formation of the Central Labor Union and the prominent participation of Mexicans in it. Although the Central Labor Union reported many difficulties by 1921, it is worth noting that Mexican unionism was already an established fact. Under trying circumstances, Idar could still report in 1920 that "organized labor is slowly advancing in numerical strength over the unorganized." The establishment of a union of bakers, the initiation of a union label campaign, and the prospects of new jobs for the large number of unemployed workers in the construction of new buildings in the downtown area gave him reason to submit a hopeful report.[78]

While on the border, Idar also mixed labor diplomacy with organizing on both sides of the international line. For instance, during the latter part of 1921 he initiated a move to establish better relations between the United Brotherhood of Carpenters and Joiners of America and its counterpart in Mexico. He traveled to Aguascalientes to confer with carpenters' unions interested in establishing ties with the national union. His subsequent work among carpenters on both sides of the border provided the brotherhood the theoretical right to call itself an international union. A week after returning from Aguascalientes, Idar reported the installation of Carpenters' Union No. 993 in Piedras Negras, Mexico. Also joining in the ceremonies was another Eagle Pass carpenters' union that Idar organized, as well as unionists representing the machine shops from Piedras Negras.[79]

Idar continued visiting the border area during the early part of 1922. He spent two months further organizing railroad workers from Piedras Negras. The ensuing negotiations between the workers and the company on the preferred location of the railway shops led Idar to solicit the assistance of D. W. Tracy, the vice president of the Brotherhood of Electrical Workers, and Francisco A. Moreno, president of the Central Committee of the Mexican Miners' Union, La Rosita, Coahuila, and delegate to the 1918 PAFL conference. Their collaboration, according to the United States consul, resulted in placing the union of railroad workers "in control of the situation and the railroads will accept the recommendations of the labor heads as to where the railroad shops will be located." His informants claimed that Idar had received "considerable ovations from the laboring classes and that daily committees [of workers] are waiting outside his hotel to see him."[80]

Idar's visits to the border and his organizing ventures into Mexico were in keeping with the AFL's interest in extending the influence of U.S. labor. As previously noted, this influence was important in convincing Mexican unionists to assist the AFL in discouraging Mexican workers from entering the United States. The AFL was able to compel them to cooperate in this matter primarily because Idar had established friendly relations with unionists in the states of Coahuila, Nuevo León, and Chihuahua. His report of "a tour through Mexico" during the summer of 1921, for instance, included detailed information about organizing activity in the northern region, a report that denoted familiarity with the Mexican unionists and their work. It also noted the appealing prospect of collaboratively organizing trade unions: "We have invitations to organize local unions at Monterrey, San Pedro de las Colonias, and Juárez, Mexico."[81]

Idar's involvement in the area of labor diplomacy also included relations between the AFL and CROM. He participated as an advance man and translator for numerous PAFL activities, including the federation's conferences. He played a particularly important role in the jointly sponsored 1925 immigration conference that formalized further the understandings between the labor federations on the issue of regulating Mexican immigration. AFL president Green assigned Idar, along with Vargas, who was now a labor attaché with the Mexican Embassy, to the AFL delegation.[82]

Idar also organized in the San Antonio area immediately after the PAFL conference. From his offices in San Antonio he began an impressive regional organizing campaign that resulted in the chartering of numerous Mexican organizations. Idar's work in the San Antonio area benefitted greatly from the large volume of publicity that the *Pan American Labor Press* gave to the idea of a labor alliance in the hemisphere, to the AFL's brand of craft unionism, and to the federation's new policy of incorporating Mexican workers. One of the paper's principal features was a series of verbatim reports on the proceedings of the first P A F L conference. Articles by Murray, Idar, Vargas, and such Mexican labor leaders as Antonio Villarreal contributed to rising expectations that the new A F L policy would result in the improvement of conditions of Mexicans in the United States. These articles, as well as the published testimonies of Mexican unionists in the P A F L conference, encouraged unionization and improved relations with Anglos by defending the Mexican as an organizable worker and dependable unionist. The San Antonio labor paper, *El Unionista,* also played a key role in Idar's organizing campaigns.

El Unionista, published between 1919 and 1922, was the official organ for several mixed and separate Mexican unions in San Antonio: the Brotherhood of Maintenance of Way Laborers and Railroad Workers No. 1588; the Boot and Shoe Workers' Union No. 195; the Bakers and Confectionery Workers' International Union of America No. 185; and the International Hod Carriers and Building Laborers' Union of America No. 93. The paper gave wide publicity to the organizing activities of these unions in the city and in the outlying areas. It also provided important articles on the merits of unionism and on the new opportunity to join the A F L. The editor of *El Unionista,* Ramón Torres Delgado, was an established leader in the area. In 1910 he had been one of the editors of *El Progreso,* the official organ for La Liga Mexicana headquartered in San Antonio. La Liga Mexicana agitated during the 1900s for the overthrow of the Díaz regime and for improvements in the condition of the Mexican community in Texas, in particular pecan shellers from the city.[83]

The earliest public mention of Idar as an A F L organizer in San Antonio was made by *El Imparcial de Texas* in 1919 when it announced that Mexicans were joining the A F L in increasing numbers. Idar had been busy installing unions, "that were previously isolated and working of their own volition." Now that the war was over, returning veterans were demanding their old jobs, and Mexicans were seeking the security of an A F L charter. As in Laredo, affiliation with the national federation became a necessary political step for many independent workers' organizations. Also, inter-organizational cooperation was evident in San Antonio.[84]

Accompanying the chartering of independent workers' organizations into A F L unions was the tendency to maintain the original mutual aid societies as dual associations. These groups provided Mexican workers the necessary autonomy and control while participating in the ethnically mixed city and state federations. This expression of independence meant that the Mexican workers reserved the right to revert back to their own alliances until the AFL assured them complete acceptance. This was the case with the shoeworkers, bakers, and typographers organized by Idar and also with other local Mexican unionists. Idar, for instance, organized the Boot and Shoe Workers' Union No. 195 from members of a mutual aid society of Mexican shoe workers who were especially sensitive to the past indifference of the AFL. According to *El Unionista,* La Sociedad Porfirio Díaz, Mutua de Zapateros "until now had not received the support of organized labor in the United States." The union obtained its charter and subsequently negotiated contracts with sixteen shops in the city. The Sociedad Porfirio Díaz, however, continued to operate as an independent workers' organization.[85]

Also present in San Antonio during 1919 and 1920 were organizations of retail clerks, laundry workers, meatcutters, and tailors that obtained charters during the early organizing campaigns. These unions combined their organizing efforts with AFL mixed unions and independent workers' organizations, including La Sociedad Morelos, Mutua de Panaderos, La Sociedad Artes Gráficas, the Bakers and Confectionery Workers International Union of America No. 185, a union of typographical workers, and the Brotherhood of Maintenance of Way Laborers and Railroad Workers No. 1588.[86]

Dances and other public functions were favorite collaborative activities. Here the unions could provide entertainment, facilitate socializing, raise needed funds, and publicize their organizing efforts in the city. One such dance was organized to raise funds for *El Unionista.* The sponsoring unions and independent workers' organizations included bakers, tailors, clerks, shoeworkers, common laborers, meatcutters, laundresses, and railroad shop and maintenance workers. Two weeks later, the organizations planned yet another dance. This time, the purpose was to generate funds for Local 195. The twentieth-year celebration of the hod-carriers' union resulted in yet another type of event that brought together all the sister organizations in an expression of solidarity and fraternity. The public function was "a literary and musical celebration," a popular form of commemoration that mutual aid societies planned for such solemn occasions. The program opened with musical pieces by an orchestra directed by "profesor" Angel Moreno and the reading of the organization's constitutional preamble by the secretary, Ramón Frausto. Speeches by persons representing other workers' organizations followed. A dance during the evening finished the festivities.[87]

The organizing success in San Antonio denoted an optimistic spirit that Idar, the always animated organizer, captured when he urged a meeting of retail clerks to advance "our labor movement," beyond current confines. He reminded them of the "pressing need" to build unity and fraternity among all workers regardless of color, race, religious background, or citizenship. He invited the retail clerks to take the initiative and organize both Mexicans and Anglos in all the other business establishments in the city. The time was ripe, and workers could be encouraged to join in even greater numbers. Idar pointed to the success of Local 195 in securing its members the unprecedented salary of thirty-seven dollars a week. Local 93, on the other hand, had a record number of members "perfectly united and organized under the presidency of the active and untiring comrade Marcos Perales" and an able group of officers in the executive committee. The hodcarriers' union, like other Mexican locals, offered its most appealing attraction with the mutualist services that it offered its prospective members. Each member normally contributed a dollar immediately after the death of a fellow unionist to assist the widowed family. The union also maintained a fund to support members unable to work because of illness. The mutualist services that successful Mexican unions offered, according to Idar, were to continue with enthusiasm and with "far-reaching ties of fraternal love in order to avoid divisions among us."[88]

Some of these unionists joined with Idar in organizing and chartering separate unions of agricultural workers in San Antonio and in the outlying area that had previously produced socialist unions. The first one to be organized was the Agricultural Workers' Union, at Fentress. In February, 1920, Torres Delgado and Reyes Estrada traveled to Fentress and participated in the union's first organizational meeting. Idar helped organize similar unions at San Marcos, Luling, Seguín, Steples, Martindale, and in other "outlying areas." One of these unions was Farm Laborers' Union, No. 17547. Miguel Pavia, mentioned previously as a PLM sympathizer who led a group of disaffected workers out of La Agrupación Protectora Mexicana, also organized an AFL union of Mexican agricultural workers.[89] Further south, at McAllen, workers answered the organizing call regularly voiced by *El Unionista* and sister newspapers from South Texas by forming unions of masons, carpenters, and common laborers. San Antonio unionists participated in the affiliation ceremonies of one of these organizations, Carpenters' Union No. 2222.[90]

Idar continued operating out of San Antonio in the 1920s. Over the years he participated in the formation of additional unions in the city. In 1924, for example, he helped establish a federal labor union and unions of boilermakers, painters, and cement finishers. The following year, he reported organizing all-Mexican unions of hatters, carpenters, and bakers. Idar also worked among mine and smelter workers during the latter part of 1925 and may have been responsible for the organization of at least one of their unions.[91]

Idar traveled to El Paso in 1920 to assist Mexican bakery workers in obtaining an AFL charter. He returned to the border city two years later to assist the striking railroad shop workers. He played a particularly important role in keeping the strikers united, according to J. W. Kelley, organizer for the International Association of Machinists, who reported that "the full history of the strike . . . will never be written unless due and proper credit is given to Bro. Idar." He also went to Houston in 1922, organizing at least one union of Mexican workers. The union, Federal Labor Union No. 17727, was established in the bustling Mexican neighborhood of Magnolia Park. Soon thereafter, he again left San Antonio for his first visit to Corpus Christi, a place that was to occupy his attention during the 1920s. One of his assignments was to organize unions of Mexican railroad workers in Kingsville and in other locations in the area. Most of his reports from Corpus Christi and the last one that he submitted from the Rio Grande Valley failed to specify whether he was organizing separate Mexican unions, although he always expressed an interest in the local Mexican work force. An increased number of Mexican workers may have reached the skilled ranks, and they may have participated in ethnically mixed unions organized by Idar. On the other hand, he may have been disposed to downplay the ethnicity of the new unionists, in keeping with his concerns over the divisiveness of racial thinking.[92]

The Corpus Christi Trades Council had just been organized in anticipation of a campaign that sought to capitalize on the growth of the local economy. Deep-water dredging and construction attracted workers to the city and, according to Idar, "organized labor should come early here to promote the firm establishment of the trade union movement." Idar accompanied the international representative of the carpenters' union and reported that he was attempting to organize locals of auto mechanics, cooks, and waiters.[93]

Four years later he returned to assist in reorganizing the Corpus Christi Trades Council. Idar also participated in efforts to organize unions of musicians, bakers, and caterers. He apparently established a working relationship with a federation of restaurant workers similar to his connection with the international union of carpenters. He assisted in the formation of a state council of culinary workers during the 1926 TSFL convention. While in Corpus Christi, Idar installed a local of catering workers and attended to the formation of unions of electrical workers, painters, and longshoremen. He also expressed an interest in organizing carpenters and laundry workers. The development of the city's port facilities promised a bright future for labor in Corpus Christi. It "was destined to be a great port city, and organized labor is here to stay."[94]

Idar's organizing reports for the late 1920s continued to reflect a confident and encouraging tone. He announced in 1927 that he was off to Los Angeles "to cooperate in the organization of a quarter million Mexicans who reside in that locality." He did not leave, however, without first visiting the Rio Grande Valley, a place that like Corpus Christi and Los Angeles "held great promise for the trades union movement." His report from the Rio Grande Valley may have been overly optimistic. Yet it had all the elements contained in the charge that Gompers gave him in 1918 — discourage immigration, promote the selective incorporation of Mexican workers into the trade union movement, collaborate with local unionists, and improve relations within the state federation.[95]

Conclusion

Low Mexican participation in the AFL and the TSFL characterized the early 1900s. The rise in immigration and the ensuing growth of the urban work force intensified competition among workers and strengthened even further the resolve of organized labor to defend its privileged position in a racially-defined labor market.

The record of Mexican incorporation was impressive, primarily due to the work by Clemente Idar and to the response of Mexican workers, rather than a truly committed strategy of incorporation by the TSFL and the AFL. One of the most interesting twists in this story is that Mexican organizers like Idar and the organizations that acquired AFL charters continued to include Mexican nationals. The all-inclusive organizing strategy adopted by Mexican AFL unions notwithstanding, developments outside their community played a more determining role.

Although labor market forces played a major role in convincing labor to incorporate Mexicans, political decisions at the highest levels of organized labor gave the decision policy definition and strategic meaning. The decision to organize Mexicans, in other words, was part of a larger design that strengthened the political influence of the AFL and furthered the cause of craft unionism along the border and in Mexico. Discrimination against Mexican workers was a central issue in the building of an international labor alliance. The promise to organize them allowed the AFL the chance to negotiate its proposal for restricting Mexican immigration. Ironically, CROM's intercession on behalf of all Mexican workers resulted in the implementation of an organizing policy that excluded Mexican nationals.

The policy to incorporate Mexicans was intended principally to protect Anglo workers and to safeguard the interests of craft unionism. For Mexicans, however, it represented an historic moment for change. Some may have been so taken by the gesture that they joined in the highly optimistic assessment made by Torres Delgado that "the prejudices of yesteryear have disappeared."[96] Prejudices had not disappeared, but change was so significant that he could imagine them gone. In the racially-charged environment of Texas, incorporation meant more than an AFL charter and the valuable support that Mexican unionists could expect. It represented acceptance and, very possibly, an opportunity to improve the condition of the entire community. These kinds of meanings provide an explanation for the almost sudden entry of an impressive number of Mexican workers into the AFL.

Chapter Eight

The Mexican Worker in a Changing World

Industrialization was the single most important factor that shaped the living and working conditions of Mexican workers during the early 1900s and that precipitated their organizing responses. The imperialist expansion of the United States during the early and middle years of the nineteenth century and the disruptive yet eventual incorporation of southwestern regions into the national economy of the United States made possible the process of industrialization in the Southwest. The Texas and United States wars against Mexico and the subsequent military pacification of the Southwest made way for accelerated development and a massive shift of land ownership away from Mexican hands. The Civil War and undeclared hostilities between Mexicans and Anglos in South Texas retarded industrialization. However, once the railways extended their reach to the border and connected the economies of the United States and Mexico, South Texas more rapidly began to exhibit characteristics associated with other developing regions.

For the Mexican community, the process involved proletarianization, segregation, and continued economic and political losses. The immigrant population grew rapidly, and the Mexican work force became concentrated in the bottom occupational sectors of the newly developing ranching, farming, railway, mining, service, and manufacturing industries. Mexicans thus entered the twentieth century a subordinated minority and bottom segment of the rural and urban working class.

Large numbers of Mexican immigrants were drawn into Texas as the economy continued to grow and expand. The chaos of the Mexican Revolution also contributed to the immigrant flow during the 1910s, and the size of the Mexican community of South Texas significantly increased. Meanwhile, persistent and widespread practices of occupational and wage discrimination reinforced inequality for both U.S.-born and Mexico-born Mexicans. The numerical growth and geographical expansion of the Mexican population and the occupational concentration of its workers accompanied a general climate of social discrimination and racial conflict. Farmers and Anglo urban workers attempted

197

to gain control over the labor market by promoting discriminatory practices in the work place and the union hall. The organizing responses by Mexicans also contributed to tensions and conflicts.

Contrary to the views of some historians, Mexicans sought improvements and even transformations in the economy and in society. They took spontaneous, informal, and ad hoc measures to provide mutual support and to improve their condition. More formal and deliberate mutualist and protest actions led to the formation of organizations and regional alliances. Although these actions represented different stages of political development, mobilization often meant the simultaneous appearance of distinct organizational forms and strategies. The San Diego revolt registered the most radical response and underscored the importance of binational relations in explaining the diffusion of political ideas to and from Mexico. Political influences from Mexico were important in shaping Texas-Mexican politics, especially since the Mexican community was relatively isolated from the dominant Anglo society.

Mexican workers' organizations generally expressed a working-class focus and orientation as part of a broad concern for the condition of the entire Mexican community. These organizations were the logical choices for Mexicans who wished to collectivize their power as workers because the Anglo labor federations generally excluded them or practiced racial discrimination. Mexicans, however, did not form alternative institutions simply because the dominant society did not accommodate their interests and concerns. Mutual aid societies and Spanish-language newspapers also reflected cultural tastes and dispositions that were entertained in their own right.

Independent workers' organizations that recruited Mexican workers and spoke on their behalf included mutual aid societies, Masonic orders, and cooperative agencies. Sometimes these functioned independently of each other, although they most often participated in informal cooperative endeavors and in formal networks that occasionally functioned beyond the borders of the state. They usually offered their membership basic social services, including death and illness insurance, job placement assistance, and legal help. They also sponsored public events that reinforced a Mexicanist identity, provided a source of entertainment, and offered a means to further organize the Mexican community. Mutualistas, in particular, played an important civic role in establishing private schools and Spanish-language newspapers. As such, these representative organizations served basic material and political needs and mirrored ongoing philosophical and ideological strains of thought.

Mexicans manifested nationalist and working-class sentiments and envisioned a range of ideas from improvements in their condition as

Mexicans and as workers to the transformation of society in the United States and in Mexico. Although Mexicans exhibited political-ideological differences and divisions, most of their organizations agreed on the need for broadly based unity in the community and for concerted actions on its behalf. An ethic of mutuality that reflected the popular working-class values of fraternalism, cooperation, and altruism expressed a sense of righteous purpose. This ethic was reflected in the activities of the mutual aid societies, organizations that adopted strict rules of moral comportment among its members. Intellectuals added to the communitarian trend a political meaning with their translations of mutualism into calls for unionism and working-class unity. Although most Mexican organizations that welded mutualist principles with the unionist cause remained independent, some became affiliates of Anglo labor federations.

The history of Federal Labor Union No. 11953 sheds light on the earliest known cause in which a Mexican workers' organization officially discarded its independent status for a charter of affiliation from the A F L. Despite its formal association with the larger federation, the F L U maintained its membership in the network of local associations and expanded its recruiting concerns beyond the local Mexican community to include an expressed interest in building an international federation of workers from the Americas. Locally it attempted to establish a city-wide labor federation of craft unions and assisted workers that were organizing in the nearby mining communities. The F L U was short-lived, yet it recorded a salient point of reference in the history of Mexican organized labor in Texas.

The union's affiliation with the A F L suggests that the U.S. labor federation played an influential role. The A F L provided financial assistance, advice, representation during strike negotiations, and support for the reorganization of the union in 1910. In addition, the F L U pursued a course of organizational development that conformed to practices by other federal labor unions within the A F L. In Laredo this meant that all Mexican workers, regardless of gender, skill, or occupation, entered the A F L by way of a federal labor union despite the fact that Anglo railway brotherhoods and craft unions also existed in the city. Federal labor unions were expected to build their own craft unions by reorganizing their constituency into separate unions according to the craft skills of the workers.

The F L U had a prior history as an independent workers' organization. In other words, the impetus for organizing the union and for defining and formulating its guiding principles originated in Laredo with a probable influence from across the border. Though Laredo may not have been a haven for a socialist union like the FLU, the community encouraged labor organizing among Mexican workers. The union's leaders were already expressing a fully elaborated and coherent ideology and publishing an impressive labor paper when the AFL charter was obtained. This suggests that the FLU's most formative influences originated in Laredo and across the international line. Immediate influences were evident when unions and other community organizations of Laredo and Nuevo Laredo joined with the FLU in sponsoring public programs and staging organizing drives in both cities. Moreover, widespread collaboration with different types of Mexican organizations indicates shared outlooks and values.

Mexican socialists in the interior of the state also maintained binational ties and played a prominent organizing and propagandizing role in their communities. Mexican unions of mostly farm renters and laborers from the cotton belt area initially operated as dual organizations affiliated with federations of mutual aid groups and the PLM. Some of these mutualistas and PLM clubs joined the Socialist Party's labor federations at the same time that they participated in the precursory activity of the Mexican Revolution. The resulting network of Mexican socialist unions also maintained an active interest in broadening their organizing work to include other Mexican workers in the Southwest and in Mexico. Like the FLU, these groups participated in Mexican community affairs; they had a specialized focus, yet they were broadly concerned with the welfare of the entire Mexican community. Although their parent organization was not as far removed as was the AFL from the FLU, Mexican agricultural unions usually led a separate life within the Renters' Union and the Land League. Initially, the Socialist Party took notice of Mexican organizers, with their organizing initiatives and requests for charters. The Anglo socialist leadership subsequently made impressive pronouncements in favor of organizing Mexicans, gave official support to the campaign to free José Angel Hernández, and elected other organizers like F. A. Hernández to important positions within the party and its labor federations.

All of these events occurred at a time when the TSFL was officially endorsing resolutions to encourage the exclusion of Mexican workers. Despite this important difference in the attitude of Anglo labor toward Mexican workers, the socialist leadership as well as the rank and file demonstrated ambivalence concerning the effective incorporation of Mexican agricultural workers. It usually fell on the Mexican organizers to maintain the network of exising Mexican unions, organize new groups, translate and distribute important socialist literature, and establish a Spanish-language socialist newspaper. Mexican agricultural unions joined the socialist federations in impressive numbers. No doubt the active encouragement of the Anglo socialists influenced this development. Also, exclusion and discrimination in the TSFL must have prompted Mexican agricultural unions to seek affiliation where they were most welcome. More importantly, the PLM, which did not provide a labor federation of its own, actively encouraged Mexicans to join the socialist federation. At least two Mexican Land League organizers, José Angel Hernández and Antonio Valdez, maintained leadership positions in PLM circles.

Differences and similarities were evident between the FLU and the Mexican socialist unions. Membership for each numbered about a thousand semiskilled and skilled workers. The membership of the socialist unions was more rural and was dispersed over a large area, while the FLU's was urban and concentrated. The socialist unions had an industrial organizational structure. The FLU, on the other hand, attempted to form craft unions from its membership. Both the FLU and the socialist unions professed international socialism, although the latter also explicitly endorsed nationalist revolutionary principles. The FLU pursued a strategy of "boring from within" the AFL, and although it advocated socialism, it essentially functioned as a bread-and-butter union. The agricultural socialists adopted the Texas Socialist Party's official plan of land distribution, land rental policy, and international socialist political organizing. They also embraced the PLM cause and participated prominently in the precursory activity of the Mexican Revolution. Both types of ideological expressions coincided with the ascendancy of socialist labor movements in Mexico and in the southwestern part of the United States between 1900 and 1920. Mexicans from Texas thus represented a point of confluence that offered an opportunity for building socialist working-class unity on an international scale.

Despite rapid increases in membership and capable theorists and activists within their ranks, the FLU and the socialist unions eventually expired. The FLU suffered from universal debilitating factors historically encountered by labor unions. A poverty stricken membership, a rigid economy, organizational weaknesses, tactical errors, anti-socialist feelings, and a runaway shop all combined to defeat the union. Similar economic, social, organizational, and tactical problems—as well as widespread racism outside and ambivalence within the Texas Socialist Party, the Renter's Union, and the Land League—hampered the Mexican socialists. In both cases important Mexican political figures critiqued the socialist leanings of the unions. Laredo, unlike the more ethnically mixed cotton belt area, offered Mexican unionists a more culturally secure and politically supportive environment.

The AFL was indifferent, and the TSFL was practically opposed to admitting Mexican workers into their ranks throughout most of the 1900–20 period. Once the AFL announced plans to actively recruit them, and despite the fact that the TSFL remained inhospitable, Mexican workers' organizations began to formally request AFL charters in earnest. The earlier history of this marriage had not shown promising results. The FLU remained isolated from the TSFL and distant from the AFL. Local No. 93 was similarly isolated and moved along mainly under its own volition. Mexican workers who joined mixed unions were made to feel unwelcome by the exclusive use of English, discrimination in union hiring halls, and anti-Mexican attitudes. Consequently, most Mexican workers' organizations remained independent or sought affiliation with the socialist federations.

The appointment of Clemente Idar as the official Mexican organizer in 1918 and the public propaganda carried by the *Pan American Labor Press* and *El Unionista* contributed significantly to the almost sudden increase of Mexican participation in the AFL and TSFL. Samuel Gompers, however, appointed Idar to respond to CROM pressures and to placate Anglo labor, which was convinced Mexican workers would become job competitors and strikebreakers on a massive scale. As a consequence, Idar implemented a dual strategy. He coordinated all-inclusive organizing efforts within the Mexican community during his first years as an AFL organizer. At the same time, he promoted a more public and selective organizing campaign that conformed with the AFL's declared policy and with Gompers's nativist viewpoint as well as with his own developing ethnic orientation. One of Idar's most important contributions to the issue of labor control involved active support for the repatriation movement of the postwar period. Idar's work thus represented a pragmatic accommodation to forces beyond his control as well as a reflection of his views on the need to promote unionism and control Mexican immigration.

Most of the Mexican unions that obtained AFL charters with Idar's assistance had previously been independent workers' organizations. Some of these may have been Land League and PLM affiliates. Idar chartered agricultural workers' unions in the same towns that had earlier registered Mexican Land League locals. Torres Delgado and Pavia, who had been active members in the PLM, assisted Idar in chartering Mexican unions. Possible links with the Land League and the PLM notwithstanding, the fact that Mexican workers' organizations readily responded to Idar's overtures indicates that the determining factor in increasing Mexican participation was the AFL's new organizing policy.

The AFL's newfound interest in practicing solidarity among Mexican workers in Texas was a sudden departure from the past. We can only conjecture on the possible gains that the labor movement in Texas could have achieved if this effort had been made sooner or if the AFL's deeds had been more consistent with its promises. Equally intriguing possibilities might also have resulted from a more active organizing effort by Anglo TSFL members. The earlier incorporation of Mexican workers and a pace-setting application of the principle of solidarity within and without the TSFL could have eased tensions and provided the experience necessary to organize a large body of workers under the flag of worker solidarity.

Gompers's declaration in favor of incorporating Mexican workers dealt appropriately with a deteriorating situation among organized labor in Texas. The open-shop movement had become an especially formidable obstacle, and Anglo workers feared that employers would not stop short of recruiting Mexican workers to break strikes, depress wages, and displace unwanted workers. The deportation and repatriation of Mexicans was offered as an alternative strategy. The solution was based on the questionable premise that organized labor could best stand divided. The AFL's new organizing policy provided a more rational strategy that would have prepared organized labor for subsequent opportunities to incorporate a growing number of Mexican workers.

At one level, one can attribute the slow and ineffective incorporation of Mexican workers to the fact that Anglo labor was making its initial efforts to accommodate a growing labor force that was ethnically mixed, geographically dispersed, and occupationally differentiated. Actually, incorporation was retarded by general organizing indifference, discrimination, and exclusion. Despite an expressed interest in practicing workers' solidarity at a time when unity was essential, Mexican workers met stiff resistance from Anglo workers, especially within the more conservative AFL and TSFL. The practice of conditional solidarity initiated a period of gradual incorporation that achieved a measure of success primarily as a result of the initiatives by Mexican workers and organizers.

Like all histories, the current study raises questions that are as important as the ones that it has addressed. Questions regarding the issues of self-organization, identity, and social incorporation in particular take on special meaning in light of comparable studies for subsequent periods. For instance, what were the underlying factors that contributed to self-organization? Also, did the prevailing Mexicanist identity and strategy begin to lose currency—as Christian, García, and de Leon suggest—and did the eventual ascendancy of its Mexican American or ethnic counterpart signal a major cultural transformation in the community? Moreover, to what extent did the process of social incorporation—partly evident in the increased participation of Mexican workers in the A F L and the T S F L—reflect and reinforce an ongoing process of acculturation and what David Montejano terms a relaxation of social relations in urban areas?

Mexicans were not unlike other workers who sought to survive hardships and secure better conditions through collective action. Although the immigrant mentality may have discouraged such a strategy, up to a point, Mexican workers invariably recognized the wisdom of collectivizing their energies for mutual support, protest, and unionist purposes. The industrialization of the economies of northern Mexico and the southwestern part of the United States, aside from introducing the possibility of joining two expanding labor movements, provided a catalyst for self-organization among Mexican workers in Texas. First of all, the growth and concentration of Mexicans in urban centers and agricultural areas facilitated communication and organization. This process involved the back-and-forth migration of workers and political activists. Second, the growth and concentration of the Mexican work force in the lower occupations and in given industrial sites encouraged the development of an awareness of common interests. Third, generalized discrimination and inequality contributed significantly to a unifying Mexicanist identity.

Clearly, discrimination and inequality were major obstacles to self-organization as well as to interethnic alliances and the internationalization of the class struggle. The scarcity of financial resources, a weak bargaining position as unskilled workers, and the propensity by employers, especially agriculturalists, to maintain large labor pools of potential strikebreakers no doubt discouraged Mexicans from collectivizing their labor power. Popular anti-Mexican sentiments also led to red-baiting tactics, exclusionary practices by some Anglo unions, and occupational discrimination that placed both U.S.-born and Mexico-born workers beyond the organizing reach of Anglo labor.

Discrimination and inequality, however, also contributed to the formation of formal and informal collectivities, as well as to the taking of spontaneous actions of defense and protest. The mutual aid form of organization, for instance, minimally represented a formal attempt to help the immigrant adjust socially and culturally to life in the United States and to provide workers the basic material assistance needed to survive their condition of poverty and hardship. Discrimination and inequality also resulted in a sense of moral indignation, a point of oppositional unity, in short, a common cause for Mexicans as Mexicans and as workers speaking on behalf and in defense of their entire community. As a consequence, workers' grievances became unifying issues inseparable from other important concerns in the community. Workers' organizations, on the other hand, played a key integrative role alongside other community organizations with their pronouncements of a just cause and their appeals for unity. Common origins, combined endeavors, and shared goals among Mexican workers' organizations and other community groups made Mexican labor activity an integral part of the general socio-political movement.

The isolation of workers' alliances helps explain why the workers frequently looked toward Mexico for influence and support. This does not mean, however, that they lent a receptive ear to political movements in Mexico only as a result of indifference or even exclusion by Anglo labor. The Mexican community was culturally disposed to identify and to seek solidarity with social movements and workers' organizations in Mexico due to the historic ties with the homeland, ties reinforced by the large waves of Mexican immigration during the early 1900s. Moreover, numerous exiled political groups actively directed the attention of Mexicans to the south. Additionally, revolutionary ferment in Mexico involved a growing labor movement that imbued Mexican communities in Texas with a nationalist resolve to combat what Sara Estela Ramírez called those "horrible germs that destroy the work of mutualism." The result was the establishment of different types of workers' organizations exhibiting the broad ideological spectrum evident in Mexico.

Workers' alliances appeared in places with high Mexican population concentrations, including the border area that extends from Brownsville to Laredo, the southwestern portion of the cotton belt area below Austin and San Antonio, and in cities like San Antonio and Laredo. Ranch workers were conspicuously absent from these organizations, most probably because of their isolation and the more effective methods of control that ranch owners used on them. Urban areas facilitated self-organization and unionization because workers were concentrated and thus were able more easily to form and maintain workers' associations. The presence of well-established Anglo labor unions and the work of political exiles in inland cities also encouraged Mexicans to organize. Workers in border cities like Laredo, on the other hand, benefitted from their ties with Mexico. Self-organization among Mexicans in the cotton belt seemed the most improbable since they faced the most debilitating obstacles. This area, however, registered one of the highest number of Mexican tenants, that is, workers sufficiently stable and relatively able financially to maintain their organizations. Moreover, the P L M and then the Texas Socialist Party maintained an organizing focus among Mexican workers in the area.

The response by Mexican workers to the overtures of the Texas Socialist Party, the AFL, and the TSFL demonstrates that many of them seriously entertained the idea of joining with Anglo labor either to promote worldwide working-class unity or simply to share in the political and material benefits of affiliation. The great majority of Mexican workers, however, sought more traditional organizational forms, including mutual aid societies, cooperatives, and other types of independent workers' organizations. This prevailing mutualist trend in part reflected a preindustrial or artisanal tradition reinforced by immigration from Mexico. Two additional factors bolstered this tradition in a more immediate and determining manner. First, workers and the community at large desperately needed basic social and cultural services; consequently, organizations of a mutualist character proliferated. Second, segregation meant that Mexicans had to establish their own alternative institutions because they could only depend on themselves for survival. This explains why workers' organizations often chose to forego the adoption of specialized, that is, exclusively unionist, functions. These organizations normally maintained their traditional forms until local struggles or the possibility of an alliance with Anglo labor required more adversarial postures and a union-type structure. On the other hand, when opportunities for interethnic alliances failed to meet expectations, Mexican workers' organizations reverted to the familiar mutual aid type.

The broad ideological spectrum evident in Mexican organizational life often reflected political motivations that went beyond the material and spiritual needs of the membership and the immediate community. Strategies often involved plans to build networks of organizations that spoke of regional unity to combat racial violence, discrimination, and inequality. On some occasions, mutualistas and unionists entertained the idea of building an international working-class movement in conjunction with labor in Mexico and in other parts of the United States. Above all, Anglo labor's lack of interest, the broad needs of the Mexican community, and the prevailing moralistic and nationalistic political culture contributed to a focus on the community's general welfare. When conditions in the workplace worsened, on the other hand, independent Mexican workers' organizations made explicit their focus and orientation on Mexicans as workers. Political influences from outside the Mexican community demonstrated that beyond immediate conditioning and precipitating factors associated with the workplace, workers' organizations benefited from alliances with individuals and groups, both from Mexico and from the United States, emphasizing unity among the entire working class.

One of the most challenging enterprises in this study was the conceptualization of a Mexicanist political culture. It was clear from the outset that Mexican political life was dynamic and complex. Equally evident were unifying moralistic and nationalistic principles that gave the prevailing Mexicanist identity a sense of purpose and meaning. Working-class mutualist values and an exalted sense of being Mexican, in other words, gave coherence to the varied world of Mexican politics. This Mexicanist identity manifested popular underlying values in the community and a singular point of unity among different groups, including workers who embraced varied political strategies and ideologies. These findings and formulations challenge prevailing views.

Historians have given inadequate attention to Mexican culture as a basis for political action, preferring to treat it in a highly abstract fashion as an almost purely identificational phenomenon with relatively unclear connections to the world of politics. The conventional culturalist approach focuses on different types of organizations that appear over time and reflect points in an acculturation process between a Mexicanized working-class and an Americanized middle-class identity and outlook. Although both of these subcultures and their corresponding organizations are said to coexist especially after the 1930s, the latter are said to have increasingly supplanted the former much as in the case of European-origin immigrant groups who became Americanized and integrated into society. L U L A C and other middle-class organizations may have continued ascribing to moralistic principles in their organizing appeals; however, they also confined their attention to the U.S.-born at the same time that they claimed constitutional rights with patriotic force. One of the major problems in the utilization of this framework is that it places greater importance and value on the politics of the more Americanized. Mario García, the major exponent of this view, for instance, downplays the role of agency and a combative spirit among working-class Mexicans who were allegedly burdened by the presence of large numbers of fearful and contented immigrants.[1]

García treats the more Mexicanized culture of the so-called "immigrant generation" as a case of cultural lag, a stage of arrested development awaiting the emergence of a U.S.-born and upwardly mobile Mexican sector sufficiently acculturated to effectively seek equal treatment and respect for itself as well as for the entire community. García adds that political participation was low and that Mexicans were primarily interested in surviving rather than challenging their condition. Montejano gives credence to García's argumentation by granting little attention to the world of Mexican politics, on the grounds that it was generally ineffective during the pre–World War II period.

Historians such as José Amaro Hernández, Arnoldo de Leon, Ricardo Romo, and Alberto Camarillo, on the other hand, explicitly treat

Mexican culture as functional and desirable in its own right, as well as a basis for community struggles.[2] They do not, however, add much depth to a discussion that essentially assumes an enabling relation between culture and politics without the corresponding substantive evidence and explanation. For example, they fail to say what Mexican political culture was, and they do not explain how fundamental cultural values of working-class origins contributed to refined political outlooks and persisted as sources of collective identity across time as well as among immigrant, U.S.-born, poor, and upwardly mobile Mexicans. The lack of definition and analysis has resulted in an impressionistic interpretation of the connection between culture and politics, a point of inquiry of proven importance in U.S. immigrant and labor history.[3]

Although this study does not attempt to explain the well-known fact that mutualista organizations declined in numbers beginning sometime during the Second World War, it is necessary to address the view that a Mexicanist identity on which they were based also faded in importance as U.S.-born Mexicans increased in numbers and importance. A Mexicanist or all-inclusive identity that political leaders often employed in making their organizing appeals did suffer erosion as leaders from the emerging middle class began to embrace a narrow ethnic identity and organizing focus, as well as an emphasis on constitutional rights theoretically guaranteed to them by virtue of their citizenship. The emergence of this new orientation during the early 1900s, however, suggests that political and economic circumstances, rather than major cultural transformations in the community, often determined which identity and strategy a leader embraced.

Emilio Flores's testimony before the Industrial Commission and his subsequent report in *La Prensa* involved more than a disingenuous move intended to hide his opposition to immigration and the PLM. The Dallas hearings encouraged him to reveal privately held views that were out of step with prevailing ideas in La Agrupación and in the Mexican community. Without this opportunity, Flores may not have expressed his exaggerated ethnic identity. The commission members were soliciting information on the causes of industrial strife and agrarian discontent and provided Flores the receptive audience he did not have at home.

The case of de la Luz Saenz also underscores the need to examine the circumstances that circumscribed or limited the political world within which the emerging ethnic leadership operated. Wartime rhetoric and improved job opportunities, rather than a sudden ethnic birth, contributed to de la Luz Saenz's elaboration of a strategy of incorporation that called for equality on the basis of contributions at the home and war fronts. LULAC leaders later embraced this strategy and emphasized wartime contributions as expressions of loyalty to flag and country. Although one can only conjecture as to the extent to which L U L A C leaders reflected or led public opinion, they departed substantially from de la Luz Saenz's identity and loyalty formulations. He clearly expressed a Mexicanist identity and loyalty to the principles of democracy, justice, and fair play. The war gave rise to an expressed hope in incorporation that de la Luz Saenz expressed in Mexicanist terms. On the other hand, the persistence of discrimination and inequality particularly evident among the forgotten Mexican veterans during the postwar period discouraged de la Luz Saenz from promoting the conservative and accommodating brand of politics that L U L A C subsequently found so appealing.

Idar's experiences provide further explanation for the emergence of ethnic politics. Idar drifted away from the Mexicanist world of his father and his youth because of an opportunity made possible by the new policy of the A F L. Idar had strongly identified with the plight of Mexican nationals, although he always may have been inclined to side with U.S.-born Mexicans if encouraged to make the choice. When the A F L offered him the unprecedented chance to implement its new policy, he urged Mexican trade unionists to incorporate Mexican nationals. However, while in Anglo circles like the T S F L conventions, he increasingly elected to become the kind of ethnic labor leader that would give political emphasis to citizenship. Idar did not abandon Mexican immigrants. In fact, he urged their incorporation while organizing in Mexican communities. He also did not deny that his allegiance as a trade unionist was with the U.S.-born and naturalized. This represented a division within the Mexican community that no doubt deepened as Mexican trade unionists organized as U.S.-born workers. The experiences of the Mexican workers who gained entry into the A F L on the basis of a selective organizing strategy that shunned Mexican nationals no doubt strengthened an incipient ethnic identity and its corresponding organizing focus. The decision to join under these circumstances and even Idar's conversion, however, was made possible by Anglo labor's attempt to regain control over the labor market and to undermine leftist politics, and not necessarily by a sudden cultural transformation among U.S.-born Mexicans.

Incorporation experiences—which were increasingly repeated as Jim Crowism began to fall apart in the 1940s—undoubtedly reflected and reinforced a growing adherence to an ethnic identity and organizing focus. New opportunities in an increasingly open society contributed to an attendant decline of traditional alternative institutions such as mutualistas. Repression and cooptation of the labor left, on the other hand, deprived Mexican workers of an opportunity to embrace more inclusive forms of organization and more critical views of the socio-economy. My point is that a culturalist approach that does not take into account political and economic circumstances offers an incomplete explanation of Mexican political culture, especially the determining role that the leadership played in guiding political thought and organizing strategy. The reemergence of leftist labor organizing and a Mexicanist political orientation as challenges to the craft unionism of the AFL and the conservativism of LULAC during the 1930s minimally underscore persistent inequality and the continuing importance of a more inclusive identity and organizing strategy.

To conclude, industrialization was the single most important development that shaped the condition of the Mexican community and that precipitated its political and cultural responses during the early 1900s. The community was undergoing a critical period of development characterized by discrimination, inequality, and extreme hardship, as well as by racial conflict and internal divisions. Mexicans responded in a variety of ways. These responses manifested a working-class ethic of mutuality and nationalist and working-class demands that ranged from improvements in immediate conditions to the radical transformation of society in the United States and Mexico. Mexican workers' organizations consistently sought to build alliances with labor throughout Texas and Mexico. Indifference, exclusion, and discrimination by Anglo labor, however, often impaired the development of interethnic alliances. Some of the more leftist-oriented groups—the Texas Socialist Party and the PLM—issued the strongest appeals for an internationalist workers' struggle that disregarded ethnic differences. The period surrounding the First World War witnessed the demise of these groups and the ascendancy of the conservative AFL and TSFL, with their insubstantial efforts to incorporate Mexican workers into the trade labor movement. Full and effective incorporation that would involve large numbers of Mexican workers on the basis of equality presumably had to await the continued test of time, sincerity, and will.

Appendix

Table 1.
U.S.- and Mexico-Born Mexican Population in Texas, By Decade

Year	Mexico-Born From Census	U.S.-Born[a] Calculated	Total Predicted From Model
1850	——	——	5,000[b]
1860	12,443	6,850	19,293
1870	22,510	13,988	36,498
1880	43,161	27,492	70,653
1890	51,559	53,634	105,193
1900	71,062	92,555	163,617
1910	124,238	153,093	277,331
1920	249,652	255,705	505,357

[a]The U.S.-born figures have been calculated by applying a .37 percent rate of increase registered by the total Mexican population between 1920 and 1970. The U.S.-born population in 1860 thus combines 1,850 new additions with the 5,000 U.S.-born persons from 1850. From that point on the percentage increase for every decade is added to the previous U.S.-born population. The total population is then predicted by adding the Mexico-born.

[b]The initial U.S.-born figure is from Richard Nostrand, "The Hispanic American Borderland; A Regional Historical Geography," Ph.D. dissertation, University of California, Los Angeles, 1968, p. 149.

SOURCE: Roberto Villarreal, "Model for Estimating the Spanish-Surnamed Population of Texas, 1860–1960," manuscript in author's possession. The table is an abbreviated and revised version of the original. It is based on Mexico-born figures provided by the U.S. Census and does not attempt to account for Mexicans missed by the Census or for Anglo-surnamed Mexicans.

Table 2.
Foreign-born Whites in Selected Occupations,
New Mexico, Arizona, and Texas 1900–20

Occupations	New Mexico			Arizona			Texas		
	1900	1910	1920	1900	1910	1920	1900	1910	1920
Agricultural workers	7.1	6.4	9.9	16.0	23.0	18.2	5.1	6.6	10.8
Farmers, painters, and overseers	6.5	4.6	5.1	7.8	10.8	9.7	7.9	7.3	7.4
Laborers (not specified)	8.7	14.5	16.1	40.4	50.2	51.1	16.1	16.9	24.1
Merchants and dealers (excluding wholesale)	26.2	15.4	18.3	29.4	26.3	31.1	17.1	15.7	17.5
Stockraisers, herders and drovers	3.4	5.1	3.9	13.3	13.1	9.7	18.2	15.4	11.5
Steam railroad employees	15.1	37.8	32.6	37.5	78.3	81.0	11.7	25.8	48.0
Miners and quarrymen	39.8	58.2	56.2	41.5	62.9	62.7	62.8	61.0	63.8
Carpenters and joiners	15.4	10.2	13.5	—	—	—	14.0	9.7	10.8
Servants, waiters, and waitresses	11.1	11.1	14.0	18.0	29.1	33.0	9.3	9.2	12.3
Laundresses	7.7	4.1	19.9	48.0	43.9	33.0	6.4	5.0	9.3

NOTE: Based on total population over ten years of age

SOURCE: Roden Fuller, "Occupations of the Mexican-Born Population of Texas, New Mexico, and Arizona, 1900–1920," *Journal of the American Statistical Association* 23 (March, 1928): 67.

Table 3.
Average Daily Wages Paid Mexican Workers in Texas
during the Period 1900–20, by Selected Occupations

Occupations	1900–10	1911–20
Ranch and Farm Laborers	$ .55	$ .75
Railroad Track Employees	.65	1.25
Railroad Shop Employees	1.00	1.50
Mine Workers	1.55	1.65
Public Works Laborers	1.35	1.35

SOURCE: Victor S. Clark, *Mexican Labor in the United States,* Bureau of Labor Bulletin 78 (Washington, D.C.: U.S. Bureau of Labor Statistics, 1908), 466–522; Samuel Bryan, "Mexican Immigrants in the United States," *The Survey,* September 7, 1912, 726–30; and a survey (conducted by the author) of wage data appearing in Spanish-language newspapers.

Table 4.
Types of Mexican Workers and Wages in San Antonio, 1926

Types	Number	(%)	Average Weekly Earnings
Common Laborers	618	(47.7)	$13.68
Regular Job Holders	270	(20.8)	20.18
Businessmen	87	(6.7)	21.31
Skilled Workers	280	(21.6)	22.00
Professional Workers	41	(3.2)	24.90
TOTAL	1,296		

SOURCE: William Knox, "The Economic Status of the Mexican Immigrant in San Antonio, Texas," Master's thesis, University of Texas, Austin, 1927, pp. 15–19. Figures are calculated from survey data collected by Knox among U.S.-born and Mexico-born respondents. The table applies only to the 1,296 male heads of households for which Knox provides complete data. Knox does not indicate the number of days calculated in the work week.

Table 5.
Types of Mexican Workers by Nativity in San Antonio, 1926

Types	U.S.-born	%	Mexico-born	%
Common Laborers	142	(33.5)	389	(50.1)
Regular Job Holders	125	(29.5)	115	(14.8)
Businessmen	36	(8.5)	58	(7.5)
Skilled Workers	99	(23.4)	181	(23.3)
Professional Workers	22	(5.1)	34	(4.3)
TOTALS	424		777	

SOURCE: William Knox, "The Economic Status of the Mexican Immigrant in San Antonio, Texas," Master's thesis, University of Texas, Austin, 1927, pp. 21–22. Figures are calculated from survey data collected by Knox among U.S.-born and Mexico-born respondents.

Table 6.
Occupations and Weekly Earnings by Mexican and Anglo Women by Selected Industries, El Paso, 1919

Industry	Mexicans		Anglos		Difference
Hotels, Restaurants	$ 8.96	(72)	$14.94	(83)	$ 5.98
Laundries	6.56	(252)	17.90	(26)	11.34
Manufacturing	7.91	(135)	15.60	(19)	7.69
Mercantile	10.71	(345)	18.91	(437)	8.20
Telegraph, Telephone	10.00	(1)	18.13	(256)	8.13
Miscellaneous	8.02	(38)	25.86	(123)	17.84
AVERAGES AND TOTALS	$ 8.69	(843)	$18.56	(944)	$ 9.87

SOURCE: Texas Bureau of Labor Statistics, *Sixth Biennial Report, 1919–1920* (Austin: Von Boeckmann–Jones Co., 1921), pp. 103–109.

Table 7.
Educational Background and Weekly Wages of
Mexican and Anglo Women in El Paso, 1919

Grade Level	Mexican		Anglo		Wage Difference
No Schooling	$ 7.55	(46)	$ -0-		$ -0-
First to Third	7.30	(263)	7.21	(7)	.09
Fourth to Eighth	9.39	(513)	16.04	(356)	6.65
High School	13.69	(19)	20.06	(481)	6.37
College	-0-		28.25	(55)	-0-
Business Course	15.00	(2)	25.44	(45)	10.44

SOURCE: Texas Bureau of Labor Statistics, *Sixth Biennial Report, 1919–1920* (Austin: Von Boeck-mann– Jones Co., 1921), pp. 103–109.

Table 8.
Membership Figures for Hod Carriers Union No. 93, 1909–20

	Jan.	Feb.	Mar.	Apr.	May	June	July	Aug.	Sept.	Oct.	Nov.	Dec.	Total Average
1909	28	28	30	*	*	*	*	*	*	*	*	*	28.7
1910	20	66	72	65	68	52	46	47	63	70	*	*	56.9
1911	85	77	64	56	50	50	52	48	58	59	54	54	58.9
1912	56	56	50	57	57	60	59	55	54	53	57	56	55.8
1913	56	56	61	76	79	*	69	67	*	66	65	62	65.7
1914	61	63	62	56	67	69	63	63	63	63	62	62	62.8
1915	62	58	54	54	54	56	53	52	54	52	48	49	53.8
1916	50	58	61	57	57	52	48	49	47	43	42	41	50.4
1917	40	46	44	44	47	47	52	55	*	51	53	58	48.8
1918	61	63	56	59	59	54	56	58	52	48	47	44	54.8
1919	46	42	40	40	43	69	120	183	196	217	254	257	125.6
1920	257	261	276	263	250	247	256	263	253	221	210	211	247.3

*Figures not available

SOURCE: Records of Local Unions, *International Hod Carriers and Building Laborers' Union of America No. 93, Membership Records*, 1909–20, AFL-CIO Offices, Washington, D.C.

Table 9.
Annual Initiation Figures for Local 93 by Total Membership, 1911–20

	Date of Initiation													Total Membership
	1908	1909	1910	1911	1912	1913	1914	1915	1916	1917	1918	1919	1920	
1911	11	24	55	27										117
1912	8	15	11	23	37									94
1913	7	15	7	4	24	38								95
1914	7	14	7	4	13	18	29							92
1915	6	11	5	3	9	10	17	28						89
1916	4	9	3	2	7	5	4	24	35					93
1917	3	7	3	2	5	2	2	11	13	40				88
1918	3	7	3	1	4	2	2	6	6	33	31			98
1919	3	6	3	1	4	1	1	4	3	12	11	317		366
1920	3	4	3	1	2	1	1	2	2	9	6	239	110	383

Source: Records of Local Unions, *International Hod Carriers and Building Laborers' Union of America No. 93, Membership Records*, AFL-CIO Office, Washington, D.C.

Table 10.
Mexican Delegates to the TSFL Annual Convention, 1904–20

Year	City	Name	Organization
1904	Houston	Joe Gómez	Musicians
1905	Thurber	Frank Caro	Meat Cutters and Federal Union
1906	Galveston	A. Gómez	Screwmen No. 217
1907*			
1908*			
1909	San Antonio	N. Guerra	Flour Mill Workers
	San Antonio	M. A. Domínguez	Carpenters 717
1910	Galveston	Andrew Sánchez	Federal Labor Union
1911	Dallas	L. J. Vargas	Leather Workers
	Waco	J. Cárdenas	Tailors
1912	Thurber	Lee Américo	Mine Workers No. 2763
1913	Thurber	Lee Américo	Mine Workers No. 2763
	Thurber	F. S. Caro	Trades Council, Brickmakers, Butchers, and Stationary Firemen
1914	Big Springs	Nieves Morales	Railway Carmen No. 14365
	Houston	J. J. Gonzales	Plummer No. 68
	Thurber	Lee Américo	Mine Workers No. 2763
	Thurber	Frank Caro	Central Labor Council, Bartenders, Butchers, and Stationary Firemen
1915	Thurber	Lee Américo	Mine Workers
1916	El Paso	P. A. Carvajal	Bartenders, Bar Porters, Tile Workers and Cigar Makers
	San Antonio	Al Galán	Stage Employees
	Thurber	Lee Américo	Mine Workers
1917	San Antonio	M. A. Domínguez	Carpenters
	San Antonio	Albert Galán	Stage Employees
	Thurber	F. S. Caro	Trade Council, Butchers, Carpenters
	Thurber	Lee Américo	Mine Workers
1918	San Antonio	Cenobio Andrade	Hod Carriers
	San Antonio	Al Galán	Stage Employees
1919	Thurber	F. S. Caro	Trade Council, Brickmakers, and Teamsters
	Thurber	Lee Américo	Mine Workers
	Waco	J. M. Patillo	Central Labor Council, Electrical Workers, and Union Label League
1920	Orange	A. W. Barrón	Central Body and Teamsters
	Orange	A. W. Barrón	Blacksmiths
	San Antonio	Frank D. Guardo	Catering Industrial Workers and Janitors
	San Antonio	A. F. Cadena	Chauffeurs and Retail Clerks
	San Antonio	R. Chiado	Railway Carmen
	Thurber	Lee Américo	Mine Workers
		F. S. Caro	Central Body and Stationary Firemen

*Spanish surnames not available

SOURCE: A survey of the *Proceedings of the Texas State Federation of Labor, 1904–1920*, by the author.

Notes

Introduction

1. For observations on the history of mobilization and popular perceptions see Rodolfo Acuña, *Occupied America: A History of Chicanos;* John R. Chávez, *The Lost Land: The Chicano Image of the Southwest;* and Peter Matthiessen, *Sal Si Puedes: Cesar Chavez and the New American Revolution.* Franklin García, past field representative for the International Meat Cutters of America, pointed out that the image of the unorganizable Mexicans abounded while they were registering one of the most impressive organizing rates in Texas during the 1940–75 period (Franklin García, interview with Emilio Zamora, Austin, Tex., June 28, 1974; transcript in author's possession).

2. Juan Gómez-Quiñones, *Sembradores, Ricardo Flores Magón y El Partido Liberal Mexicano: A Eulogy and Critique;* Juan Gómez-Quiñones and Luis Leobardo Arroyo, "On the State of Chicano History: Observations on Its Development, Interpretations, and Theory, 1970–1974," *Western Historical Quarterly* 7 (Apr., 1976): 155–85; and Emilio Zamora, *El Movimiento Obrero Mexicano en el Sur de Texas, 1900–1920.*

3. Victor S. Clark, *Mexican Labor in the United States,* U.S. Bureau of Labor Bulletin No. 78; Emilio Zamora, "Chicano Socialist Labor Activity in Texas, 1900–1920," *Aztlán* 6 (Sum., 1975): 221–36.

4. For critiques on the literature on the San Diego revolt see Juan Gómez-Quiñones, "Plan de San Diego Reviewed," *Aztlán* 1 (Spr., 1970): 124–32; David Montejano, *Anglos and Mexicans in the Making of Texas, 1836–1986,* pp. 117–25.

5. Ruth Allen, *Chapters in the History of Organized Labor in Texas,* University of Texas Publication No. 4143.

6. José E. Limón, "El Primer Congreso Mexicanista de 1911: A Precursor to Contemporary Chicanismo," *Aztlán* 5 (Spr., Fall, 1974): 85–117; Gómez-Quiñones, *Sembradores.*

7. Other Texas labor histories that omit or distort the early history of Mexican labor include Grady L. Mullenix, "A History of the Texas State Federation of Labor" (Ph.D. diss., University of Texas at Austin, 1955); James Maroney, "Organized Labor in Texas, 1900–1929" (Ph.D. diss., University of Houston, 1975); F. Ray Marshall, *Labor in the South,* pp. 194–99, 230–33; Robert E. Zeigler, "The Workingman in Houston, Texas, 1865–1914" (Ph.D. diss., Texas Tech University, 1972); Charles Mac Gibson,

"Organized Labor in Texas from 1890 to 1900" (Master's thesis, Texas Tech University, 1973); Harold A. Shapiro, "The Workers of San Antonio, Texas, 1900–1940" (Ph.D. diss., University of Texas at Austin, 1952); and John D. Privett, "Agricultural Unionism among Chicanos in Texas" (Master's thesis, University of Texas at Austin, 1976).

8. Additional exceptions to the above include: George Green, "The ILGWU in Texas, 1930–1970," *Journal of Mexican American History* 1 (Spr., 1971): 144–69; Julie Leininger Pycior, "La Raza Organizes: Mexican American Life in San Antonio, 1915–1930, As Reflected in Mutualista Activities" (Ph.D. diss., University of Notre Dame, 1979); and Victor Nelson-Cisneros, "La Clase Trabajadora en Tejas, 1920–1940," *Aztlán* 6 (Sum., 1976): 239–65; Victor Nelson-Cisneros, "UCAPAWA Organizing Activities in Texas, 1935–1950," *Aztlán* 9 (Spr., Sum., 1978): 71–84.

9. The historian Mario García offers one of the most recent depictions of the unorganizable or apathetic Mexican worker. He claims that the participants in the political mobilization efforts of the early 1900s represented a minority and were thus unrepresentative of popular concerns and aspirations. He notes that immigrants were generally content with their improved condition and abstained from joining organized labor for fear of jeopardizing their jobs. Although it may be true that immigrants were inclined to reject political activity because of their vulnerability and improved condition, my findings indicate that they did not take long to familiarize themselves with their new surroundings and to respond collectively to their condition. Regarding the numbers argument, enough of them participated in workers' organizations to warrant our attention (Mario García, *Desert Immigrants: The Mexicans of El Paso, 1880–1920;* Mario García, "Americanization and the Mexican Immigrant, 1880–1930," in Ronald Takaki, ed., *From Different Shores: Perspectives on Race and Ethnicity in America,* pp. 69–77). For recent works on European-origin immigrants that dispute García's suppositions see Dirk Hoerder, ed., *Essays on Working-Class Immigrants: "Struggle a Hard Battle."*

10. Herbert G. Gutman, *Work, Culture, and Society in Industrializing America: Essays in American Working-Class and Social History,* p. 9.

11. For a review of the "new" labor history see David Brody, "The Old Labor History and the New: In Search of An American Working Class," *Labor History* 20 (Win., 1979): 111–26; David Montgomery, "To Study the People: The American Working Class," *Labor History* 21 (Fall, 1980): 485–512; Jim Green, "Culture, Politics and Workers' Response to Industrialization in the U.S.," *Radical America* 6 (Jan., Feb., 1982): 101–28; Jim Green, "Struggling with Class Struggle: Marxism and the Search for a Synthesis of U.S. Labor History," *Labor History* 28 (Fall, 1987): 497–514.

12. The British historian Edward P. Thompson has been especially influential in the reexamination of workers' history. Herbert Gutman, an American scholar of the new labor school, is credited with breaking with the narrow tradition of trade union history in the United States (Edward P. Thompson, *The Making of the English Working Class;* Gutman, *Work, Culture, and Society in Industrializing America*). The Commons school is associated with the "old" labor history that has been critiqued for its narrow ap-

proach to the study of labor history. Traditional labor scholarship associated with Commons school includes John R. Commons and Associates, *A Documentary History of American Industrial Society,* 10 vols.; John R. Commons, *History of Labor in the United States,* 4 vols.; Richard T. Ely, *The Labor Movement in America;* Selig Perlman, *A History of Trade Unionism in the United States;* and Selig Perlman, *A Theory of the Labor Movement.*

13. James Robert Green is one of the few "new" labor historians who has given more than a perfunctory treatment to Mexican labor history. Relying on my previously published work, Green offers an account of Mexican participation in the Texas Socialist Party and the Land League of America (James R. Green, *Grass Roots Socialism: Radical Movements in the Southwest, 1895–1943;* James R. Green, "Tenant Farmer Discontent and Socialist Protest in Texas, 1900–1917," *Southwestern Historical Quarterly* 81 [1977]: 133–54).

14. F. Ray Marshall, "Some Reflections on Labor History," *Southwestern Historical Quarterly* 75 (Oct., 1971): 139–57.

15. For general works that treat Mexican labor history, consult Juan Gómez-Quiñones, "The Origins and Development of the Mexican Working Class in the United States: Laborers and Artisans North of the Río Bravo, 1600–1900," in Elsa C. Frost, Michael C. Meyer, and Josefina Z. Vázquez, eds., *El Trabajo y los Trabajadores en la Historia de México,* pp. 506–17; Juan Gómez-Quiñones and David Maciel, *Al Norte Del Río Bravo (Pasado Lejano, 1600–1930);* David Maciel, *Al Norte del Río Bravo (Pasado Inmediato, 1930–1981);* and Mark Reisler, *By the Sweat of Their Brow: Mexican Immigrant Labor in the United States, 1900–1940.* Also refer to two important special journal issues on the subject: *Aztlán* 6 (Sum., 1975), and *Review* 4 (Win., 1981).

16. Selected works that contribute to the conceptualization of Mexican labor history include Gómez-Quiñones and Arroyo, "On the State of Chicano History"; and Thomas Almaguer and Albert Camarillo, "Urban Chicano Workers in Historical Perspective: A Review of the Literature," in Armando Valdez, Albert Camarillo, and Tomas Almaguer, eds., *The State of Chicano Research on Family, Labor, and Migration: Proceedings of the First Stanford Symposium on Chicano Research and Public Policy,* pp. 3–32.

17. Juan Gómez-Quiñones, "The First Steps: Chicano Labor Conflict and Organizing, 1900–1920," *Aztlán* 3 (Spr., 1972): 13–49.

18. I have benefitted primarily from Montejano's discussion on the use of farm labor controls and Greenberg's examination of trade unionism among a racially stratified working class (Montejano, *Anglos and Mexicans in the Making of Texas, 1836–1986,* pp. 197–219; Stanley B. Greenberg, *Race and State in Capitalist Development: Comparative Perspectives,* pp. 273–87).

Chapter 1

1. For histories that treat the subject of socioeconomic change in the Southwest and its effect on the Mexican community, see Tomás Almaguer, *Interpreting Chicano History: The "World System" Approach to 19th Century*

California, Institute for the Study of Social Change Working Paper No. 10; Luis Leobardo Arroyo, Victor Nelson-Cisneros, Juan Gómez-Quiñones, and Antonio Ríos-Bustamante, "Preludio al Futuro: Pasado y Presente de los Trabajadores Mexicanos al Norte del Río Bravo, 1600–1975," in Maciel, ed., *La Otra Cara de Mexico: El Pueblo Chicano*, pp. 243–77; Gómez-Quiñones and Maciel, *Al Norte Del Río Bravo;* Juan Gómez-Quiñones and Antonio Ríos-Bustamante, "La Comunidad al Norte del Río Bravo," in Maciel, ed., *La Otra Cara de Mexico*, pp. 24–73; Carey McWilliams, *North from Mexico: The Spanish-Speaking People of the United States;* Montejano, *Anglos and Mexicans in the Making of Texas;* and Leonard Pitt, *The Decline of the Californios, 1846–1890.*

2. Theodore R. Fehrenbach, *Lone Star: A History of Texas and Texans,* pp. 596–603; Frank Goodwyn, *Lone Star Land: Twentieth Century Texas in Perspective,* pp. 57–59; John Williams Knox, "The Economic Status of the Mexican Immigrant in San Antonio, Texas," (Master's thesis, University of Texas, Austin, 1927), pp. 6–13; Paul S. Taylor, *An American-Mexican Frontier: Nueces County, Texas,* pp. 71–81.

3. For a description of industrial activity and growth in Texas, see U.S. Bureau of the Census, *Abstract of the Thirteenth Census (1910), Statistics for Texas,* pp. 597, 687–794; U.S. Bureau of the Census, *Fourteenth Census of the United States (1920), State Compendium, Texas,* pp. 239–62; and Reisler, *By the Sweat of Their Brow,* pp. 128–29.

4. Southwestern Bell Telephone Company, *Economic Survey of Texas,* pp. 86–88, 96–97; Rupert Norval Richardson, *Texas: The Lone Star State,* pp. 297–98, 305–306; Matt S. Meier and Feliciano Rivera, *The Chicanos: A History of Mexican Americans,* pp. 93–95.

5. Bureau of the Census, *Fourteenth Census of the United States,* p. 7.

6. Southwestern Bell Telephone Company, *Economic Survey of Texas,* pp. 86–89, 96.

7. George Waverley Briggs, "The Housing Problem in Texas: A Study of Physical Conditions under Which the Other Half Lives," reprinted from the *Galveston-Dallas News,* Nov. 19–Dec. 19, 1911, pp. 59–70; pamphlet. Also see Alvin S. Johnson, "Mexico in San Antonio," *The New Republic,* June 24, 1916, 190–91; Chester T. Crowell, "Strange News from Texas," *The American Mercury* 4 (Mar., 1925): 323–30.

8. Montejano, *Mexicans and Anglos in the Making of Texas, 1836–1986,* pp. 113–15; Arnoldo de Leon, *Ethnicity in the Sunbelt: A History of Mexican Americans in Houston,* pp. 8–9, 23, 25–26; Guadalupe San Miguel, Jr., *"Let All of Them Take Heed": Mexican Americans and the Campaign for Educational Equality in Texas, 1910–1981,* pp. 13–17.

9. Servando I. Esquivel, "The Immigrant from Mexico," *The Outlook* 125 (May 19, 1920): 131.

10. Mattie Bell, "The Growth and Distribution of the Texas Population" (Ph.D. diss., Baylor University, 1955), pp. 166–73.

11. Mexican immigration to the United States has been a subject of much interest. The following provide a comprehensive treatment of the subject: Jorge Bustamante, "The Historical Context of Undocumented Mexican Immi-

gration to the United States," *Aztlán* 3 (Fall, 1972): 257–81; Lawrence Cardoso, "Labor Emigration to the Southwest, 1916 to 1920: Mexican Attitudes and Policy," in George C. Kiser and Martha W. Kiser, eds., *Mexican Workers in the United States: Historical and Political Perspectives;* Manuel Gamio, *Mexican Immigration to the United States: A Study of Human Migration and Adjustment;* and Juan Gómez-Quiñones, "Mexican Immigration to the United States and the Internationalization of Labor, 1848–1980: An Overview," in Antonio Ríos-Bustamante, ed., *Mexican Immigrant Workers in the United States,* Anthology No. 2, pp. 13–34.

12. The discussion on northern Mexico, particularly La Laguna region, is based on the following: Rodney D. Anderson, *Outcasts in Their Own Land: Mexican Industrial Workers, 1906–1911,* pp. 28–48; Barry Carr, *El Movimiento Obrero y la Política en Mexico, 1910–1929,* pp. 200–201; William K. Meyers, "La Comarca Lagunera: Work, Protests and Popular Mobilization in North Central Mexico," in Thomas Benjamin and William McNellie, eds., *Other Mexicos: Essays on Regional Mexican History, 1876–1910,* pp. 243–74; Ildefonso Villarello Vélez, *Historia de la Revolución Mexicana en Coahuila,* pp. 899–95; Francois Xavier Guerra, "Territorio Mimado, Mas Alla de Zapata en la Revolución Mexicana," *NEXOS* 6 (Mayo de 1983): 33–43; John Mason Hart, "U.S. Economic Hegemony, Nationalism, and Violence in the Mexican Countryside, 1876–1920," in Daniel Nugent, ed., *Rural Revolt in Mexico and U.S. Intervention,* Monograph Series 27, pp. 69–83.

13. Taylor, *An American-Mexican Frontier,* p. 114.

14. Samuel Bryan, "Mexican Immigrants in the United States," *The Survey,* Sept. 7, 1912, 727; José Hernández Alvarez, "A Demographic Profile of the Mexican Immigration to the United States, 1910–1950," *Journal of Inter-American Studies* 8 (July, 1966): 474.

15. Esquivel, "The Immigrant from Mexico," p. 131; U.S. Congress, House, Statement of Representative John C. Box, *Imported Pauper Labor and Serfdom in America, Hearings before the Committee on Immigration and Naturalization,* 67th Cong., 1st Sess., 1921, p. 18.

16. U.S. Congress, House, *Temporary Admission of Illiterate Mexican Laborers, Hearings before the Committee on Immigration and Naturalization,* H.J. Res. 271, 66th. Cong., 2nd sess., 1920, p. 7. For a discussion on the congressional debates and public opinion surrounding the issue of Mexican immigration during the second decade, consult Acuña, *Occupied America,* pp. 158–63, 185–88.

17. Bryan, "Mexican Immigrants in the United States," pp. 728–29; James L. Slayden, "The Mexican Immigrant: Some Observations on Mexican Immigration," *The Annals of the American Academy of Political and Social Science* 93 (Jan., 1921): 121–23.

18. *Temporary Admission of Illiterate Mexican Laborers,* pp. 49–50, 90.

19. J. Blaine Gwin, "Immigration along Our Southwest Border," *The Annals of the American Academy of Political and Social Sciences* 93 (Jan., 1921): 126–30.

20. Hernández Alvarez, "A Demographic Profile," p. 474; Bryan, "Mexican Immigration in the United States," pp. 726–27; Gwin, "Immigration along

Our Southwest Border," pp. 726–27; "Los Mexicanos se vienen," *Evolución,* July 24, 1910, p. 3; "El éxodo de Mexicanos ha continuado en grande escala," *La Prensa,* Sept. 25, 1914. For testimony before a congressional committee on labor agencies that shipped Mexican workers out of Texas, see U.S. Congress, Senate, Committee on Foreign Relations, *Investigation of Mexican Affairs, Hearings before a Subcommittee of the Committee on Foreign Relations,* 66th Cong., 1st Sess., 1920, vol. 3, pp. 2143–44, 2148–51, 2153–55, 2157, 2159, 2162–64.

21. Texas State Federation of Labor, *Proceedings* (Galveston: Apr. 12–16, 1910), p. 83; hereafter cited as TSFL, *Proceedings.*

22. Mario Barrera, *Race and Class in the Southwest: A Theory of Racial Inequality,* pp. 59–62; Bryan, "Mexican Immigrants in the United States," pp. 726–28; Clark, *Mexican Labor in the United States,* pp. 477–95; and Malcolm H. Townes, "The Labor Supply of Texas," (Master's thesis, University of Texas, 1923), pp. 59–75, 81–90.

23. Roden Fuller, "Occupations of the Mexican-Born Population of Texas, New Mexico, and Arizona, 1900–1920," *Journal of the American Statistical Association* 23 (Mar., 1928): 47–64.

24. Paul S. Taylor, *Mexican Labor in the United States: Dimmit County, Winter Garden District, South Texas,* University of California Publications in Economics Vol. 6, pp. 306–307; Texas State Employment Service, *Origins and Problems of Texas Migratory Farm Labor,* pp. 7, 23–25.

25. Clark, *Mexican Labor in the United States,* pp. 494–95; Clemente N. Idar, "Laredo City Offers Good Field for Organization; Letters Tell Condition in Principal Door to Mexico," *Pan American Labor Press,* Sept. 11, 1918, pp. 2–3; Knox, "The Economic Status of the Mexican Immigrant in San Antonio, Texas," pp. 40–42; "Los que emigran," *La Prensa,* Jan. 29, 1914, p. 2; "Por la humanidad y por la raza," ibid., Dec. 31, 1914, pp. 5–6.

26. "Las dificultades entre Mexicanos y Americanos en Waco, Texas," *La Prensa,* Jan. 29, 1915, p. 4; "Trabajadores Mexicanos," ibid., May 7, 1914, p. 7; "Sigue la huelga," *El Defensor del Obrero,* Nov. 25, 1906, pp. 169–70; TSFL, *Proceedings* (El Paso: June 8–12, 1914), pp. 88–89; *Temporary Admission of Illiterate Mexican Laborers,* p. 7273.

27. Bryan, "Mexican Immigrants in the United States," pp. 728–29; Clark, *Mexican Labor in the United States,* pp. 476–78.

28. Mario García, "The Chicana in American History: The Mexican Women of El Paso, 1800–1920: A Case Study," *Pacific Historical Review* 49 (May, 1980): 315–30. For additional references to the condition of Mexicana workers throughout the state and a theoretical postulation on the sexual division of labor see Barrera, *Race and Class in the Southwest,* pp. 94–99, 102–103.

29. Texas Bureau of Labor Statistics, *Sixth Biennial Report, 1919–1920,* pp. 103–109.

30. William J. Knox's study of Mexicans from San Antonio is one of the few sources that provides labor market participation data on Mexicanas. According to Knox, approximately 248, or 16 percent, of the 1,550 Mexicanas that he surveyed in 1926 worked outside their homes. The great ma-

jority of them, 70 percent, were born in Mexico (Knox, "The Economic Status of the Mexican Immigrant in San Antonio, Texas," p. 22).

Chapter 2

1. Clark, *Mexican Labor in the United States,* pp. 482–85; Jay S. Stowell, *The Near Side of the Mexican Question,* pp. 38–39. This section draws on David Montejano's excellent discussion on farm labor controls during the early 1900s. I give more emphasis, however, to the mobility of Mexican workers as one of numerous organizing initiatives that shaped political relations in rural and urban areas. I also give added attention to the massive migration into the cities and to the prominent role that organized labor played in defending the established order (see Montejano, *Mexicans and Anglos in the Making of Texas, 1836–1986*).

2. Charles M. Harger, "The New Era of the Ranch Lands," *The American Review of Reviews* 44 (Nov., 1911): 580–82; Thomas A. Hickey, "The Land Renters Union in Texas," *International Socialist Review,* Sept., 1912, 239–44; Charles W. Holman, "The Tenant Farmer, Country Brother of the Casual Worker," *The Survey,* Apr. 17, 1915, 62–64; Frank Putnam, "Texas in Transition," *Collier's,* Jan. 22, 1910, 15.

3. For a description of industrial activity and growth in Texas, see *Abstract of the Thirteenth Census (1910), Statistics for Texas,* pp. 597, 687–794; Bureau of the Census, *Fourteenth Census of the United States,* pp. 239–62; and Reisler, *By the Sweat of Their Brow,* pp. 128–29.

4. *Corpus Christi Caller,* Feb. 15, 1885, quoted in Taylor, *An American-Mexican Frontier,* p. 105.

5. *Corpus Christi Caller,* Jan. 14, 1898, quoted in ibid., p. 105.

6. *Corpus Christi Caller,* Dec. 2, 1909, quoted in ibid., p. 105.

7. *The Gulf Coast Magazine,* Summer, 1905, 34.

8. *Star Gardens* (Kansas City, Mo.: Rio Grande Valley Investment Co., ca. 1915), p. 9.

9. Fehrenbach, *Lone Star,* pp. 687–89; C. L. Cline, "The Rio Grande Valley," *Southwest Review* 25 (Apr., 1940): 241; Carey McWilliams, *Ill Fares the Land: Migrants and Migratory Labor in the United States,* pp. 209–10.

10. Harger, "The New Era of the Ranch Lands," pp. 580–82; Taylor, *An American-Mexican Frontier,* p. 83.

11. Rex Willard, *Status of Farming in the Lower Rio Grande Irrigated District of Texas,* U.S. Department of Agriculture Bulletin No. 665, p. 21.

12. Ibid., pp. 1–24; Dorothy Lee Pope, *Rainbow Era on the Rio Grande,* pp. 63–67.

13. Charles B. Austin, *Studies in Farm Tenancy,* University of Texas Bulletin No. 21, pp. 19–23; Lewis H. Haney and George S. Wehrwein, eds., *A Social and Economic Survey of Southern Travis County,* University of Texas Bulletin No. 65, pp. 25–26; U.S. Commission on Industrial Relations, *Final Report and Testimony,* 10:8952, 8954, 9222–26.

14. Ruth Allen, "The Socialist Party in Texas," Ruth Allen Papers on Labor

Movements in Texas, Eugene C. Barker Texas History Center, University of Texas, Austin, pp. 36–37; Stuart Jamieson, *Labor Unionism in American Agriculture,* U.S. Bureau of Labor Statistics, Bulletin No. 836, pp. 260–61. Also refer to the numerous letters from Mexican renters and laborers submitted to the Commission on Industrial Relations by E. O. Meitzen, an officer of the Texas Socialist Party, in Commission on Industrial Relations, *Final Report,* 10:9282–88.

15. Max S. Handman, "The Mexican Immigrant in Texas," *Political and Social Science Quarterly* 7 (June, 1926): 35–36; Robert H. Montgomery, "Keglar Hill," *The Survey,* May 1, 1931, 171–95. All references to Keglar Hill are based on the Montgomery article.

16. Montgomery, "Keglar Hill," p. 194.

17. Ibid., p. 195.

18. For findings similar to those described by Montgomery, see George S. Wehrwein, "Social Life," in Haney and Wehrwein, eds., *A Social and Economic Survey of Southern Travis County,* pp. 53–55.

19. Handman, "The Mexican Immigrant in Texas," p. 335. For additional views on the alleged docility of the Mexican immigrant see Clark, *Mexican Labor in the United States;* and E. F. Bainford, "Industrialization and the Mexican Casual," *Proceedings of the Fifth Annual Convention of the Southwestern Political and Social Science Association.*

20. *Temporary Admission of Illiterate Mexican Laborers,* pp. 16, 28, 30.

21. Historians have begun to amend the traditional view of the newcomer mentality among European-origin immigrants with research that points to a high degree of labor agitation, homeland politics, and community-building activities. For samples of this recent work see Hoerder, ed., *Essays on Working-Class Immigrants.*

22. Lawrence A. Cardoso, *Mexican Emigration to the United States, 1897–1931, Socio-Economic Patterns,* pp. 56–70.

23. Reisler, *By the Sweat of Their Brow,* pp. 128–29; Clark, *Mexican Labor in the United States,* pp. 484, 489, 496–501.

24. *Temporary Admission of Illiterate Mexican Laborers,* p. 30.

25. Clark, *Mexican Labor in the United States,* p. 477.

26. Taylor, *An American-Mexican Frontier,* p. 139.

27. Ibid., pp. 113, 128, 133. Also see Clark, *Mexican Labor in the United States,* for similar observations.

28. Clark, *Mexican Labor in the United States,* pp. 471–72.

29. Taylor, *An American-Mexican Frontier,* pp. 112–13, 127–28, 137, 139; Commission on Industrial Relations, *Final Report,* 10:9258. I address the topics of rural workers' organizations and spontaneous strike activity in chapter 3.

30. Montejano, *Anglos and Mexicans in the Making of Texas,* pp. 214–18.

31. David J. Saposs, "Self-Government and Freedom of Action in Isolated Industrial Communities," field report to U.S. Commission on Industrial Relations, microfilm, p. 24.

32. Reisler, *By the Sweat of Their Brow,* pp. 25–26. Reisler suggests that German intrigue may have been exaggerated since some of the persons circulating the rumors sought to force the Mexican sharecroppers to sell their cotton at reduced prices.

33. Quoted in Taylor, *An American-Mexican Frontier,* p. 140.

34. Texas Bureau of Labor Statistics, *Twelfth Biennial Report, 1931–1932,* pp. 26–29.

35. Ibid.; Montejano, *Mexicans and Anglos in the Making of Texas,* pp. 208–13. Montejano dates the beginning of governmental control over labor mobility with the establishment of the Emigrant Labor Law. It was in fact preceded by the farm labor distribution program beginning in 1918.

36. Slayden, "The Mexican Immigrant," p. 123; Cardoso, *Mexican Emigration to the United States,* p. 114.

37. Leonard Watkins, "Farm Labor," in Haney and Wehrwein, eds., *A Social and Economic Survey of Southern Travis County,* pp. 129–39.

38. Taylor, *An American-Mexican Frontier,* p. 130.

39. Ibid.

40. TSFL, *Proceedings* (Galveston: Apr. 12–16, 1910), p. 117.

41. Texas Bureau of Labor Statistics, *Fifth Biennial Report, 1917–1918,* pp. 29–31. For a historical analysis of protective labor legislation in the United States see Alice Kessler-Harris, *Out of Work: A History of Wage Earning Women in the United States,* pp. 120–24.

42. "La ley del jornal mínimo para mujeres," *La Vanguardia,* Feb. 3, 1921, p. 2. Unless otherwise noted, the author has translated the Spanish-language texts used in this study.

43. The numerous organizing reports that appear in the published proceedings of the TSFL reflect a widespread fear of the alleged Mexican threat.

44. Taylor, *An American-Mexican Frontier,* p. 160.

45. TSFL, *Proceedings* (Houston: Apr. 24–28, 1916), p. 114, (Fort Worth: May 21–25), p. 112.

46. TSFL, *Proceedings* (Houston: Apr. 24–28, 1916), p. 113.

47. Unidentified Mexican printer, interview with Manuel Gamio, San Antonio, Tex., ca. 1928, Manuel Gamio Papers, Bancroft Library, University of California, Berkeley.

48. For a history of the influential role that the brotherhoods played in promoting labor legislation in Texas, see "Brief History of Labor Legislation in Texas," Texas Bureau of Labor Statistics, *Eighth Biennial Report, 1923–1924,* pp. 19–27.

49. *Imported Pauper Labor and Serfdom in America,* pp. 10–17. Congressman John C. Box, of Texas, submitted correspondence and newspaper articles that reflected widespread opposition to Mexican labor by Anglo workers, including organized labor from Galveston and Fort Worth. Beginning in the first decade and especially during the second, organized labor faced an open-shop movement in these cities as well as in San Antonio (Allen, *Chapters in the History of Organized Labor in Texas,* pp. 228–45; Harold

Shapiro, "The Labor Movement in San Antonio, Texas, 1865–1915," *The Southwestern Social Science Quarterly* 36 [Sept. 1955]: 160–75).

50. TSFL, *Proceedings* (Fort Worth: May 21–25, 1917), p. 112.

51. Malcolm H. Harris, "The Labor Supply of Texas," (Master's thesis, University of Texas, 1922), pp. 75–76; *La Vanguardia*, Mar. 31, 1921, p. 4.

52. TSFL, *Proceedings* (Cleburne: Apr. 26–May 1, 1920), p. 127.

53. Reisler, *By the Sweat of Their Brow,* pp. 51–52.

54. *International Oil Worker*, Sept., 1920, quoted in Allen, *Chapters in the History of Organized Labor in Texas,* p. 233.

55. "Mexican Rights in the United States," *The Nation,* July 12, 1922, 53. Also see "Noticias amenazantes aparecieron en Eastland," *La Vanguardia,* Feb. 24, 1921, p. 1; "Neff ordena que se de la debida protección a Mexicanos," ibid., Feb. 24, 1921, pp. 1, 2; "Eastland Citizens Protest Presence of Mexican Laborers," *Austin American-Statesman,* February 6, 1921; "Night Riders Raid Mexican Camps," *Ranger Daily Times,* reprinted in *Imported Pauper Labor and Serfdom in America,* pp. 14–15.

56. "Labor Conditions; Results of Admission of Mexican Laborers Under Departmental Orders For Employment in Agricultural Pursuits," *Monthly Labor Review,* Nov. 1920, pp. 221–23, quoted in Reisler, *By the Sweat of Their Brow,* p. 36.

57. John Stone, interview with Paul S. Taylor, Carrizo Springs, Tex., ca. 1929, Paul S. Taylor Papers, Bancroft Library, University of California, Berkeley; Mr. Kennedy, interview with Paul S. Taylor, San Antonio, Tex., ca. 1929, Taylor Papers; J. H. Means, interview with Paul S. Taylor, San Antonio, Tex., ca. 1929, Taylor Papers.

58. Watkins, "Farm Labor," p. 138.

59. "Activities and Results," *The San Antonian: A Journal of Community Service,* Mar. 1920, 1; Slayden, "The Mexican Immigrant: Some Observations on Mexican Immigration," p. 124. C. F. Russi, a TSFL vice-president from San Antonio, reported to the federation that he suspected the chamber of collaborating with employers to depress wages by encouraging immigrants to come to San Antonio. He did not claim, however, that immigrants were displacing U.S.-born workers. Moreover, the arrival of large number of immigrants did not seem to have affected the Anglo unions. Russi claimed that organized labor in the city had registered a 25 percent increase in its membership (TSFL, *Proceedings* [Beaumont: May 19–24, 1919], p. 51).

60. Allen, *Chapters in the History of Organized Labor in Texas,* p. 128; Ralph W. Steen, *Twentieth Century Texas: An Economic and Social History,* pp. 115–16; James C. Maroney, "Labor's Struggle for Acceptance: The Houston Worker in a Changing Society, 1900–1929," in Francisco A. Rosales and Barry J. Kaplan, eds., *Houston: A Twentieth Century Urban Frontier,* pp. 34–57.

61. Allen, *Chapters in the History of Organized Labor in Texas,* p. 129; Richardson, *Texas,* p. 417.

62. Allen, *Chapters in the History of Organized Labor in Texas,* pp. 129–36; "A Brief History of Labor Legislation in Texas," in Texas Bureau of Labor Statistics, *Eighth Biennial Report, 1923–1924,* pp. 19–27.

63. TSFL, *Proceedings* (Austin: May 13–17), p. 72.

64. TSFL, *Proceedings* (Galveston: Apr. 12–16, 1910), pp. 17–18.

65. Ibid., pp. 83–84, 88.

66. TSFL, *Proceedings* (Palestine: May 6–10, 1912), p. 16.

67. Ibid., p. 111.

68. Maroney, "Organized Labor in Texas, 1900–1929," p. 37; TSFL, *Proceedings* (Fort Worth: May 21–25, 1917), p. 83, (San Antonio: Mar. 18–23), p. 83, (Beaumont: May 19–24, 1919), p. 115; "Una mujer pide que se haga justicia a los trabajadores Mexicanos," *La Prensa*, Jan. 10, 1915, pp. 1, 8; "Provocan a los Mexicanos que residen en Waco los Americanos," ibid., Jan. 12, 1915, pp. 4, 5.

69. "La propaganda anti-Mexicana de las uniones de trabajadores," ibid., Jan. 13, 1915.

70. TSFL, *Proceedings* (Houston: Apr. 19–23, 1926), pp. 24–25.

71. For a discussion on the lobbying efforts of the AFL, see Reisler, *By the Sweat of Their Brow*, pp. 34–35, 67–70. For a review of nativist reactions to immigrants, the congressional debates on immigration, and immigration policies during the 1910s and 1920s, see Gómez-Quiñones, "Mexican Immigration to the United States," pp. 22–25.

72. TSFL, *Proceedings* (Palestine: May 6–10, 1912), p. 16.

73. Ibid. See the following for reports and resolutions on immigration: TSFL, *Proceedings* (Cleburne: Apr. 26–May 1, 1920), pp. 31, 51, 126–27, (Galveston: Apr. 12–16, 1921), p. 127, (Port Arthur: Apr. 21–25, 1924), pp. 84–85, (Amarillo: May 25–28, 1925), p. 33; American Federation of Labor, *Reports of Proceedings of Annual Conventions* (Atlantic City: June 9–23, 1919), p. 242, (Denver: June 13–25), p. 87, (Montreal: June 7–19), p. 104. Also see *Imported Pauper Labor and Serfdom in America*, pp. 10–17.

74. TSFL, *Proceedings* (Cleburne: Apr. 26–May 1, 1920), p. 31.

75. Reisler, *By the Sweat of Their Brow*, pp. 210–14.

76. Ibid., pp. 169–79. See the following for analysis on the Pan American Federation of Labor, the international labor organization established by the AFL in cooperation with labor leaders from Latin American countries: Sinclair Snow, *Samuel Gompers and the Pan American Federation of Labor*; Harvey A. Levenstein, *Labor Organizations in the United States and Mexico: A History of Their Relations*; and Lewis L. Lorwin, *The International Labor Movement: History, Policies, Outlook*.

Chapter 3

1. Histories of Mexicans in the United States have examined mutual aid societies, unions, informal responses, and even indifferent behavior to organization. Each provides an important part of the total picture. However, as partial treatments they offer incomplete assessments and often lead to questionable inferences or conclusions. For example, Mario García's emphasis on a contented immigrant mentality and David Montejano's focus

on changing ethnic relations give little play to the numerous types of community organizations that such historians as Arnoldo de Leon have studied. The studies by de Leon, on the other hand, do not adequately treat formative influences from Mexico. My own work on Mexican socialist activity has examined the development of unionism in isolation of other organized workers' actions.

2. Copy of ultimatum sent to George Wethers, foreman of the L.I.T. Ranch at Tascosa, Oldham County, Ruth Allen Papers on Labor Movements in Texas. Also see Allen, *Chapters in the History of Organized Labor in Texas,* pp. 33–41; and McWilliams, *North from Mexico,* p. 190.

3. Anonymous, "Notes" based on membership rolls of the Longshoremen's Association, Ruth Allen Papers on Labor Movements in Texas. Also see James V. Reese, "The Evolution of an Early Texas Union: The Screwmen's Benevolent Association of Galveston, 1866–1891," *Southwestern Historical Quarterly* 75 (Oct., 1971): 158–85. Although African Americans normally organized their own separate organizations, their participation denoted a relatively open circle of workers that may explain why Mexicans gained entry. Interracial relations among New Orleans dockworkers during the same period suggests that the industrial nature of production in the docks encouraged such alliances as well as racial conflicts within workers' organizations (Daniel Rosenberg, *New Orleans Dockworkers: Race, Labor, and Unionism, 1892–1923*).

4. "Laborers Rejoicing, The City Alive with Visiting and Local Knights of Labor," *San Antonio Daily Times,* July 22, 1886, Ruth Allen Papers on Labor Movements in Texas. The Knights also demonstrated their sympathy towards Mexicans in New Mexico, where they were allied with two regional organizations, Las Gorras Blancas and El Partido del Pueblo Unido. Mexican organizers with the Knights established at least twenty local assemblies in northern New Mexico during the 1880s (Robert J. Rosenbaum, *Mexican Resistance in the Southwest, "The Sacred Right of Self-Preservation,"* pp. 118–24).

5. "Thurber on Strike," *The United Mine Workers' Journal,* Sept. 24, 1903; Mary Jane Gentry, "Thurber: The Life and Death of a Texas Town," (Master's thesis, University of Texas, 1946).

6. Eugene V. Debs, "A Valiant Foeman," *Social Democratic Herald,* Aug. 13, 1903, p. 1.

7. Confidential Dispatch, August 2, 1910, U.S. Department of State, Records Relating to Internal Affairs of Mexico, 1910–1929, Record Group 59, National Archives, Washington, D.C.

8. Joe Priest, Secret Service Agent, to Secretary of State, Sept. 28, 1909, RG 59, Department of State Records; newspapers and circulars by the Political Refugee Defense League can be found in the John Murray Papers, Bancroft Library, University of California, Berkeley.

9. For an examination of the favorable view of the Mexican revolution by American socialists, see Ivie E. Cadenhead Jr., "The American Socialists and the Mexican Revolution of 1910," *The Southwestern Social Science Quarterly* 43 (Sept., 1962): 103–17. Also see documents and testimony by Lázaro Gutiérrez de Lara, John Kenneth Turner, John Murray, and Mary

"Mother" Jones in U.S. Congress, House, Committee on Rules, *Hearings on H. J. Res. 201, Providing for a Joint Committee to Investigate Alleged Persecutions of Mexican Citizens by the Government of Mexico.*

10. Quoted from *The Javelina* in Taylor, *Mexican Labor in the United States,* p. 351.

11. Although English-language newspapers credited the lone Anglo in the group with being the leader, he seems to have been an adventurer who joined the group after it was organized and on its way to Mexico ("Pretendían libertar a los contrabandistas de Carrizo Springs," *La Prensa,* Nov. 27, 1913, p. 4). For a history of the PLM in the Southwest, particularly its organizing work in the state of Texas see Gómez-Quiñones, *Sembradores.*

12. Taylor, *Mexican Labor in the United States,* p. 351.

13. Ibid.

14. Guerra, "Territorio Mimado," pp. 34–38. For an examination of the issue of binational relations between Mexican communities and the role that political exiles played in the Southwest during the nineteenth and twentieth centuries, see Juan Gómez-Quiñones, "Notes on an Interpretation of the Relations between the Mexican Community in the United States and Mexico," in Carlos Vásquez and Manuel García y Griego, eds., *Mexican-U.S. Relations: Conflict and Convergence,* pp. 417–39; Robert Case, "La Frontera Texana y Los Movimientos de Insurrección en México, 1850–1900," *Historia Mexicana* 14 (1965): 415–52; Charles C. Cumberland, "Mexican Revolutionary Movements from Texas, 1906–1912," *Southwestern Historical Quarterly* 52 (Jan. 1949): 301–24; Hart, "U.S. Economic Hegemony," pp. 69–83.

15. See two works by Américo Paredes for discussions on the distinct cultural identity of the binational cultural region extending from the mouth of the Rio Grande River to the two Laredos: *With His Pistol in His Hand: A Border Ballad and Its Hero,* pp. 7–15; and *A Texas-Mexican Cancionero: Folksongs of the Lower Border,* pp. 3–5.

16. Marcelo Rodea, *Historia del Movimiento Obrero Ferrocarrilero, 1890–1943,* pp. 87–90, 98–100; Esther Shabot A., "La Unión de Mecánicos Mexicanos y la Huelga de 1906," *Memoria del Segundo Coloquio Regional de Historia Obrera,* pp. 163–237; Anderson, *Outcasts in Their Own Land,* pp. 90–92.

17. Anderson, *Outcasts in Their Own Land,* pp. 90–91, 117; Leininger Pycior, "La Raza Organizes; Mexican American Life in San Antonio," p. 135.

18. Emory E. Bailey, ed., *Who's Who in Texas: A Biographical Directory* (Dallas: Who's Who Publishing Company, 1938), p. 191.

19. "Un obrero que lucha por el buen nombre de su patria," *La Prensa,* June 19, 1913, p. 8; "Fiesta," ibid., Dec. 23, 1914, p. 1.

20. Alfredo Navarrete, *Alto a la Contrarevolución,* pp. 93–96.

21. Anderson, *Outcasts in Their Own Land,* p. 90.

22. Limón, "El Primer Congreso Mexicanista de 1911, pp. 85–117; Nicasio Idar, president, and José María S. Martínez, secretary, Sociedad Mutualista "Hijos de Juárez" to Junta Patriótica, Feb. 3, 1904, Asunto Ricardo Flores

Magón, 1901–1906, Secretaría de Relaciones Exteriores, México, D.F. Nicasio also published *La Revista,* a Masonic paper, served as an officer of the Masonic lodge Benito Juárez, and was a member of the most popular mutualist organization in the city, Sociedad Mutualista Hijos de Juárez.

23. Rodea, *Historia del Movimiento Obrero Ferrocarrilero,* pp. 82–83.

24. "Murio ayer un conocido líder del trabajo," *La Prensa,* Jan. 28, 1934, p. 12. For a running debate on the merits of socialism and unionism between Nicasio Idar and the leadership of Federal Labor Union No. 11953, see "El socialismo," *El Defensor del Obrero,* Sept. 13, 1906, p. 88, and "Socialismo," Sept. 30, 1906, ibid., p. 105.

25. For a history of the Pan American Federation of Labor, see Snow, *Samuel Gompers and the Pan American Federation of Labor.*

26. Chapter seven addresses the organizing work by Idar during the 1920s.

27. Guerra, "Territorio Mimado," pp. 41–45; Peter V. N. Henderson, "Mexican Rebels in the Borderlands, 1910–1912," *Red River Valley Historical Review* 2 (Sum., 1975): 207–19; Barry Carr, "Las Peculiaridades del Norte Mexicano, 1880–1927: Ensayo de Interpretación," *Historia Mexicana* 22 (Enero, Marzo, 1973): 320–46. Historians agree that the northern Mexico region played a significant role in the revolution, in large part because Texas offered political exiles the necessary refuge and organizing opportunities.

28. For historical interpretations of the PLM, see Gómez-Quiñones, *Sembradores;* and James D. Cockcroft, *Intellectual Precursors of the Mexican Revolution, 1900–1913.* A copy of the 1906 PLM plan appears in Arnaldo Córdova, *La Ideología de la Revolución Mexicana; La Formación del Nuevo Régimen,* pp. 405–27. For documentary information on Mexican exiled politics in South Texas during the first decade, see the large number of consular and military reports as well as intercepted correspondence involving PLM sympathizers in the following: RG 59, Department of State Records; Ricardo Flores Magón Papers, Federal Records Center, Fort Worth, Texas; Ricardo Flores Magón Papers, Silvestre Terrazas Collection, Bancroft Library, University of California, Berkeley.

29. Gómez-Quiñones, *Sembradores,* p. 27; Edingardo Aguilar and Salvador Hernández, "Notas Sobre Magonismo, 1900–1915," *Memoria del Segundo Coloquio Regional de Historia Obrera,* pp. 123–62.

30. Evidence of widespread support for the PLM in Texas is contained in correspondence intercepted by government authorities. See Asunto Ricardo Flores Magón, 1901–1909, and Ricardo Flores Magón Papers, Terrazas Collection. The first collection includes mostly correspondence from Texas sympathizers between 1901 and 1906. Cities like Laredo and San Antonio and the cotton belt area registered the highest concentrations of PLM supporters. For descriptions of revolts and participation of PLM sympathizers from Texas see Ildefonso Villarello Vélez, *Historia de la Revolución Mexicana en Coahuila,* pp. 88–90, 95–98, 101–104; Aguilar and Hernández, "Notas Sobre Magonismo, 1900–1915," pp. 139–44.

31. Quoted in William K. Meyers, "La Comarca Lagunera, p. 258.

32. Ibid., pp. 261–62.

33. Clark, *Mexican Labor in the United States,* p. 496; "En bien de nuestra Raza, una carta interesante," *La Prensa,* Apr. 18, 1915, pp. 3, 8.

34. Taylor, *An American-Mexican Frontier,* pp. 113, 133, 137–38.

35. Commission on Industrial Relations, *Final Report,* 10:9258.

36. Ernesto Galarza, "Mexicans in the Southwest: A Culture in Process," in Edward H. Spicer and Raymond H. Thompson, eds., *Plural Society in the Southwest,* pp. 284–85; Arnoldo de Leon, *The Tejano Community, 1836–1900,* pp. 60–61.

37. "Mexican Journeys to Bethlehem," *The Literary Digest,* June 2, 1923, 105–106.

38. Leonard L. Watkins, "Farm Labor," in Haney and Wehrwein, *A Social and Economic Survey of Southern Travis County,* p. 131.

39. "Tratan de organizarse los trabajadores Mexicanos de San Antonio," *La Prensa,* July 4, 1917.

40. "Los Mexicanos de Gonzales, Tex., elevaron una solicitud," ibid., Nov. 7, 1914, p. 1.

41. "Provocan a los Mexicanos que residen en Waco los Americanos," ibid., Jan. 2, 1915, pp. 4, 5.

42. XYZ, "La situación de nuestros compatriótas," *La Prensa,* Jan. 14, 1915, p. 6.

43. Clemente Idar, "El movimiento de repatriación," *El Unionista,* Dec. 30, 1920, p. 2.

44. Copy of newspaper in Ruth Allen Papers, Labor Archives, University of Texas, Arlington.

45. J. Lee Stambaugh and Lillian J. Stambaugh, *The Lower Rio Grande Valley of Texas,* p. 172.

46. J. L. Allhands, *Railroads to the Rio,* pp. 130–31. For comments on Mexican labor in the Rio Grande Valley and the low wages, see Allhands's work, *Gringo Builders,* pp. 165–66, 257–59.

47. "A Cotulla Episode," *The Borderland of Two Republics,* May 11, 1906, p. 7; Asunto Disturbios en Artesia Wells, 1909, Secretaría de Relaciones Exteriores, México, D.F.

48. Josef J. Barton, "Land, Labor, and Community in Nueces: Czech Farmers and Mexican Laborers in South Texas, 1880–1930," in Frederick C. Luebke, ed., *Ethnicity on the Great Plains,* pp. 190–209; Cardoso, *Mexican Emigration to the United States,* p. 40.

49. Barton, "Land, Labor, and Community in Nueces," pp. 199–209.

50. This framework is an adaptation of Edward P. Thompson's definition of English working-class organizations from the early nineteenth century. Thompson's definition referred to organizations outside a modern industrial setting and consequently beyond the influence of an adversarial process that involved formal and institutionalized bargaining over wages and working conditions between workers and employers. The organizations that we are examining exhibited a working-class focus and orientation and oc-

casionally functioned in a union-like manner (Thompson, *The Making of the English Working-Class,* p. 21).

51. De Leon, *The Tejano Community,* pp. 194–96; Leininger Pycior, "La Raza Organizes: Mexican American Life in San Antonio," pp. 35, 42–47.

52. Arnoldo de Leon, *Ethnicity in the Sunbelt: A History of Mexican Americans in Houston,* Monograph Series No. 7, pp. 9–13. La Sociedad Vigilancia was a statewide federation with headquarters in San Antonio. The Houston organization was the second recorded chapter. (Alonso Flores (president) and Jesús E. Galindo (secretary) to Venustiano Carranza, September 22, 1915, Venustiano Carranza Papers, Centro de Estudios de Historia de México, México, D.F.).

53. *Austin City Directory, 1912–1913,* p. 50; *Austin City Directory, 1914,* p. 50; "El Cinco de Mayo en Austin," *La Prensa,* May 8, 1913, p. 4; ibid., Mar. 19, 1914, p. 2; ibid., Jan. 8, 1915, p. 5; ibid., July 29, 1915, p. 4.

54. Confidential Dispatch, Aug. 2, 1910, RG 59, Department of State Records.

55. The organization's newspaper, *El Progreso,* carried the all-encompassing nationalist motto in its masthead that anticipated the one adopted by La Liga Mexicanista established during El Congreso Mexicanista: "De la Raza! Por la Raza! Para la Raza." "Mexicans Cheer Díaz," *San Antonio Daily Express,* Sept. 11, 1910, p. 5, "Mexicans Will Celebrate," ibid., Aug. 15, 1910, p. 12; "Interesante folleto," *La Crónica,* Aug. 6, 1910, p. 4.

56. Leininger Pycior, "La Raza Organizes: Mexican American Life in San Antonio," pp. 112, 115, 126, 131, 164, 233.

57. Ibid., pp. 22–26.

58. Ibid., pp. 55, 147–53; "Sociedad Protectora de Mexicanos de los Estados Unidos," *La Prensa,* July 30, 1914, p. 2. González later secured employment as legal counsel with the Mexican consulate in San Antonio. He also became a leading figure in the League of United Latin American Citizens after its formation in 1929.

59. "Nueva sociedad mutualista," *La Prensa,* Oct. 2, 1913, p. 2.

60. Leininger Pycior, "La Raza Organizes: Mexican American Life in San Antonio," p. 214.

61. *La Prensa,* Mar. 19, 1914, p. 3.

62. "Desarrollo notable del Club Cooperativo Mexicano de Floresville," ibid., Sept. 1, 1915, p. 5.

63. Ibid., Nov. 13, 1913, p. 2; "Nueva mesa directiva," ibid., Jan. 1, 1914, p. 7.

64. Quedó organizada la Unión de Sembradores Mexicanos," ibid., Apr. 18, 1915, p. 4; "Quedó establecida una Sociedad de Agricultores Mexicanos en Fall, Tex.," ibid., July 21, 1915, p. 5; "Unión de Agricultores Mexicanos," ibid., Apr. 29, 1915, p. 3.

65. "Quedó establecida La Unión de Sembradores Mexicanos," ibid.

66. "Convocatoria," *La Crónica,* June 18, 1910, p. 5; "Voto de gracias," *La Prensa,* July 30, 1914, p. 5; "Notas de Pearsall," *La Crónica,* June 18, 1910, p. 6; "Círculo," ibid., Aug. 19, 1910, p. 3; "Aniversario de la Soc. Carmen Romero Rubio de Díaz de Sras y Sritas," ibid., Mar. 16, 1911, p. 6.

67. Leonor Villegas de Magnón to Venustiano Carranza, May 12, 1915, Carranza Papers. Villegas de Magnón included the following documents in her correspondence: Francisco Álvarez Tostado, "A Los Hijos de Cuauhtémoc, Hidalgo y Juárez en Texas," Nov. 26, 1914; Juana Ríos to Junta Femenil Pacifista, May 11, 1915; Jovita Idar, María Villarreal, and Leonor Villegas de Magnón to Sra. María de Jesús Pérez, May 11, 1915.

68. "Recepción," *El Defensor del Obrero,* Sept. 30, 1906, p. 108; "Excursión," *El Defensor del Obrero,* Oct. 30, 1906, pp. 113–14; "Big Time at Minera; Miners' Union No. 12340 to be Inaugurated There Tomorrow; Special Excursion Train Will Be Run to Take a Large Delegation From This City; Nuevo Laredo Band Will Go For the Occasion," *The Laredo Times,* July 7, 1907, p. 2.

69. "Colocación de la primera piedra para el edificio del Instituto Domínguez," *La Crónica,* Feb. 22, 1916, p. 4.

70. "Toil Will Be Celebrated; Local Unions to do Honor to Curse of Eden Next Monday, All Laredo Will be Shut Up and Day will be Given to Parade and Fete," *The Laredo Times,* Sept. 1, 1907, p. 1.

71. "Por la Unión de Impresores," *La Crónica,* Nov. 16, 1918, p. 1.

72. "A los cocheros de Brownsville," ibid., May 25, 1911, p. 3; "Nuevas elecciones," ibid., May 11, 1911, p. 4; "Una cuestión importante," ibid., June 22, 1918, p. 1; "Aniversario de la Sociedad Carmen Romero Rubio de Díaz de Señoras y Señoritas," ibid., March 16, 1911, p. 6; "Instalación," ibid., Oct. 8, 1911, p. 1.

73. "Pago de una póliza," ibid., Jan. 22, 1910, p. 3; "Instalación," ibid., Oct. 8, 1911, p. 2; *La Prensa,* Jan. 7, 1915, p. 3, "Voto de gratitud," ibid., Jan. 8, 1915, p. 6.

74. "Oración fúnebre," *La Crónica,* Mar. 2, 1911, p. 3.

75. Serodes to Constantineau, Nov. 27, 1908, Chatillon to Constantineau, Apr. 19, 1911, Serodes to Constantineau, Apr. 7, 1912, Jean Joseph to Antonine, Apr. 21, 1915, La Liga de Protección Mexicana, *Reglamento de La Liga de Protección Mexicana* (Oblate Archives, 1884–1913, Missionary Oblate of Mary Immaculate at San Antonio, Texas). I wish to thank Dr. José Roberto Juárez for making available to me his research notes from the Oblate Archives.

76. Asunto Catarino Garza, Del Tribunal del Segundo Circuito de la Corte Federal de Texas, Secretaría de Relaciones Exteriores, México, D.F.; Virgil N. Lott and Virginia M. Fenwick, *People and Plots on the Rio Grande,* p. 46; "Cuatro periodistas Mexicanos en Texas en el siglo XIX," *La Prensa,* Feb. 13, 1938, p. 4. For a discussion of the concept of the Mexican regional community as an expanding basis for social organization in northern New Mexico and southern Colorado, see Sara Deutsch, *No Separate Refuge: Culture, Class, and Gender on an Anglo-Hispanic Frontier in the American Southwest, 1880–1940.*

77. "Sociedad Latino Americana de Auxilios Mutuos: A todos los cuerpos sociales residentes en Texas, que la presente miren," *El Demócrata Fronterizo,* May 12, 1906, pp. 1–2.

78. Limón, "El Primer Congreso Mexicanista de 1911," pp. 85–118; *Primer Congreso Mexicanista, Laredo, Texas, Verificado los Días 14 al 22 de Septiembre, 1911; Discursos y Conferencias, Por La Raza y Para la Raza.* At least twenty-four official delegates representing the following towns and cities attended the meeting: Brownsville, San Benito, Kingsville, Rio Grande City, Beeville, Ciudad Camargo (Tamaulipas), Falfurrias, San Antonio, Gonzales, Rockport, Darwin, Bay City, Sarita, Mission, Alice, Victoria, Berclair, Laredo, Nuevo Laredo, Méndez (Tamaulipas), Houston, and San Ignacio.

79. Two months before El Congreso Mexicanista and weeks after this incident, *La Crónica* carried an article on the lynching with the following announcement: "There is nothing else but to organize" ("Valiente cobardía de los linchadores de Thorndale, Texas; Los Estados Unidos y México nada pueden hacer para el castigo de los criminales; represalias; única solución posible," July 13, 1911, p. 1).

80. At least one chapter of the federation was established in Laredo within a month after El Congreso Mexicanista. The organizing meeting was held at the Sociedad de Obreros hall, chaired by Nicasio Idar, and attended by delegates representing La Sociedad Hijos de Juárez, Logia Benito Juárez, Logia Ignacio Zaragoza, Logia Caballeros de Honor No. 14, Sociedad Mutua de Trabajadores, Sociedad de Obreros Igualdad y Progreso ("Gran Liga Mexicanista De Beneficencia y Protección," *La Crónica,* Oct. 5, 1911, p. 1).

81. See the following for a discussion of the most important issues raised by the revolt: Charles C. Cumberland, "Border Raids in the Lower Rio Grande Valley, 1915," *Southwestern Historical Quarterly* 57 (Jan., 1954): 285–311; Gómez-Quiñones, "The San Diego Revolt Reviewed," pp. 124–32. The most recent work that discusses the revolt is Montejano, *Anglos and Mexicans in the Making of Texas, 1836–1986,* pp. 117–25. For a personal account of the revolt by one of the insurgents, see Ignacio Muñoz, *La Verdad Sobre los Gringos.*

82. Report, Gen. Frederick Funston, to Secretary of State, June 15, 1915, RG 59, Department of State Records, Randolph Robertson, Vice Consul, Monterrey, to Secretary of State, June 9, 1916, RG 59, Department of State Records.

83. Cumberland, "Border Raids," pp. 301–24; William M. Hager, "The Plan of San Diego: Unrest on the Texas Border in 1915," *Arizona and the West* 5 (Win., 1963): 327–36; James A. Sandos, "The Plan of San Diego: War and Diplomacy on the Texas Border, 1915–1916," *Arizona and the West* 14 (Spr., 1972): 5–24. Exceptions to the conventional interpretation include: Gómez-Quiñones, "The San Diego Revolt Reviewed," and Rodolfo Rocha, "The Influence of the Mexican Revolution on the Mexico-Texas Border, 1910–1916," (Ph.D. diss., Texas Tech University, 1981).

84. Montejano, *Anglos and Mexicans in the Making of Texas, 1836–1986,* pp. 127–28.

85. Allen Gerlach, "Conditions Along the Border—1915, The Plan de San Diego," *New Mexico Historical Review* 63 (July, 1968): 195–212; S. H. Evans, Customs Collector, Eagle Pass, to Secretary of the Treasury, January 31, 1916, RG 59, Department of State Records. A translated copy of

the first plan appears in the Gerlach article. A Spanish-language copy of the second plan, which incorporates the first plan and thirteen new clauses, accompanies the Evans document.

86. Evans to Secretary of the Treasury, January 31, 1916, RG 59, Department of State Records.

Chapter 4

1. Foley, et al., *From Peones to Políticos,* pp. 48–51, 66–68. It is obvious that the majority of Mexicans did not participate directly in the organizational life of their communities. Other authors have accorded much attention to obstacles that inhibited self-organization and discouraged protest activity. A recent study of the Winter Garden area, for example, has pointed out that isolation, a highly oppressive political environment, and the possible internalization of negative Anglo perceptions led to a low organizing rate and a noncombative nature. My predilection is not to refute these observations, although my previous chapter demonstrates that self-organization did take place in both rural and urban areas. My preference is to explain instances of self-organization rather than to reexamine the claims of poor self-organization.

2. Spanish-language newspapers and mutual aid societies frequently used the term *Mexicanista* to express a unitary sense of community and a form of cultural nationalism. I use the term throughout this chapter because it captures the collectivist working-class spirit of the times. For a provocative comparative examination of an important organizational expression of this Mexicanist outlook and the cultural nationalism of the recent Mexican civil rights movement, see José E. Limón, "El Primer Congreso Mexicanista," pp. 85–117.

3. Thompson, *The Making of the English Working Class,* pp. 418–25. For an excellent discussion on the issue of culture as a basis for Mexican political action, see Juan Gómez-Quiñones, "On Culture," *Revista Chicano-Riqueña* 5 (Primavera, 1977): 29–47.

4. Report by Luis Recinos, Gamio Papers.

5. Slayden, "The Mexican Immigrant," p. 125; Nemesio García Naranjo, *Memorias: Nueve Años de Destierro,* Vol. 8 (Monterrey, México: Talleres de "El Porvenir," 1982), p. 158; Johnny Solís, interview with Paul S. Taylor, San Antonio, Tex., ca. 1929, Taylor Papers.

6. Chávez, *The Lost Land,* pp. 113–16. This publication is one of the most recent intellectual histories that treats this tension and the emerging ethnic identity.

7. Carole E. Christian, "Joining the American Mainstream: Texas's Mexican Americans during World War I," *Southwestern Historical Quarterly* 92 (Apr., 1989): 559–95.

8. José de la Luz Saenz, *Los México-Americanos en la Gran Guerra y Su Contingente en Pro de la Democracia, La Humanidad y La Justicia.* The publication includes articles that de la Luz Saenz wrote as a war correspondent for *La Prensa,* letters from the front to relatives and friends, and observations on the Mexican community during the post-war period.

9. Ibid., p. 112.

10. Ibid.

11. Ibid., p. 291.

12. Leininger Pycior, "La Raza Organizes: Mexican American Life in San Antonio," pp. 173–75.

13. Alonzo B. Garrett to Secretary of State, Aug. 13, 1915, RG 59, Department of State; Antonio Lozano, Mexican Consul at Laredo, to J. A. Fernández, Consul General in San Antonio, Mar. 21, 1913, in Josefina E. de Fabela, ed., *Documentos Históricos de la Revolución Mexicana,* 14:132–33; Arthur J. Rubel, *Across the Tracks: Mexican-Americans in a Texas City,* p. 43.

14. Querido Moheno, *Sobre El Avia Sangrienta,* pp. 263–64.

15. Gómez-Quiñones, *Sembradores,* pp. 6–7; Douglas W. Richmond, "La guerra de Texas se renova: Mexican Insurrection and Carrancista Ambitions, 1900–1920," *Aztlán* 11 (Spr., 1980): 1–32.

16. Alonzo B. Garrett to Secretary of State, Aug. 13, 1915, RG 59, Department of State Records.

17. Ibid.

18. Ricardo Flores Magón, *Semilla Libertaria,* Tomo 2, p. 116.

19. Leticia Barragán, Rina Ortiz and Amanda Rosales, "El mutualismo en el siglo XIX," *Historia Moderna* 3 (Octubre de 1977): 2–10. For a description of this type of organization as an incipient union structure among railroad workers in Mexico see Navarrete, *Alto a la Contrarrevolución,* pp. 116–20.

20. For studies on Mexican communities and organizational life in Texas see de Leon, *Ethnicity in the Sunbelt* and Leininger Pycior, "La Raza Organizes: Mexican American Life in San Antonio."

21. Report by Luis Recinos, Gamio Papers.

22. T. M. Paschal to Enrique Ornelas, Mexican Consul in San Antonio, Feb., 1907, RG 59, Department of State Records. Paschal prepared another report for the Mexican consulate on June 26, 1908, that reaffirmed his original findings.

23. Los niños mexicanos y las escuelas americanas," *La Prensa,* Apr. 14, 1915, p. 3.

24. Letter to Indalecio Canamas, editor of *El Fenix,* from Simón G. Domínguez, May 15, 1908, Simón G. Domínguez Letter Press, 1904–1925, Eugene C. Barker Texas History Center, University of Texas, Austin.

25. Ibid. Also see "La Orden de Caballeros de Honor ampara al Mexicano en el estado de Texas," *La Crónica,* Dec. 3, 1910, p. 2.

26. "Círculo," *La Crónica,* Aug. 19, 1910, p. 3.

27. John Murray, "Hands Across the Border," Murray Papers.

28. Ibid.

29. For a scholarly treatment of Gregorio Cortez and the variants of the ballad that have survived see Paredes, *With His Pistol in His Hand: A Border Ballad and Its Hero.*

30. "Rasgos biográficos de Pablo Cruz; extinto fundador de 'El Regidor'," *El Regidor,* Aug. 18, 1910, p. 1; "El Guarda del Bravo," ibid., May 26, 1904, p. 11. Cruz regularly published lists of contributors from throughout the state. He also printed the expenditures of the attorneys contracted to defend Cortez and identified persons and organizations that were leading local efforts in the campaign.

31. "El león despierta," *La Crónica,* July 13, 1911, p. 6.

32. Clemente N. Idar, "El Congreso Mexicanista triunfa: se discute nuestro proyecto," ibid., Apr. 13, 1915, p. 1.

33. "Cobarde, infame e inhumano lynchamiento de un jovencito Mexicano en Thorndale, Milam, Co., Texas; el mundo entero esta pendiente de tan salvaje crimen y hasta ahora no se sabe lo que el Cónsul Mexicano haya hecho en el asunto, pero es de creerse que dará un informe parecido al que dio cuando se le ordenó la investigación del asunto de la exclusión de los niños Mexicanos de las escuelas públicas," ibid., June 29, 1911, p. 1. The editors of *La Crónica* were making specific reference to the lynching of a young boy and also expressing their recurring critique of discrimination and violence against the Mexican community in Texas.

34. "A los señores delegados al Congreso Mexicanista," *La Crónica,* Sept. 14, 1911, p. 2.

35. Limón, "El Congreso Mexicanista de 1911," pp. 85–117. The assembly heard presentations by unattached individuals, a representative of the City of Laredo, and spokespersons for the following organizations: Sociedad de Obreros, Igualdad y Progreso (Laredo); Sociedad, Hijos de Juárez (Laredo); and La Agrupación Protectora Mexicana (San Antonio). The article by Limón includes some of the speeches delivered at the conference.

36. F. E. Rendon, "Conferencia," *Primer Congreso Mexicanista, Discursos Y Conferencias: Por La Raza Y Para La Raza,* pp. 7–8.

37. Hortencia Moncayo, "Discurso," ibid., p. 15. Ms. Moncayo may have been a teacher of "La Purisima," a private Mexican school.

38. Señora Soledad Flores de Peña, "Discurso," ibid., pp. 24–25.

39. Lisandro Peña, "Heroes Anónimos," ibid., p. 13.

40. This discussion is based on the following documents: Sociedad Benevolencia Mexicana, *Constitución y Leyes,* 1875; Sociedad de Obreros, Igualdad y Progreso, *Reglamento General,* 1890; Sociedad Mutualista Hidalgo y Juárez, *Reglamento,* 1900; Gran Liga Mexicanista de Beneficiencia y Protección, *Constitución* and *Reglamento;* Sociedad Unión de Jornaleros, *Reglamento General,* 1915; Sociedad Mutualista, Hijos de Juárez, *Reglamento General,* 1891; Sociedad de Conductores y Obreros Unidos, Fe y Adelanto, *Reglamento General,* 1918; Sociedad Mutualista Protectora Benito Juárez, *Reglamento General,* 1920. The years following the titles are the dates when the organizations were founded. The last organization was from San Benito, although its constitution was printed in Brownsville.

41. My remarks on Ramírez are based on the following works: Emilio Zamora, "Sara Estela Ramírez: Una Rosa Roja en el Movimiento," in Adelaida del Castillo and Magdalena Mora, eds., *Mexican Women in the United States:*

Struggles Past and Present; Inez Hernández Tovar, "Sara Estela Ramírez: The Early Twentieth Century Texas Mexican Poet," (Ph.D. diss., University of Houston, 1984); Mathilde Rodríguez Cabo, *La Mujer y La Revolución,* pp. 20–22; Lucina G. Villarreal, "Mujeres de la Revolución," *El Popular,* Apr. 29, May 1, 4, 6, and 7, 1939; Teodoro Hernández, "Las Tinajas de Ulua," *El Universal Gráfico,* Aug. 23, 1943, p. 162. The last three publications place Ramírez among the leading female historical figures of the early 1900s. According to Rodríguez Cabo, Ramírez "was a defender of women and fought for their spiritual and economic liberation, and established some mutual aid organizations for women."

42. For an examination of these private schools and the role that young immigrant Mexicanas played, see Emilio Zamora, "Las Escuelitas: A Texas-Mexican Search For Educational Excellence," *Los Tejanos: Children of Two Cultures.*

43. A copy of her presentation appears in Zamora, "Sara Estela Ramírez; Una Rosa Roja en el Movimiento," p. 168. The PLM paper described La Corregidora as "one of the few newspapers that can be truly called liberal; its mature ideas teach at the same time that they strengthen convictions, and the healthy patriotism that informs its articles brings growing enthusiasm and love for the motherland which suffers so much under the yoke of despotic leaders" ("La Corregidora," *Regeneración,* Oct. 7, 1901, p. 9).

44. The following commentary draws from three of José María Mora's articles that appeared in *El Defensor del Obrero* and the speech that he presented at El Congreso Mexicanista. These works are representative of his writings: "Un comentario," *El Defensor del Obrero,* November 25, 1906, pp. 173–75; "La ley debe ser igual para todos los hombres," ibid., Jan. 20, 1907, pp. 225–27; and "Discurso pronunciado por su autor, el Sr. J. M. Mora, delegado por La Sociedad de Obreros, Igualdad y Progreso," in *Primer Congreso Mexicanista, Discursos y Conferencias, Por La Raza Y Para La Raza,* pp. 16–18. The typographical union is discussed in Chapter 7.

45. Mora, "La ley debe ser igual para todos," *El Defensor del Obrero,* Jan. 20, 1907, p. 225.

46. Mora was making reference to the famous textile strike in Mexico that precipitated the Mexican Revolution and to the defeat of Federal Labor Union No. 11953. For a treatment of the early phase of the labor movement in Mexico, see Moisés González Navarro, *El Porfiriato, La Vida Social,* vol. 4, in Daniel Cosío Villegas, ed., *La Historia Moderna de México.*

47. Mora, "El Sr. J. M. Mora," *Primer Congreso Mexicanista,* p. 17.

48. Ibid., p. 16

49. Ibid., p. 17.

Chapter 5

1. For an examination of the federal labor unions and the AFL exclusivist organizing strategy, see Philip S. Foner, *The Policies and Practices of the American Federation of Labor, 1900–1909,* Vol. 3, pp. 198–200.

2. Fehrenbach, *Lone Star,* pp. 604–605; Virgil N. Lott and Mercurio Mar-

tínez, *The Kingdom of Zapata,* p. 211; Joseph B. Wilkinson, *Laredo and the Rio Grande Frontier,* pp. 362–65.

3. Wilkinson, *Laredo and the Rio Grande Frontier,* p. 376.

4. Ibid., pp. 376–77; Fehrenbach, *Lone Star,* p. 605; *General Directory of the City of Laredo,* 1900, p. 9; *The Laredo Times,* Special Anniversary Issue, July, 1906, p. 1; Letter, Captain, First Cavalry, to Adjutant-General, U.S. Army, Aug. 26, 1907, RG 59, Department of State Records. The following are the population figures for Laredo: 1900—15,000, 1906—16,000, 1907—17,000.

5. "Sigue la huelga," *El Defensor del Obrero,* Nov. 25, 1906, pp. 169–70.

6. *El Defensor del Obrero,* Feb. 17, 1907, p. 252.

7. Clark, *Mexican Labor in the United States,* p. 478; Richard U. Miller, "American Railroad Unions and the National Railways in Mexico; An Exercise in Nineteenth Century Proletarian Manifest Destiny," *Labor History* 15 (Spr., 1974): 239–60.

8. Prócoro F. Gutiérrez, "Adelante, adelante," *El Demócrata Fronterizo,* Apr. 28, 1906, p. 2.

9. *El Defensor del Obrero,* Feb. 17, 1907, p. 252; "Separación," ibid., Apr. 14, 1907, p. 312.

10. Moisés Poblete Troncoso, *El Movimiento Obrero Latino Americano,* p. 215; Anderson, *Outcasts in Their Own Land,* pp. 79, 90, 174.

11. Juan Gómez-Quiñones, *Sembradores,* pp. 27–28; José E. Limón, "El Primer Congreso Mexicanista de 1911," pp. 85–117; Cockcroft, *Intellectual Precursors of the Mexican Revolution,* pp. 118–19.

12. Valadés, "Las Revolucionarias," *La Prensa,* Apr. 15, 1933, pp. 11, 12, 14; "Circular," *El Defensor del Obrero,* Jan. 6, 1907, p. 211. Gutiérrez de Mendoza and Acuña y Rosete were leading participants in the early years of the PLM and were part of the exiled group that arrived in Laredo in 1904. Prior to their arrival, the former had published *Vésper* in Mexico City and had established relations with Ramírez, who endorsed the PLM as early as 1901.

13. Newspaper holdings for the period between July 1, 1906, and May 26, 1907, are available in the Eugene C. Barker Texas History Center, University of Texas, Austin.

14. The Jewish federation may have been the United Hebrew Trades organization. *El Defensor* called the federation "La Unión de oficiales Hebreos del Estado de N. York," or the Hebrew Union of the State of New York ("A todas las uniones obreras de los Estados Unidos," July 8, 1906).

15. José C. Valadés, "Vida Política de Da. Juana B. J. de Mendoza," *La Prensa,* Mar. 12, 1933, pp. 2, 5; José C. Valadés, "Las Revolucionarias," ibid., Apr. 15, 1933, pp. 11, 12, 14.

16. "La huelga de los obreros," *El Demócrata Fronterizo,* Dec. 15, 1906, p. 1. *El Demócrata Fronterizo,* published by Justo Cárdenas, was founded in 1886, making it in 1906 one of the oldest Spanish-language newspapers in the state (Stanley R. Ross, *Fuentes De La Historia Contemporanea de México,* vol. 1, p. xxxvi).

17. "La huelga de los obreros," *El Demócrata Fronterizo,* Dec. 15, 1906, p. 1.

18. *El Demócrata Fronterizo,* Mar. 3, 1906, p. 4.

19. Ibid.

20. "Labor Day Is Honored; Biggest Celebration in History of Laredo's Labor Unions," *The Laredo Times,* Sept. 1, 1906, p. 7.

21. "Gran paseo cívico," *El Defensor del Obrero,* Sept. 2, 1906, p. 77.

22. "Labor Day is Honored," *The Laredo Times,* Sept. 1, 1906, p. 7.

23. "Toil Will Be Celebrated; Local Unions To Do Honor To Curse of Eden Next Monday; All Laredo Will Be Shut Up and Day Will Be Given to Parade and Fete," *The Laredo Times,* Sept. 1, 1907, p. 1.

24. "Recepción," *El Defensor del Obrero,* Sept. 30, 1906, p. 108. The following orators and organizations participated in the celebration: A. C. Tamez (Federal Labor Union No. 11953), Simón G. Domínguez (La Sociedad Mutualista, Hijos de Juárez), José María Mora (Unattached), Aureliano Ramos (La Sociedad de Obreros, Igualdad y Progreso), and Emilio Flores (La Sociedad de Señoras y Señoritas).

25. "Barbarismos," *La Crónica,* Nov. 12, 1910, p. 1.

26. "Esfuerzo supremo, la idea mueve," ibid., Sept. 3, 1910, p. 3.

27. Ibid.

28. "La política en Brownsville," ibid., Dec. 13, 1910, p. 4.

29. Guevara was living at Nuevo Laredo by the time of El Congreso. He may have been the same Rafael E. Guevara that participated prominently in Nuevo Laredo political and labor circles after the demise of the FLU. Among Guevara's many accomplishments was his appointment to the city council by Carranza's constitutional government. Guevara represented Sociedad Concordia from Nuevo Laredo and Alvarado La Sociedad de Obreros, Igualdad y Progreso at El Congreso Mexicanista (Ayuntamiento Provisional Constitucional [Nuevo Laredo] to Venustiano Carranza, Feb. 1915, Carranza Papers; *Primer Congreso Mexicanista,* pp. 4–5).

30. "'La Revista' y 'El Defensor del Obrero,'" *El Defensor del Obrero,* Aug. 19, 1906, p. 61; "El socialismo," ibid., Aug. 19, 1906, pp. 98–101; "Un comentario," ibid., Nov. 25, 1906, pp. 173–74; ibid., Feb. 17, 1907, pp. 248–50; "Insultos, eh.?" ibid., Mar. 31, 1907, pp. 295–97; "Gielfos y gibelinos," ibid., Apr. 7, 1907, pp. 301–302; "War, War," ibid., Apr. 7, 1907, pp. 310–11; Juan C. Galván, "Volver a la carga," *El Demócrata Fronterizo,* July 28, 1906, pp. 1–3; Juan C. Galván, "Definitivo punto final," ibid., Aug. 11, 1906, pp. 1–2. Nicasio Idar was the editor of *La Revista.*

31. Ed Idar, "The Labor Movement in Laredo," p. 1, 1936 typescript, Ruth Allen Papers on Labor Movements in Texas; *El Demócrata Fronterizo,* Mar. 3, 1906, p. 4, and Sept. 6, 1907, p. 4; "Excursión," *El Defensor del Obrero,* Oct. 30, 1906, p. 114; "Sigue la huelga," ibid., Nov. 25, 1907, pp. 264–65; Dwight F. Henderson, "The Texas Coal Mining Industry," *Southwestern Historical Quarterly* 68 (Oct., 1964): 214. In 1909 the TSFL included 183 affiliated organizations with a total membership of 11,296 or a per organization average membership of 61.7. The union's membership in Laredo exceeded this average.

32. The Mexican National probably established its administrative construction and maintenance facilities at Laredo to facilitate its linkage with other United States–based railroads like the Texas Mexican and the International and Great Northern (Fehrenbach, *Lone Star,* pp. 604, 605; Wilkinson, *Laredo and the Rio Grande Frontier,* pp. 362–76).

33. Idar, "The Labor Movement in Laredo," pp. 1–3; "Los talleres suspenden sus trabajos, huelga pendiente, cargos infundados," *El Defensor del Obrero,* Nov. 18, 1906, pp. 164–65; "El trabajo todo lo vence," ibid., Feb. 8, 1907, p. 239; "Nueva dificultad," ibid., Mar. 17, 1907, pp. 277–78; "Arreglo satisfactorio," ibid., Mar. 24, 1907, pp. 285–86.

34. "Los talleres suspenden sus trabajos," *El Defensor del Obreros,* Nov. 18, 1906, pp. 164–65; "Sigue la huelga," ibid., Nov. 25, 1906, pp. 169–70.

35. "Another Strike," *The Laredo Times,* Nov. 18, 1906, p. 7.

36. "Los talleres suspenden sus trabajos," *El Defensor del Obrero,* Nov. 18, 1906, p. 166.

37. "Machinists Strike at National Shops," *The Laredo Times,* Jan. 28, 1906, p. 8; "May Yet Move Shops," ibid., Dec. 2, 1906, p. 2.

38. "National's Shops in This City; Machinists Strike and Removal of Shops to Mexico," ibid., Nov. 4, 1906, p. 3.

39. "Los talleres suspenden sus trabajos," *El Defensor del Obrero,* Nov. 18, 1906, p. 166.

40. "Sigue la huelga," ibid., Jan. 25, 1906, p. 170.

41. Ibid., p. 169.

42. Ibid.

43. "A Citizen's Meeting," *The Laredo Times,* Dec. 16, 1906, p. 4; "The National Shops Closed Two Months," ibid., Jan. 20, 1907, p. 4; "Odios de raza," *El Defensor del Obrero,* Jan. 20, 1907, p. 228.

44. "Odios de raza," *El Defensor del Obrero,* Jan. 20, 1907, p. 228.

45. Ibid.

46. Ibid., p. 231.

47. "Violated the Injunction; Eight Strikers Given Terms in the County Jail," *The Laredo Times,* Feb. 3, 1907, p. 3; "Trouble at the Shops; Workman Attacked and a Number Were Badly Hurt," ibid., Feb. 3, 1907, p. 11; and "Little Locals," ibid., Feb. 10, 1907, p. 7.

48. "Trouble at the Shops; Workman Attacked and a Number Were Badly Hurt," ibid., Feb. 10, 1907, p. 7.

49. *El Demócrata Fronterizo,* Dec. 15, 1906, p. 1.

50. "Little Locals," *The Laredo Times,* Feb. 10, 1907, p. 6; "Cause for Rejoicing," ibid., Feb. 10, 1907, p. 8.

51. "Little Locals," ibid., Mar. 31, 1907, p. 4.

52. *El Defensor del Obrero,* Feb. 17, 1907, pp. 251–52.

53. "Nueva dificultad," ibid., Mar. 17, 1907, pp. 277–78; "Arreglo satisfactorio," ibid., Mar. 17, 1907, p. 280.

54. "Sigue de amor la llama," ibid., Mar. 24, 1907, pp. 285–86.

55. Ibid. The union resumed operations by April, 1907. Its newspaper did not mention a strike during the period between April 14 and May 26, 1907, the date of the last issue held in the Eugene C. Barker Texas History Center. *El Demócrata Fronterizo* and Ed Idar attributed the demise of the union to the removal of the railroad shops across the river to Nuevo Laredo during a strike that occurred in September, 1907. Information on this strike is unavailable ("Little Locals," *The Laredo Times,* Apr. 14, 1907, p. 2; "More Labor Troubles; It Is Said That Machine Shop Laborers Will Ask Another Raise," ibid., Sept. 20, 1907, p. 2).

56. Favio Barbosa Cano, *La CROM De Luis N. Morones a Antonio J. Hernández,* p. 136.

57. *El Demócrata Fronterizo,* Oct. 13, 1906, p. 2, and Nov. 24, 1906, p. 2.

58. *Report of Proceedings of the Twenty-Sixth Annual Convention of the AFL,* held at Minneapolis, Minn., p. 69.

59. *El Defensor del Obrero,* Feb. 17, 1907, pp. 251–52.

60. Ibid., Feb. 17, 1907, p. 252.

61. Ibid., May 12, 1907, p. 348.

62. "Excursión," ibid., Oct. 30, 1906, p. 114; "Villano ultraje," ibid., Nov. 18, 1906, pp. 162–63; "Sigue la huelga," ibid., Nov. 25, 1906, pp. 169–70; "Por las minas," ibid., Mar. 3, 1907, pp. 264–65. For a history of one of these mining communities, see Janet Roy, "The Life of Minera, Texas," *Southwestern Historical Quarterly* 49 (Apr., 1946): 510–17.

63. "Por las minas," *El Defensor del Obrero,* Mar. 17, 1907, pp. 264–65.

64. "Trouble at the Shops; Workmen Attacked and a Number Were Badly Hurt," *The Laredo Times,* Feb. 3, 1907, p. 11; "Dispersed the Mob," ibid., Feb. 3, 1907, p. 12; *El Defensor del Obrero,* Feb. 17, 1907, p. 252.

65. The four-part explanatory scheme is borrowed from C. Wright Mills, *The Marxists,* pp. 12–14. Unless otherwise noted, the discussion in this section is based on articles appearing in *El Defensor del Obrero.*

66. R. E. Guevara, "Discurso, pronunciado por su autor el domingo 11 del actual, en la fiesta de la inauguración del Teatro Concordia," *El Defensor del Obrero,* Nov. 18, 1906, p. 158.

67. "Nuestro programa," ibid., July 1, 1906, n.p.

68. "Entre amantes," *El Defensor del Obreros,* Oct. 30, 1906; "Entre amigas," ibid., Feb. 24, 1907, p. 252; "Entre Amantes," ibid., Feb. 17, 1907, p. 242.

69. Emilio Zamora, "Las Escuelitas," pp. 5–6. Private Mexican schools, like other institutions in the community, reflected the direct influence of Mexico. This is evident in the emphasis that they gave public speaking, as well as poetry recitals, musical presentations, and theatrical performances, in their elementary and secondary school curriculum.

70. José María Mora, "El Obrero, leído en la noche de la celebración del día 2 del presente," *El Defensor del Obrero,* Aug. 19, 1906, pp. 66–67.

71. Julian Buitrón, "Discurso pronunciado la noche del 2 de Septiembre, con motivo de la celebración del día de Trabajo," ibid., Aug. 19, 1906, pp. 65–66.

72. Rodolfo Menéndez, "La Taberna," ibid., Nov. 3, 1906, p. 141.

73. Juan G. Holguín Burboa, "El Obrero," ibid., Aug. 29, 1906, p. 68.

74. J. M. Borrego, "Trabajo," ibid., Feb. 24, 1907, p. 251.

75. Ruperto J. Aldana, "La huelga," ibid., Mar. 3, 1907, p. 263.

76. Un obrero, "Poder del siglo XX," ibid., Apr. 21, 1907, p. 311.

77. Un obrero, "Al Obrero," ibid., May 12, 1907, pp. 342–43.

78. Also see the following by "Un obrero": "El propietario y el obrero," ibid., Apr. 14, 1907, p. 304; "Revanchas naturales," ibid., Apr. 7, 1907, p. 294; "Obreros y burgueses," ibid., Mar. 31, 1907, pp. 286–87.

79. Joaquín Dicenta, "El andamio," ibid., Nov. 25, 1906, pp. 171–72.

Chapter 6

1. For readings on the Texas Socialist Party and Mexican participation in the party, the Renters' League, and the Land League, see Allen, "The Socialist Party in Texas"; Green, *Grass-Roots Socialism;* Green, "Tenant Farmer Discontent"; and Zamora, "Socialist Labor Activity in Texas, 1900–1920." The approximate number of Mexican socialist unions is based on a survey of articles and letters that appeared in the Socialist Party newspaper, *The Rebel,* and in *La Prensa* between 1911 and 1916.

2. "Land League Organizer Arrested," *The Rebel,* Oct. 23, 1915, p. 1; "Quedó establecida una sucursal de la 'Liga Tierra de América,'" *La Prensa,* July 2, 1915, p. 6.

3. "Mexican Renters in Line," *The Rebel,* Feb. 21, 1914, p. 4.

4. "Renters' Union," ibid., Apr. 5, 1913, p. 3.

5. Thomas A. Hickey, "The Land Renters Union in Texas," *International Socialist Review,* Sept. 1912, pp. 239–44; "The Industrial Commission," *The Rebel,* Mar. 20, 1914, p. 1; "Land League of America," *The Rebel,* Nov. 21, 1914, p. 2; "Our Fifth Anniversary," *The Rebel,* July 1, 1916, p. 2; Charles W. Holman, "Preliminary Report on the Land Question in the United States," field report to the U.S. Commission on Industrial Relations, pp. 56–60; "The Land League of America Met Today," *Waco Daily Times-Herald,* Nov. 13, 1915, p. 6; Covington Hall, "With 'Pope' Hickey in Texas," *International Socialist Review,* Dec. 1915, pp. 378–80. The socialist challenge refers to the Socialist Party of America and its well-known leader, Eugene V. Debs, who represented the dual socialist strategy of organizing under the banner of the party and affiliated workers' organizations.

6. Holman, "Preliminary Report on the Land Question in the United States," p. 65.

7. "Bulletin; Texans Protest against the Imprisonment of Mexican Patriots," Aug. 25, 1909, John Murray Papers. The unions included Painters Local No. 142, Painters Local No. 172, Paperhangers Local No. 736 and Carpenters Local No. 717. The state federation also passed a supporting resolution during its annual convention (TSFL, *Proceedings* [San Antonio: May 11–14, 1909], p. 58).

8. Green, *Grass Roots Socialism,* pp. 327–35.

9. César Canseco to Secretaría de Relaciones Exteriores, Feb. 19, 1912, Josefina E. de Fabela, ed., *Documentos Históricos de la Revolución Mexicana*, pp. 453–54; "Land League Organizer Arrested," *The Rebel,* Oct. 23, 1915; "Hernández Goes Free," ibid., Jan. 22, 1916; "La policía disuelve una junta de socialistas en Houston," *La Prensa,* Jan. 1, 1914, p. 5; and "Pretendían libertar a los contrabandistas de Carrizo Springs," *La Prensa,* Nov. 27, 1913, p. 4.

10. "Correspondence," *The Rebel,* July 18, 1914, p. 3; and "The Renting Situation," ibid., Sept. 12, 1914, p. 1.

11. "Land League of America," ibid., Feb. 13, 1915, p. 2.

12. "Renters' Union," ibid., May 17, 1913, p. 3; "Renters' Union," ibid., May 31, 1913, p. 3; "Renters' Union," ibid., May 10, 1913, p. 3; and "The State Convention," ibid., p. 1. The articles titled "Renters' Union" were based on reports by organizers. They are a valuable source of information on F. A. Hernández, since he frequently had organizing news to report.

13. "Renters' Union," ibid., May 13, 1913, p. 4; "Renters' Union," ibid., Sept. 13, 1913, p. 3; "Mexican Renters in Line," ibid., Feb. 21, 1914, p. 4.

14. Green, *Grassroots Socialism,* p. 331; "Our Rebs," *The Rebel,* July 8, 1911, p. 3; "Renters' Union," ibid., May 17, 1913, p. 3; "Land League of America," ibid., Feb. 13, 1915, p. 2.

15. "Land League Organizer Arrested," *The Rebel,* Oct. 23, 1915, p. 1.

16. "State News, Land League of America," ibid., Jan. 30, 1915, p. 3.

17. "Renters' Union," ibid., May 17, 1913, p. 2.

18. "Lott Man Is Elected President of Land League," *Waco Daily-Times Herald,* Mar. 14, 1915, p. 11.

19. Consult the following for histories of the PLM: Michael E. Casillas, "Mexicans, Labor, and Strife in Arizona, 1896–1917," (Master's thesis, University of New Mexico, 1979); Cockcroft, *Intellectual Precursors of the Mexican Revolution, 1900–1913;* Arnaldo Córdova, *La Ideología de la Revolución Mexicana;* and Gómez-Quiñones, *Sembradores.*

20. Lowell L. Blaisdel, *The Desert Revolution: Baja California, 1911.*

21. For information on the support that the PLM received in Laredo and other Texas cities see José C. Valadés, "Vida Política de Da. Juana B. J. de Mendoza," *La Prensa,* Mar. 12, 19, 26 and Apr. 2, 9, 1933; and Eugenio Martínez Nuñez, *Juan Sarabia; Apóstol y Mártir de la Revolución Mexicana,* pp. 111–12. Also see the archival collection with intercepted PLM correspondence from the cotton belt that was mentioned in a previous chapter.

22. See copies of *Regeneración* and other PLM newspapers for evidence of PLM interest in and support for local Mexican struggles. I refer to some articles throughout this chapter in which Flores Magón demonstrates this interest and support.

23. C. Felipe Vega to Secretaría de Relaciones Exteriores, June 2, 1908, in de Fabela, ed., *Documentos Históricos de la Revolución Mexicana,* 10:53; Gómez-Quiñones, *Sembradores,* pp. 55–56.

24. "Judge Releases P. Dávila, No Ground for Holding Him Is Shown at Hear-

ing," *San Antonio Daily Express,* Oct. 20, 1909, p. 1; Casimiro H. Regalado to Ricardo Flores Magón, June 26, June 29, July 12, 1906, Carranza Papers.

25. Antonio de P. Araujo to Ricardo Flores Magón, Oct. 11, 1906, Flores Magón Papers, Terrazas Collection; Eulogio M. García to Ricardo Flores Magón, June 4, 1906, Asunto Ricardo Flores Magón.

26. Eulogio M. García to Ricardo Flores Magón, June 4, 1906, Asunto Ricardo Flores Magón; Francisco Reyes to Ricardo Flores Magón, July 25, 1906, and Florentino Quintanilla to Ricardo Flores Magón, June 22, 1906, Flores Magón Papers, Terrazas Collection; Ildefonso Villarello Vélez, *Historia de la Revolución Mexicana en Coahuila,* pp. 89–90; Everardo J. Acevedo to A. L. Apple, May 28, 1906, Carranza Papers.

27. L. M. Caudue to "Queridos Hermanos," Oct. 9, 1906, Terrazas Collection.

28. Enrique Ornelas to Secretaría de Relaciones Exteriores, Nov. 27, 1908, in de Fabela, ed., *Documentos Históricos de la Revolución Mexicana,* pp. 143–44.

29. See letters from PLM sympathizers to Flores Magón in Asunto Ricardo Flores Magón.

30. Quoted in Gómez-Quiñones, *Sembradores,* pp. 85–86. The letter, dated March 4, 1911, was signed by Margarita Andejas, Domitila Acuña, Severina Garza, María Cisneros, Concepción Martínez, and Carmen Luján.

31. RG 59, Department of State Records; "Fueron aprendidos dos oradores Mexicanos," *La Prensa,* Aug. 31, 1915, p. 8; Guillermina Bringas and David Mascareno, *Esbozo Histórico de la Prensa Obrera en México,* p. 33; and James Weinstein, *The Decline of Socialism in America, 1912–1925,* p. 101.

32. "Está de venta en los siguientes puntos de distribución en Texas," *Reforma, Justicia y Libertad,* June 15, 1908, p. 2.

33. Ornelas to Secretaría de Relaciones Exteriores, ibid., Feb. 11, 1907.

34. Rosendo Salazar and José G. Escobedo, *Las Pugnas de la Gleba,* pp. 44–45; José G. Escobedo, *Notas Biográficas,* pp. 31–32; testimony of Gutiérrez de Lara, *Hearings on House Resolution 201,* pp. 20–27; "La familia de Gutiérrez de Lara no ha podido confirmar aun la noticia de su muerte," *La Prensa,* Feb. 15, 1918, p. 1.

35. John Kenneth Turner, *Barbarous Mexico;* Cockcroft, *Intellectual Precursors of the Mexican Revolution,* p. 127. Gutiérrez de Lara accompanied Turner in 1908 and 1909 into Mexico to gather information for the articles published in *The American Magazine* and later converted into a book. The editors of *La Prensa,* however, claimed that Gutiérrez de Lara wrote the book but allowed Turner to take author credit because he feared reprisals. "The true author of that book was Lazaro Gutiérrez de Lara. He compiled the data. He wrote it. All Turner did was to translate it into English, sign it and distribute it" ("La familia de Gutiérrez de Lara no ha podido confirmar aun la noticia de su muerte," *La Prensa,* Feb. 15, 1918, p. 1).

36. Tendulo R. Beltrán, Cónsul General, San Antonio, to Venustiano Carranza, Feb. 18, 1915, Carranza Papers.

37. Casillas, "Mexicans, Labor, and Strife in Arizona, 1896–1917," p. 93; Villarello Vélez, *Historia de la Revolución Mexicana en Coahuila,* pp. 35, 221.

38. Francisco Hernández, *La Clase Obrera En La Historia de México, De La Dictadura Porfirista a Los Tiempos Libertarios,* pp. 136–37.

39. Lázaro Gutiérrez de Lara to Thomas Hickey, Mar. 8, 1915, Commission on Industrial Relations, *Final Report,* 10:9,272. This was a letter of introduction to the secretary of the Socialist Party in Texas. For a report on a public meeting that featured Gutiérrez de Lara see "Se efectúa un mitín político en el salón de actos del mercado," *La Prensa,* Apr. 3, 1915, p. 1.

40. Quoted by Amado G. Hernández, "Fiesta del trabajo en Uhland, Texas," *Regeneración,* May 11, 1912, p. 1.

41. Ibid.

42. Ibid.

43. "El mitín de Gurley," *Regeneración,* Sept. 12, 1910, p. 3. The date on this issue is clearly mistaken. It carries another article that refers to the September 11, 1913, incarceration of *Los Mártires,* leading one to speculate that the correct year was 1913 or 1914.

44. "Instalación," *La Prensa,* Oct. 8, 1911, p. 2; "Agrupación Protectora Mexicana de San Antonio, Texas," *La Crónica,* Sept. 22, 1911, p. 2; "Agrupación Protectora Mexicana! Circular," ibid., July 13, 1911, p. 2; "Agrupación Protectora Mexicana," ibid., July 13, 1913, p. 2. For historical accounts of La Agrupación, see Jamieson, *Labor Unionism in American Agriculture,* pp. 260–61; and Emilio Flores Testimony, Commission on Industrial Relations, *Final Report,* 10:9200–9205.

45. Flores Testimony, Commission on Industrial Relations, *Final Report,* 10:9200.

46. "Sociedad Protectora de Mexicanos en los Estados Unidos," *La Prensa,* July 30, 1914, p. 2.

47. "Agrupación Protectora Mexicana," *La Crónica,* Aug. 1911, p. 4; "Ecos de las Fiestas Patrias," *La Prensa,* Oct. 2, 1913, p. 2.

48. "La Agrupación Protectora Mexicana tiene en proyecto importantes mejoras," *La Prensa,* July 22, 1915, p. 6.

49. Flores Testimony, Commission on Industrial Relations, *Final Report,* 10:9200. Flores based his testimony on data that he secured through a questionnaire that he sent to each of the organizations' chapters. The questionnaire inquired about each chapter's history, the condition of Mexican workers in Texas, their experiences crossing the border and in the courts, their relationship with landlords, and their treatment by Anglos ("La Agrupación Protectora Mexicana," *La Prensa,* Mar. 17, 1915, p. 3).

50. Flores Testimony, Commission on Industrial Relations, *Final Report,* 10:9200–9204.

51. Ibid., 10:9200–9201.

52. Ricardo Flores Magón, "En defensa de los Mexicanos," *Regeneración,* Sept. 12, 1910, p. 3. As noted in note 43, the correct year of publication for this issue of *Regeneración* was either 1913 or 1914.

53. Ibid.

54. Ibid.

55. Flores Testimony, Commission on Industrial Relations, *Final Report,* 10: 9200–9201.

56. "En bien de nuestra raza, una carta interesante," *La Prensa,* Apr. 28, 1915, pp. 3, 8.

57. Flores Testimony, Commission on Industrial Relations, *Final Report,* 10: 9204.

58. Gómez-Quiñones, *Sembradores,* pp. 61–65; Richmond, "La guerra de Texas se renova: Mexican Insurrection and Carrancista Ambitions, 1900–1920," pp. 1–32.

59. "Pretendían libertar a los contrabandistas de Carrizo Springs," *La Prensa,* Nov. 27, 1913, p. 4.

60. "Lo del complot contra los Estados Unidos carece absolutamente de fundamento," *La Prensa,* Feb. 24, 1915, p. 1; "Otro Mexicano aprendido por sedicioso," ibid., Sept. 4, 1915, p. 6.

61. Gómez-Quiñones, *Sembradores,* pp. 55–56. Also see articles appearing in *Regeneración* that reported on campaign activities in Texas.

62. "A todos los compañeros," *Regeneración,* Sept. 12, 1914, p. 3.

63. "Un grupo de Mexicanos amenaza al gobernador Colquitt," *La Prensa,* Nov. 20, 1913, p. 1.

64. Green, *Grass Roots Socialism,* p. 331; Holman, "Preliminary Report on the Land Question in the United States," p. 62. Also see "Landlord Violence," *The Rebel,* Oct. 17, 1914, p. 3; "Hernández Goes Free," ibid., Jan. 22, 1916, p. 1.

65. "Un grupo de Mexicanos amenaza al gobernador Colquitt," *La Prensa,* Nov. 20, 1913, p. 2; "Pretendían libertar a los contrabandistas de Carrizo Springs," ibid., Nov. 27, 1913, p. 4.

66. "Pretendían libertar a los contrabandistas de Carrizo Springs," ibid., Nov. 27, 1913, p. 4.

67. Ibid., Sept. 10, 1915, p. 1.

68. "The Newspaper Liars," *The Rebel,* June 5, 1915, p. 3.

69. Ibid.

70. Ibid.

71. "Mexican Secret Societies Formed to Regain Texas," *Austin American-Statesman,* Aug. 13, 1915, p. 1; "Del público, son amantes del orden los Mexicanos que residen en el condado de Guadalupe," *La Prensa,* Sept. 2, 1915, p. 1; "La nueva ley sobre arrendamiento de tierras y los obreros mexicanos," ibid., Mar. 3, 1915, p. 4.

72. "Hernández Goes Free," *The Rebel,* Jan. 22, 1916, p. 1. Also see the following on the arrest of Hernández: Zamora, "Chicano Socialist Labor Activity in Texas, 1900–1920," pp. 229–30; Mario D. Longoria, "Revolution, Visionary Plan, and Marketplace: A San Antonio Incident," *Aztlán* 12 (Autumn, 1981): 218–20.

73. "Land League Organizer Arrested," *The Rebel,* Oct. 23, 1915, p. 1.

74. "Mexican Papers Refused Benefits of U.S. Mails," *San Antonio Express,* Sept. 1, 1915, p. 2.

75. Ibid.

76. "Plan to Incite Uprising Here Nipped by Police," ibid., Aug. 31, 1915, p. 2. It has been necessary to use the clearly awkward translation of this article since Hernández's paper is unavailable.

77. "Hernández Goes Free," *The Rebel*, Jan. 22, 1916, p. 1; "Land League Convention," *The Rebel*, Dec. 4, 1915, p. 2.

78. "Fueron aprehendidos dos oradores populares Mexicanos," *La Prensa*, Aug. 31, 1915, p. 8; "Aprehensiones por las autoridades federales," ibid., Sept. 2, 1915, p. 6; "Land League," *The Rebel*, Sept. 25, 1915, p. 3; "Land League Organizer Arrested," ibid., Oct. 23, 1915, p. 1; and "Hernández Goes Free," ibid., Jan. 22, 1916.

79. "The State Convention," *Waco Daily-Times Herald*, Mar. 14, 1915, p. 11; "Land League Convention," *The Rebel*, Dec. 4, 1915, p. 2.

80. "Land League Convention," *The Rebel*, Dec. 4, 1915, p. 1.

81. "State Office News," *The Rebel*, May 27, 1916, p. 4. Reports to *The Rebel* and letters submitted as exhibits indicate that Mexican organizers continued initiating political work beyond the point of official recognition and apparent support.

82. "Land League Organizer Arrested," ibid., Oct. 23, 1915, p. 1; "La Conferencia Obrera de Laredo, Texas," *Pan American Labor Press*, Dec. 13, 1918, p. 3.

83. For a participant's observations concerning the repression of the Texas socialists, see the following: Typescript, Carl P. Brannin Papers, Vertical File Collection, No. 11, Labor Archives, University of Texas, Arlington, p. 49; and Carl P. Brannin, Oral History Collection, vol. 2, ibid., p. 22.

Chapter 7

1. For a brief account of Idar's life, see "Murió ayer un conocido líder del trabajo," *La Prensa*, Jan. 24, 1934, p. 12.

2. Robert W. Glover and Allan G. King, "Organized Labor in Texas," in Louis J. Rodríguez, ed., *Dynamics of Growth; An Economic Profile of Texas*, pp. 136–56. For readings on the leftist challenge, see Melvyn Dubofsky, *We Shall Be All;* Joseph Conlin, *Bread and Roses Too;* Philip S. Foner, *The Policies and Practices of the American Federation of Labor, 1900–1909*, Vol. 3; Philip S. Foner, *The AFL in the Progressive Era, 1910–1915*, vol. 5 of *History of the Labor Movement in the United States;* and John H. M. Laslett, *Labor and the Left*.

3. Mullenix, "A History of the Texas State Federation of Labor," pp. 77, 82–83; Glover and King, "Organized Labor in Texas," pp. 143–52; "State Labor Convention," *Dallas News*, Jan. 1, 1900, copy in Ruth Allen Papers on Labor Movements in Texas.

4. Mullenix, "A History of the Texas State Federation of Labor," p. 197; W. E. Leonard, "The Population of Texas and Its Potentialities as a Labor Force," in Lewis H. Haney, ed., *Bulletin of the University of Texas* 3 (Jan. 10, 1915): 54; Steen, *Twentieth Century Texas*, pp. 416–17; Allen, *Chapters in the History of Organized Labor in Texas*, pp. 151–52. For comparable national

growth trends in the AFL see: Sanford Cohen, *Labor in the United States,* pp. 95–99.

5. "La Sociedad Mutualista Mexicana Artes Gráficas," *La Prensa,* Feb. 5, 1917.

6. "La Sociedad Morelos del ramo de panadería," ibid., Sept. 7, 1917; "Se solucionó la huelga de panaderos," ibid., Nov. 26, 1918; Leininger Pycior, "La Raza Organizes: Mexican American Life in San Antonio," pp. 137–38.

7. Leininger Pycior, "La Raza Organizes: Mexican American Life in San Antonio," pp. 130–31.

8. "Acta primordial de la Unión Internacional de Trabajadores, No. 93," *El Unionista,* Apr. 15, 1920, p. 3; Charter, International Hod Carriers and Building Laborers' Union of America, Affiliated April 13, 1903, in union's offices, San Antonio, Texas; Membership receipt for Cenobio Andrade, 1906, in Asunto Ricardo Flores Magón.

9. "Acta Primordial de la Unión Internacional de Trabajadores, No. 93," *El Unionista,* Apr. 15, 1920, p. 3.

10. "Una convocatoria a los obreros de la Unión de Jornaleros Mexicanos," *La Prensa,* June 10, 1915, p. 8; International Hod Carriers and Building Laborers Union of America No. 93, Membership and Financial Records, Records of Local Unions, AFL-CIO Library, Washington, D.C.

11. "Por La Unión Empleados de Comercio," Oct. 18, 1919, *El Unionista,* p. 1; International Hod Carriers and Building Laborers' Union of America No. 93, 1919, Financial Report, Records of Local Unions, AFL-CIO Library, Washington, D.C.

12. Earle Sylvester Sparks, "A Survey of Organized Labor in Austin" (Masters' thesis, University of Texas at Austin, 1920), p. 143.

13. Minute Books of Galveston Labor Council, vol. 5, 1917–1920, May 28, June 11, and June 15, 1917, Labor Archives, University of Texas at Arlington, Arlington, Texas.

14. "Festividad," *La Crónica,* Jan. 5, 1911, p. 2; "Fiesta," *La Prensa,* Dec. 23, 1914, p. 1. Local No. 2832 appeared in 1911, and local No. 14722 in 1914.

15. TSFL, *Proceedings* (San Antonio: May 11–14, 1909), p. 16.

16. Minute Books of United Brotherhood of Carpenters and Joiners of America No. 14, vol. 8, Apr. 29, 1913–Mar. 23, 1915, pp. 17–18, and vol. 11, Jan. 7, 1919–Dec. 23, 1919, p. 116, Labor Archives, University of Texas at Arlington, Arlington, Texas; "Local Union Directory," *Weekly Dispatch,* Jan. 2, 1915, p. 2; "La conferencia obrera de Laredo, Texas," *La Prensa,* Jan. 28, 1934, p. 12.

17. *El Unionista* carried numerous articles that reveal increased unionist activity in San Antonio during the war. These unions and others regularly printed organizing and fund raising reports in the labor paper.

18. TSFL, *Proceedings* (Beaumont: May 14–17, 1906), p. 7.

19. Minute Books of Austin Trades Council vol. 1, Nov. 8, 1904–Mar. 31, 1908 and vol. 2, Apr. 14, 1908–Sept. 27, 1910, Labor Archives, University of Texas at Arlington, Arlington, Texas; Minute Books of Galveston Labor

Council vol. 2, Apr. 14, 1908–Sept. 27, 1920, vol. 4, 1914, 1917, and vol. 5, 1917–1920, ibid.

20. TSFL, *Proceedings* (Beaumont: May 14–17, 1906), p. 20.

21. "Thurber on Strike," *The United Mine Worker's Journal,* Sept. 24, 1903, p. 1. A copy of this and other pertinent research documents and notes are in the Ruth Allen Papers on Labor Movements in Texas, Eugene C. Barker Texas History Center.

22. Although beyond the scope of this study, it is worth noting that the AFL's new policy in favor of organizing U.S.-born and naturalized Mexicans also resulted in the formation of Mexican unions in El Paso during the second decade. One of the most impressive results was the formation of an all-women union, the Laundry Workers' Union, which waged an unsuccessful strike in 1919 (Mario García, "The Chicana in American History: The Mexican Women of El Paso, 1880–1920: A Case Study," *Pacific Historical Review* 49 [May, 1980]: 331–37).

23. Taylor, *Mexican Labor in the United States,* pp. 354–55.

24. Cardoso, *Mexican Emigration,* p. 97; Report by Luis Recinos, p. 7, Gamio Papers.

25. Idar, "Laredo City Offers Good Field For Organization," *Pan American Labor Press,* Sept. 11, 1918, p. 2.

26. Antonio I. Villarreal, "Letter From Villarreal To Labor Men," *Pan American Labor Press,* Sept. 13, 1918, p. 4.

27. "La conferencia obrera de Laredo, Tex.," *La Prensa,* Dec. 14, 1918, p. 5. Another Mexican delegate to the same labor conference, Francisco A. Moreno, claimed he had organized Mexican workers in Texas during 1915. It cannot be determined if Moreno was a member of Rico's delegation. Nevertheless, Moreno's observations on the relationship between Mexican workers and organized labor in Texas corroborated Rico's statements. For a history of the PAFL, consult Snow, *Samuel Gompers.*

28. Idar, "The Labor Movement in Laredo," in Ruth Allen Papers on Labor Movements in Texas. For additional observations on discrimination against Mexican workers within mixed unions especially regarding the exclusive use of English, see "Meetings for Mexican Workers Should be Conducted in Spanish Language," *Pan American Labor Press,* Oct. 30, 1918, p. 4; and John Murray, "Report of John Murray, Secretary, Pan American Federation of Labor Conference Committee," *Pan American Labor Press,* Nov. 11, 1918, p. 2.

29. TSFL, *Proceedings* (Galveston: Apr. 12–16, 1910), pp. 113–14; (El Paso: June 8–12, 1914), pp. 88–89.

30. Dr. A. G. García, "Jornales y el trabajo," *La Vanguardia,* Mar. 31, 1921, p. 2.

31. Foner, *The Policies and Practices of the American Federation of Labor, 1900–1909,* pp. 261–81.

32. TSFL, *Proceedings* (Waco: Apr. 15–19, 1911), p. 40; Samuel Gompers, "Reasons for Immigration Restrictions," *American Federationist* 23 (Apr., 1916): 253–56.

33. Organized labor from Mexico turned to U.S. workers and the AFL at the height of tensions with appeals for unity against war and continuing capitalist influence. U.S. and Mexican labor representatives subsequently signed an agreement endorsed by the executive council of the AFL. According to this pact, Mexican labor agreed to cooperate fully while the AFL pressured its government against military intervention. Gompers also sent a fact-finding commission to Mexico in 1916 to gauge the opinion of labor on a formal hemispheric alliance ("Appeal to U.S. Workers," *International Labor Forum* [1916]; "To the Executive Council of the American Federation of Labor [July 3, 1916]; "Report of the Executive Council of the AFL," *AFL Proceedings,* in Murray Papers).

34. AFL, *Report of Proceedings* (Buffalo: Nov. 12–24, 1917), pp. 63–65; and "Arizona Labor for Laredo Meeting and Pan American Federation," *Pan American Federation of Labor,* Oct. 16, 1918, p. 81; Levenstein, *Labor Organizations in the U.S. and Mexico,* pp. 50–62.

35. John Murray, "Mexico—The Day After the War; What the Coming International Labor Conference May Mean in the Life of Nations," *American Federationist* 25 (Nov., 1918): 985–88; "Aid Mexicans to Organize Says A.F. of L.," *Pan American Labor Press,* Sept. 25, 1918, pp. 3–4.

36. "American Federation of Labor," *American Federationist* 32 (July, 1925): 553–56; ibid. 32 (Oct., 1925): 921–25. Subsequent meetings by the AFL-CROM commission revealed that Green's strategy for containing immigration had not worked. AFL leaders from the Southwest led a strong opposition to the AFL-CROM agreement, while CROM lost its standing with the death of president Alvaro Obregón. As a result, the AFL began to more forcefully seek quota legislation. The breakdown of the AFL-CROM agreement may explain why the issue of incorporating Mexicans lost its original impetus and did not advance beyond the appointment of Idar. It also may have contributed to the decision to restrict Idar's organizing attention to U.S.-born and naturalized Mexicans (Reisler, *By the Sweat of Their Brow,* pp. 169–73; Cardoso, *Mexican Emigration to the United States,* p. 135).

37. Bernard Mandel, *Samuel Gompers,* pp. 453–58; Snow, *Samuel Gompers,* pp. 119–20; James Weinstein, *The Corporate Ideal in the Liberal State, 1900–1918,* pp. 217–18, 240–41; Memorandum, June 24, 1916, Press and Miscellaneous, Samuel Gompers Papers, AFL-CIO Library, Washington, D.C.; "Outline of Plans of the American Alliance for Labor and Democracy," Dec., 1918, President's Office, Reports and Reference Materials, AFL Papers, AFL-CIO Library, Washington, D.C. The National Council on Defense was created in 1916 as part of Wilson's preparedness program. The American Alliance was established in 1917 as a propaganda arm of the Committee on Public Information.

38. C. N. Idar to Secretary of State, Nov. 19, 1917, RG 59, Department of State Records.

39. Ibid.

40. See the following for reports on public meetings organized to discourage Mexicans from leaving Texas: "Plan Counteracts Propaganda Scaring Mexicans," *San Antonio News,* Sept. 7, 1918, p. 1; "Propaganda Among Mexicans Causing Hundreds to Leave," *San Antonio Express,* Sept. 7, 1918, p. 1;

"Preparing to Entertain the Numerous Delegates," *The Laredo Times,* Oct. 25, 1918, p. 1.

41. Consult the following for historical accounts on CROM: Marjorie R. Clark, *Organized Labor in Mexico;* Rocío Guadarrama, *Los Sindicatos y La Política en México: La CROM, 1918–1928.* CROM represented a political departure from the leftist COM, the national labor federation that preceded it. The new labor federation was established in 1917 with the active support and encouragement of president Carranza who sought to recruit labor to promote industrial peace and reconstruction.

42. "La conferencia de obreros," *Evolución,* Oct. 10, 1918, p. 1; "Representatives Coming For Big Meeting Tomorrow," *The Laredo Times,* Oct. 7, 1918, p. 1; "Two Thousand Delegates Will Attend Conference," Oct. 9, 1918, ibid., p. 1; AFL, *Report of Proceedings* (Atlantic City: June 19–23, 1919), pp. 87–91.

43. "Pan-American Federation of Labor Organized by International Labor Conference in Laredo, Texas," *Pan American Labor Press,* Dec. 4, 1918, p. 1.

44. Levenstein, *Labor Organizations in the United States and Mexico,* pp. 90–91.

45. My comments on the conference are based on the published proceedings that appear in the *Pan American Labor Press* and in the works by Snow and Levenstein.

46. Snow, *Samuel Gompers,* pp. 89–97.

47. Quoted in Levenstein, *Labor Organizations in the United States and Mexico,* p. 98.

48. PAFL, *Report of the Proceedings of the Second Congress of the PAFL* (New York: July 7–10, 1919), pp. 52–56.

49. Although Idar's jurisdiction involved Texas, Arizona, New Mexico, Oklahoma, and Mexico, he spent most of his time in Texas. See the correspondence from Gompers for details on the organizing assignments given to Idar (Letters from Samuel Gompers to Clemente Idar, Between March, 1919, and April, 1924, Letterbooks, 1919–1924, Samuel Gompers Papers, AFL-CIO Library, Washington, D.C. This source is available on microfilm). Also, refer to Idar's organizing reports that appeared in the *American Federationist.*

50. Gompers to Idar, Apr. 9 and 24, 1924, Letterbooks, 1919–1924, Gompers Papers; "Labor Leader Pleads for Passage," *San Antonio Light,* May 2, 1930, p. 12.

51. Snow, *Samuel Gompers,* pp. 106–24; Levenstein, *Labor Organizations in the United States and Mexico,* p. 116.

52. William Green to John P. Frey, July 9, 1925, and William Green to Clemente Idar, July 28, 1925, Letterbooks, 1925, William Green Papers, AFL-CIO Library, Washington, D.C. The Green Papers are available on microfilm.

53. Murray was the same person who had previously represented the Committee for the Defense of the Foreign Born in its 1909 campaign in support of jailed PLM members from Texas. He was also an important intermediary that established contact between the AFL and the Mexican labor federations in preparation for the PAFL conference.

54. TSFL, *Proceedings* (Galveston: Apr. 12–16, 1921), p. 115.

55. TSFL, *Proceedings* (El Paso: Apr. 17–21, 1922), p. 41.

56. TSFL, *Proceedings* (El Paso: Apr. 17–21, 1922), pp. 87–88, 101–109. The Mexican labor leaders included Alberto Carrillo Vargas (representative of a national railroad union and CROM), Salvador Álvarez (general organizer for CROM), José Cortez (secretary of the Mexico City Labor Council), a person listed by the last name of Fernández Rodarte (personal representative of Luis N. Morones, the head of CROM), Ruiz Cayetano Pérez (representative of the Torreon Central Labor Council), and José W. Kelly (general organizer for the International Association of Machinists).

57. Ibid., p. 101.

58. Ibid., (Amarillo: May 25–28, 1925), p. 33.

59. Ibid., (Port Arthur: Apr. 21–25, 1924), p. 35.

60. Ibid.

61. Ibid., (Amarillo: May 25–28, 1925), p. 11.

62. Ibid., pp. 26–27.

63. Ibid., p. 27.

64. Ibid.

65. Letters from Samuel Gompers to Clemente Idar, Mar. 23, 1921, and to John Hart, Mar. 21, 1921, Letterbooks, 1919–24, Gompers Papers.

66. Letter from Samuel Gompers to Clemente Idar, Aug. 22, 1922, Letterbooks, 1919–24, Gompers Papers.

67. Clemente Idar, "El movimiento de repatriación," *El Unionista,* Dec. 30, 1920, p. 2; Letter from Clemente Idar to Frank Morrison, Secretary of the AFL, Letterbooks, 1919–1924, Gompers Papers. Los Angeles Consul Eduardo Ruiz reported in 1921 that on a fact-finding tour throughout the Southwest he had provided financial assistance to repatriates from Fort Worth and Dallas (Cardoso, *Mexican Emigration to the United States,* p. 101–102).

68. Idar, "El Movimiento del Repatriación," *El Unionista,* Dec. 30, 1920, p. 2.

69. Letter from Samuel Gompers to Clemente Idar, Apr. 8, 1921, Letterbooks, 1919–1924, Gompers Papers.

70. "La inmigración afecta a los salarios," *El Unionista,* May 13, 1920, p. 1.

71. Idar's organizing activities are noted in the sections titled "Organizing Expenses" in the *Proceedings* of the AFL annual conventions and in the organizing "Reports" that appear in the *American Federationist,* the AFL's official organ.

72. Idar, "Laredo City Offers Good Field for Organization," p. 1.

73. "Distinguidos leaders obreros en Laredo," *Evolución,* Sept. 25, 1918, p. 1; "Lo que serán las conferencias obreras en Laredo el próximo 13 de noviembre," ibid., Oct. 26, 1918, p. 1; "Labor fructífera de una unión, ibid., Nov. 26, 1918, p. 1.

74. "La fiesta del la Unión de Pintores," ibid., Nov. 3, 1918, p. 1, and Nov. 5, 1918, p. 1.

75. "Se organizan los tipógrafos de Laredo," ibid., Nov. 12, 1918, p. 2; "El unionismo en Laredo," ibid., Nov. 13, 1918, 2; "Por La Unión de Impresores," *El Demócrata Fronterizo,* Nov. 16, 1918, p. 1.

76. "Se pretende unificar dos uniones," *Evolución,* Nov. 30, 1918, 1.

77. Sociedad de Conductores y Obreros Unidos, Laredo, Texas, *Reglamento General,* p. 3.

78. *American Federationist* 27 (Aug., 1920): 768.

79. Samuel Gompers to Clemente Idar, Dec. 28, 1921, and Feb. 6, 1922, in Letterbooks, 1919–1924, Gompers Papers; *American Federationist* 29 (Mar., 1922): 230.

80. William P. Blocker to Secretary of State, Jan. 24, 1922, RG 59, Department of State Records; "Organized Heads Here on Railroad Shops, Matters Make Outlook Appear Good," *Eagle Pass News Guide,* Jan. 19, 1922 (copy of article accompanied Blocker's report).

81. *American Federationist* 29 (July, 1922): 523. For evidence of Idar's continuing communications with railroad unions from Mexico, see also Samuel Gompers to Clemente Idar, Oct. 24, 1922, Letterbooks, 1919–1924, Gompers Papers.

82. "American Federation of Labor," *American Federationist* 32 (July, 1925): 553–56; 32 (Oct., 1925): 921–25.

83. *El Progreso,* Jan. 8, 1920, RG 59, U.S. Department of State Records. Another San Antonio newspaper, *El Diario,* also promoted unionism alongside *El Unionista.* The editor was José Reyes Estrada, an officer of the typographical workers' union, La Sociedad Artes Gráficas, and a former writer for *El Unionista* ("Nuevo periódico diario," *El Unionista,* Sept. 30, 1920, p. 3).

84. "El obrerismo unionado se va abriendo paso," *El Unionista,* Feb. 24, 1921, p. 2.

85. "El contrato de La Unión de Zapateros," *El Unionista,* Oct. 4, 1919, p. 1; "Los zapateros se organizan," *El Unionista,* Oct. 18, 1919, p. 1.

86. "Gracias," *El Unionista,* Jan. 22, 1920, p. 1; *American Federationist* 28 (June, 1921): 518; ibid., (Nov., 1921): 982.

87. "Gracias," *El Unionista,* Jan. 2, 1920, p. 1; "Baile de zapateros," ibid., Feb. 5, 1920, p. 3; "Con toda pompa La Unión de Jornaleros celebrará el XX aniversario de su instalación con una velada," ibid., Apr. 15, 1920, p. 1.

88. "Por la Unión 'Empleados de Comercio'," ibid., Oct. 18, 1919, p. 2; "Quiere Ud. ingresar a alguna de nuestras uniones?" ibid., Dec. 18, 1919, p. 3; "La Unión de Jornaleros ayuda a los jornaleros Mexicanos emigrados," ibid., Mar. 11, 1920, p. 1.

89. "Los agricultores de Fentress, Texas, se organizan," ibid., Feb. 12, 1920, pp. 1, 4; "Fentress, Texas," ibid., Feb. 26, 1920, p. 2; "Seran organizados los agricultores Mexicanos de Fentress, Texas," ibid., Sept. 23, 1920, p. 1; "El movimiento obrero entre los labradores de Texas," ibid., Nov. 18, 1920, p. 2; Miguel Pavia, "Convocatoria," ibid., Apr. 29, 1920, p. 3; *American Federationist* 28 (Feb., 1921): 162; ibid. (Aug., 1921): 686.

90. "El movimiento obrero de McAllen, Texas," *El Unionista,* Oct. 25, 1919, p. 1; "Unión local de Carpinteros No. 2222, de McAllen Texas," ibid., Nov. 18, 1920, p. 4. The following newspapers maintained fraternal relations with *El Unionista: El Latino-Americano* (Alice); *El Mañana* (McAllen); *El Porvenir* (Brownsville) ("Colegas que nos visitan," *El Unionista,* Dec. 11, 1919, p. 1).

91. *American Federationist* 31 (Jan., 1924): 100; ibid. (Mar., 1924): 184; ibid., 32 (Apr., 1925): 270; ibid., 32 (July, 1925): 594; ibid., 32 (Sept., 1925): 831.

92. "Los panaderos de El Paso, Texas, se organizan," *El Unionista,* Feb. 12, 1920, p. 1; J. W. Kelley to Samuel Gompers, Sept., 1922, and Samuel Gompers to Clemente Idar, May 17, 1923, in Letterbooks, 1919–1924, Gompers Papers.

93. *American Federationist* 31 (Aug., 1924): 100; ibid. (Mar., 1924): 678.

94. *American Federationist* 33 (June, 1926): 754; ibid. (Aug., 1926): 1011; ibid. (Sept., 1926): 1128.

95. *American Federationist* 34 (Feb., 1927): 242; ibid. (May, 1927): 621.

96. *El Unionista,* Sept. 13, 1915, p. 1.

Chapter 8

1. Mario García, *Desert Immigrants: The Mexicans of El Paso, 1880–1920;* Mario García, *Mexican Americans: Leadership, Ideology, and Identity, 1930–1960.*

2. José Amaro Hernández, *Mutual Aid For Survival: The Case of the Mexican American;* Albert Camarillo, *Chicanos in a Changing Society: From Mexican Pueblos to American Barrios in Santa Barbara and Southern California, 1848–1930;* de Leon, *The Tejano Community, 1836–1900;* de Leon, *They Called Them Greasers;* de Leon, *Ethnicity in the Sunbelt;* Ricardo Romo, *History of a Barrio: East Los Angeles.*

3. For views on the important mediating role that immigrant voluntary associations played as cultural institutions in community and labor struggles, see Hoerder, ed., *Essays on Working-Class Immigrants.*

Bibliography

Government Sources

Clark, Victor S. *Mexican Labor in the United States.* U.S. Bureau of Labor Bulletin No. 78. Washington, D.C.: U.S. Bureau of Labor Statistics, 1908.

Jamieson, Stuart. *Labor Unionism in American Agriculture.* U.S. Department of Labor Bulletin No. 836. Washington, D.C.: Government Printing Office, 1945.

Texas Bureau of Labor Statistics. *Biennial Reports.* Austin: Von Boeckman-Jones, 1917–32.

Texas State Employment Service. *Origins and Problems of Texas Migratory Farm Labor.* Austin: Farm Placement Service Division, 1940.

U.S. Bureau of the Census. *Abstract of the Thirteenth Census (1910), Statistics for Texas, Containing Statistics of Population, Agriculture, Manufacturers, and Mining for the State, Counties, Cities, and Other Divisions.* Washington, D.C.: Government Printing Office, 1913.

————. *Fourteenth Census of the United States (1920), State Compendium, Texas, Statistics of Population, Occupations, Agriculture, Irrigation, Drainage, Manufacturers, Mines, and Quarries for the State, Counties, and Cities.* Washington, D.C.: Government Printing Office, 1925.

U.S. Commission on Industrial Relations. Field Reports. Wisconsin Historical Society, Madison, Wisconsin.

————. *Final Report and Testimony,* Vol. 10. Washington, D.C.: Government Printing Office, 1916.

U.S. Congress, House. *Imported Pauper Labor and Serfdom in America: Hearings Before the Committee on Immigration and Naturalization,* 67th Cong., 1st sess., 1921.

————. *Temporary Admission of Illiterate Mexican Laborers: Hearings before the Committee on Immigration and Naturalization,* H.J. Res. 271, 66th Cong., 2d. sess., 1920.

————. Committee on Rules. *Hearings on H.J. Res. 201, Providing for a Joint Committee to Investigate Alleged Persecutions of Mexican Citizens by the Government of Mexico.* Washington, D.C.: Government Printing Office, 1910.

U.S. Congress, Senate. Committee on Foreign Relations. *Investigation of Mexican Affairs, Hearings before a Subcommittee of the Committee on Foreign Relations,* 66th Cong., 1st sess., 1920. Vol. 3.

U.S. Department of State. Records Relating to Internal Affairs of Mexico, 1910–1929, Record Group 59, National Archives, Washington, D.C.

Archival and Other Primary Sources

Allen, Ruth. Papers. Labor Archives, University of Texas, Arlington, Texas.
————. Papers on Labor Movements in Texas. Eugene C. Barker Texas History Center, University of Texas, Austin, Texas.
American Federation of Labor. Records of Local Unions. AFL-CIO Library, Washington, D.C.
————. Reports and Reference Materials. President's Office. AFL-CIO Library, Washington, D.C.
————. *Reports of Proceedings of Annual Conventions, 1900–1921.* Washington, D.C.: AFL, 1900–21.
Asunto Catarino Garza, Del Tribunal del Segundo Circuito de la Corte Federal de Texas. Secretaría de Relaciones Exteriores, Sección de Archivo General, México, D.F.
Asunto Disturbios in Artesia Wells, 1909. Secretaría de Relaciones Exteriores, Sección de Archivo General, México, D.F.
Asunto Ricardo Flores Magón, 1901–1906. Secretaría de Relaciones Exteriores, Sección de Archivo General, México, D.F.
Austin City Directory, 1912–1913. Austin: Morrison and Fourney, 1914.
Austin City Directory, 1914. Austin: Morrison and Fourney, 1914.
Brannin, Carl B. Papers, Vertical File Collection and Oral History Collection. Labor Archives, University of Texas, Arlington, Texas.
Carranza, Venustiano. Papers. Centro de Estudios de Historia de México, México, D.F.
Domínguez, Simón. Simón E. Domínguez Letter Press, 1904–1925. Eugene C. Barker Texas History Center, University of Texas, Austin, Texas.
Flores Magón, Ricardo, Papers. Department of State Records, Federal Records Center, Fort Worth, Texas.
————. Papers. Silvestre Terrazas Collection, Bancroft Library, University of California, Berkeley, California.
Gamio, Manuel. Papers. Bancroft Library, University of California, Berkeley, California.
García, Franklin. Interview with Emilio Zamora, Austin, Texas, June 28, 1974. Transcript in author's possession.
General Directory of the City of Laredo, 1900. Laredo: Arguindegui and McDonnell, Compilers and Publishers, 1900.
Gompers, Samuel. Papers. AFL-CIO Library, Washington, D.C.
Gran Liga Mexicanista de Beneficiencia y Protección. *Constitución.* Laredo: Tipografía de N. Idar, 1912.
Green, William. Papers. AFL-CIO Library, Washington, D.C.
International Hod Carriers and Building Laborer's Union of America No. 93. Charter. Union's Offices, San Antonio, Texas.
————. Membership and Financial Records, Records of Local Unions, AFL-CIO Library, Washington, D.C.
La Liga de Protección Mexicanista. *Reglamento.* Segunda edición. Del Rio, Tex.: Talleres Tipográficos de "El Regidor," 1912.
Minute Books of Austin Trades Council, Vol. 1 (1904–1908) and Vol. 2 (1908–10). Labor Archives, University of Texas, Arlington, Texas.
Minute Books of Galveston Labor Council, Vol. 2 (1908–10), Vol. 4

(1914–16), and Vol. 5 (1917–20). Labor Archives, University of Texas, Arlington, Texas.

Minute Books of the United Brotherhood of Carpenters and Joiners of America No. 14, Vol. 8 (1913–15) and Vol. 11 (1919). Labor Archives, University of Texas, Arlington, Texas.

Murray, John. Papers. Bancroft Library, University of California, Berkeley, California.

Pan American Federation of Labor. "Proceedings of the 1918 Pan American Federation of Labor Conference," *La Prensa*. November, 1918.

————. *Report of the Proceedings of the Second Congress of the PAFL.* Washington, D.C.: PAFL, 1919.

Primer Congreso Mexicanista, Laredo, Texas, Verificado los Días 14 al 22 de Septiembre, 1911; Discursos y Conferencias, Por La Raza y Para La Raza. Laredo: Tipografía de N. Idar, 1912.

Sociedad Benevolencia Mexicana. *Constitución y Leyes.* San Antonio, Tex.: G. F. Sigmond y Cia., 1889.

Sociedad de Conductores y Obreros Unidos, Fe y Adelanto. *Reglamento General de la Sociedad de Conductores y Obreros Unidos, Fe y Adelanto.* Laredo, Tex.: Compañía Publicista Idar, 1921.

Sociedad de Obreros, Iqualdad y Progreso. *Reglamento General Reforma de la Sociedad de Obreros, Iqualdad y Progreso.* Laredo, Tex.: Gate City Printing Office, 1891.

Sociedad Mutualista Hidalgo y Juárez. *Reglamento Interior de la Sociedad Mutualista Hidalgo y Juárez.* Alice, Tex.: Tipografia "El Genio," 1900.

Sociedad Mutualista, Hijos de Juárez. *Reglamento General de la Sociedad Mutualista, Hijos de Juárez,* Laredo, Tex., 1916 and 1924.

Sociedad Mutualista Protectora Benito Juárez. *Reglamento General de la Sociedad Protectora Benito Juárez.* Brownsville, Tex.: Preciado Publishing Co., 1926.

Sociedad Unión de Jornaleros. *Reglamento General de la Sociedad Unión de Jornaleros.* Laredo, Tex.: Imprenta de "XYZ," 1915.

Star Gardens. Kansas City, Mo.: Rio Grande Valley Investment Co., 1915.

Taylor, Paul. Papers. Bancroft Collection, University of California, Berkeley, California.

Texas State Federation of Labor. *Proceedings of Annual Conventions.* Austin, Tex.: TSFL, 1900–20.

Villareal, Roberto. "Model for Estimating the Spanish-Surnamed Population of Texas, 1860–1920." Copy in author's possession.

Newspapers and Periodicals

American Federationist (Washington, D.C.: 1916–29)
Austin American-Statesman (Austin: 1915, 1922)
The Borderland of Two Republics (Laredo: 1906)
La Crónica (Laredo: 1910–15)
El Defensor del Obrero (Laredo: 1905–1907)
El Demócrata Fronterizo (Laredo: 1905–10)
Evolución (Laredo: 1918)
Gulf Coast Magazine (Corpus Christi: 1905)

International Oil Worker (Fort Worth: 1920)
The Javelina (Asherton: 1912, 1917)
The Laredo Times (Laredo: 1905–10)
Literary Digest (1923)
Monthly Labor Review (Washington, D.C.: 1920)
The Nation (New York: 1922)
Pan American Labor Press (San Antonio: 1919–20)
El Popular (Mexico City: 1939)
El Progreso (San Antonio: 1920)
La Prensa (San Antonio: 1913–25)
Ranger Daily Times (Ranger: 1922)
The Rebel (Halletsville: 1911–16)
Reforma, Justicia y Libertad (Austin: 1908)
Regeneración (Los Angeles: 1912)
El Regidor (San Antonio: 1904–1906, 1915)
The San Antonian: A Journal of Community Service (1920)
San Antonio Daily Express (San Antonio: 1909–10)
San Antonio Daily Times (San Antonio: 1886)
Social Democratic Herald (Cincinnati: 1903)
El Unionista (San Antonio: 1919–22)
El Universal Gráfico (Mexico City: 1943)
La Vanguardia (Austin: 1921)
Waco Daily Times-Herald (Waco: 1915)
Weekly Dispatch (San Antonio: 1915)

Theses and Dissertations

Bell, Mattie. "The Growth and Distribution of the Texas Population." Ph.D. diss., Baylor University, 1955.

Casillas, Michael. "Mexicans, Labor, and Strife in Arizona, 1896–1917." Master's thesis, University of New Mexico, 1979.

García, Mario. "Obreros: The Mexican Workers of El Paso, 1900–1920." Ph.D. diss., University of California, San Diego, 1975.

Gentry, Mary Jane. "Thurber: The Life and Death of a Texas Town." Master's thesis, University of Texas, Austin, 1946.

Harris, Malcolm. "The Labor Supply of Texas." Master's thesis, University of Texas, 1922.

Hernández Tovar, Inez. "Sara Estela Ramírez: The Early Twentieth Century Texas Mexican Poet." Ph.D. diss., University of Houston, 1984.

Knox, John William. "The Economic Status of the Mexican Immigrant in San Antonio, Texas." Master's thesis, University of Texas, Austin, 1927.

Leininger Pycior, Julie. "La Raza Organizes: Mexican American Life in San Antonio, 1915–1930, as Reflected in Mutualista Activities." Ph.D. diss., University of Notre Dame, 1979.

MacGibson, Charles. "Organized Labor in Texas from 1890 to 1900." Master's thesis, Texas Tech University, 1973.

Maroney, James. "Organized Labor in Texas, 1900–1929." Ph.D. diss., University of Houston, 1975.

Mullenix, Grady Lee. "A History of the Texas State Federation of Labor." Ph.D. diss., University of Texas, Austin, 1955.

Privett, John Delmar. "Agricultural Unionism among Chicanos In Texas." Master's thesis, University of Texas, Austin, 1976.

Rocha, Rodolfo. "The Influence of the Mexican Revolution on the Mexico-Texas Border, 1910–1916." Ph.D. diss., Texas Tech University, 1981.

Shapiro, Harold Arthur. "The Workers of San Antonio, Texas, 1900–1940." Ph.D. diss., University of Texas, Austin, 1952.

Sparks, Earle Sylvester. "A Survey of Organized Labor in Austin." Master's thesis, University of Texas, Austin, 1920.

Townes, Malcolm H. "The Labor Supply of Texas." Master's thesis, University of Texas, Austin, 1923.

Vassberg, David E. "The Use of Mexicans and Mexican Americans As An Agricultural Work Force in the Lower Rio Grande Valley of Texas." Ph.D. diss., University of Texas, Austin, 1967.

Winn, Charles Carr. "Mexican Americans in the Texas Labor Movement." Ph.D. diss., Texas Christian University, 1972.

Zeigler, Robert E. "The Workingman in Houston, Texas, 1865–1914." Ph.D. diss., Texas Tech University, 1972.

Books

Acuña, Rodolfo. *Occupied America: A History of Chicanos.* New York: Harper and Row, 1988.

Allen, Ruth. *Chapters in the History of Organized Labor in Texas.* University of Texas Publication No. 4143. Austin: University of Texas, 1941.

Allhands, J. L. *Gringo Builders.* Dallas, Tex.: Privately printed, 1931.

———. *Railroads to the Rio.* Salado, Tex.: Anson Jones Press, 1960.

Almaguer, Tomás. *Interpreting Chicano History: The "World System" Approach to 19th Century California,* Institute for the Study of Social Change Working Paper No. 10. Berkeley: University of California, 1977.

Anderson, Rodney D. *Outcasts in Their Own Land: Mexican Industrial Workers, 1906–1911.* De Kalb: Northern Illinois University Press, 1976.

Araiza, Luis. *Historia Del Movimiento Obrero Mexicano.* México, D.F.: Editorial Cuauhtémoc, 1965.

Austin, Charles B. *Studies in Farm Tenancy,* Bulletin of the University of Texas No. 21. Austin: University of Texas Press, 1915.

Barbosa Cano, Favio. *La CROM De Luis N. Morones a Antonio J. Hernández.* Puebla, México: ICUAP, Editorial Universidad Autónoma de Puebla, 1980.

Barrera, Mario. *Race and Class in the Southwest: A Theory of Racial Inequality.* Notre Dame: University of Notre Dame, 1979.

Blaisdel, Lowell L. *The Desert Revolution: Baja California, 1911.* Madison: University of Wisconsin Press, 1962.

Bringas, Guillermina and David Mascareno. *Esbozo Histórico de la Prensa Obrera en México.* México, D.F.: UNAM, Instituto de Investigaciones Bibliográficas, 1988.

Camarillo, Albert. *Chicanos in a Changing Society; From Mexican Pueblos to American Barrios in Santa Barbara and Southern California, 1848–1930.* Cambridge: Harvard University Press, 1979.

Cardoso, Lawrence A. *Mexican Emigration to the United States, 1897–1931: Socio-Economic Patterns.* Tucson: University of Arizona Press, 1980.

Carr, Barry. *El Movimiento Obrero y la Política en México, 1910–1929.* México, D.F.: Ediciones Era, 1976.

Chávez, John R. *The Lost Land; The Chicano Image of the Southwest.* Albuquerque: University of New Mexico Press, 1984.

Clark, Marjorie Ruth. *Organized Labor in Mexico.* Chapel Hill: University of North Carolina Press, 1934.

Cockroft, James D. *Intellectual Precursors of the Mexican Revolution.* Austin, Tex.: Van Boeckmann-Jones Co., 1968.

Cohen, Sanford. *Labor in the United States.* Columbus, Ohio: Charles E. Merrill Books, Inc., 1966.

Commons, John R. *A Documentary History of American Industrial Society,* 10 vols. New York: Russell and Russell, 1958.

———. *History of Labor in the United States.* 4 vols. New York: Macmillan Company, 1918–35.

Conlin, Joseph. *Bread and Roses Too.* Westport, Conn.: Greenwood Publishing Company, 1969.

Córdova, Arnaldo. *La Ideología de la Revolución Mexicana: La Formación del Nuevo Régimen.* México, D.F.: Ediciones Era, 1975.

De la Cerda Silva, Roberto. *El Movimiento Obrero en México.* México, D.F.: Instituto de Investigaciones Sociales, UNAM, 1961.

De Leon, Arnoldo. *Ethnicity in the Sunbelt: A History of Mexican Americans in Houston.* Monograph Series No. 7. Houston: Mexican American Studies Program, University of Houston, 1989.

———. *The Tejano Community, 1836–1900.* Albuquerque: University of New Mexico Press, 1982.

———. *They Called Them Greasers; Anglo Attitudes toward Mexicans in Texas, 1821–1900.* Austin: University of Texas Press, 1983.

Deutsch, Sara. *No Separate Refuge: Culture, Class, and Gender on an Anglo-Hispanic Frontier in the American Southwest, 1880–1940.* New York: Oxford University Press, 1987.

Dubofsky, Melvyn. *We Shall Be All.* Chicago: Quadrangle Books, 1969.

Ely, Richard T. *The Labor Movement in America.* New York: T. Y. Crowell and Co., 1886.

Escobedo, José G. *Notas Biográficas.* México, D.F.: Señoría del Trabajo y Previsión Social, 1951.

Fabela, Josefina E. de, ed. *Documentos Históricos de la Revolución Mexicana,* Vols. 10, 14. México, D.F.: Editorial Jus, S.A., 1968.

Fehrenbach, Theodore R. *Lone Star: A History of Texas and the Texans.* New York: Macmillan Publishing Company, 1974.

Flores Magón, Ricardo. *Semilla Libertaria.* Tomo 2. México, D.F.: Grupo Cultural "R.F.M.", 1923.

Foley, Douglas E., Clarice Mota, Donald E. Post, and Ignacio Lozano. *From Peones to Políticos: Class and Ethnicity in a South Texas Town, 1900–1987.* Austin: University of Texas Press, 1988.

Foner, Philip S. *History of the Labor Movement in the United States.* 5 vols. Chicago: International Publishers, 1964–80.

———. *Organized Labor and the Black Worker.* New York: International Publishers, 1976.

———. *The Policies and Practices of the American Federation of Labor, 1900–1909,* Vol. 3. New York: International Publishers, 1981.

Foster, James C., ed. *American Labor in the Southwest, the First One Hundred Years.* Tucson: University of Arizona Press, 1982.

Gamio, Manuel. *Mexican Immigration to the United States: A Study of Human Migration and Adjustment.* New York: Dover Publications, 1971.

García, Mario. *Desert Immigrants; The Mexicans of El Paso, 1880–1920.* New Haven: Yale University Press, 1981.

———. *Mexican Americans: Leadership, Ideology, and Identity, 1930–1960.* New Haven: Yale University Press, 1989.

García Naranjo, Nemesio. *Memorias: Nueve Años de Destierro,* Vol. 8. Monterrey, Mex.: Talleres de "El Porvenir," 1982.

Gómez-Quiñones, Juan. *Sembradores, Ricardo Flores Magón y El Partido Liberal Mexicano: A Eulogy and Critique.* Monograph No. 5. Los Angeles, Calif.: UCLA Chicano Studies Research Center, 1973.

———, and David Maciel. *Al Norte del Río Bravo (Pasado Lejano, 1600–1930).* México, D.F.: Siglo Veintuno y UNAM, 1981.

———, and Victor Nelson-Cisneros. *Selected Bibliography on Chicano Labor Materials.* Los Angeles: Aztlán Publications, 1974.

González Navarro, Moisés. *El Porfiriato, La Vida Social.* Vol. 4. In *La Historia Moderna de México,* edited by Daniel Cosío Villegas. México, D.F.: Editorial Hermes, 1957.

Goodwyn, Frank. *Lone Star Land: Twentieth Century Texas in Perspective.* New York: Alfred A. Knopf, 1955.

Green, James R. *Grass Roots Socialism: Radical Movements in the Southwest, 1895–1943.* Baton Rouge: Louisiana State University, 1978.

Greenberg, Stanley B. *Race and State in Capitalist Development: Comparative Perspectives.* New Haven: Yale University Press, 1980.

Greene, Victor. *The Slavic Community on Strike: Immigrant Labor in Pennsylvania Anthracite.* South Bend, Ind.: University of Notre Dame Press, 1968.

Guadarrama, Rocío. *Los Sindicatos y La Política en México: La CROM, 1918–1928.* México, D.F.: Ediciones Era, 1981.

Gutman, Herbert G. *Work, Culture, and Society in Industrializing America: Essays in American Working-Class and Social History.* New York: Alfred A. Knopf, 1976.

Haney, Lewis H., and George S. Wehrwein, eds. *A Social and Economic Survey of Southern Travis County,* University of Texas Bulletin No. 65. Austin: University of Texas Press, 1916.

Hernández, Francisco. *La Clase Obrera en La Historia de México: De La Dictadura Porfirista a Los Tiempos Libertarios.* México, D.F.: Siglo Veintuno, 1980.

Hernández, José Amaro. *Mutual Aid for Survival: The Case of the Mexican American.* Malabar, Calif.: Robert E. Krieger Publishing Company, 1983.

Hoerder, Dirk, ed. *Essays on Working-Class Immigrants: "Struggle a Hard Battle."* De Kalb: Northern Illinois University Press, 1986.

Kessler-Harris, Alice. *Out of Work: A History of Wage Earning Women in the United States.* New York: Oxford University Press, 1982.

Kiser, George C., and Martha W. Kiser, eds. *Mexican Workers in the United States: Historical and Political Perspectives.* Albuquerque: University of New Mexico Press, 1979.

Laslett, John H. M. *Labor and the Left.* New York: Basic Books, 1970.

Levenstein, Harvey A. *Labor Organizations in the United States and Mexico: A History of Their Relations.* Westport, Conn.: Greenwood Press, 1971.

Lorwin, Lewis L. *The International Labor Movement: History, Policies, Outlook.* New York: Harper and Brothers Publishers, 1953.

Lott, Virgil N., and Virginia M. Fenwick. *People and Plots on the Rio Grande.* San Antonio: Naylor Company, 1957.

———, and Mercurio Martínez. *The Kingdom of Zapata.* San Antonio: Naylor Company, 1953.

Maciel, David. *Al Norte del Río Bravo (Pasado Inmediato, 1930–1981).* México, D.F.: Siglo Veintiuno, 1981.

Mandel, Bernard. *Samuel Gompers.* Yellow Springs: Antioch Press, 1963.

Marshall, F. Ray. *Labor in the South.* Cambridge: Harvard University Press, 1967.

Martin, Roscoe C. *The People's Party in Texas.* Austin: University of Texas Press, 1933.

Martínez Nuñez, Eugenio. *Juan Sarabia: Apóstol y Mártir de la Revolución Mexicana:* México, D.F.: Instituto Nacional de Estudios Históricos, 1965.

Matthiessen, Peter. *Sal Si Puedes: César Chavez and the New American Revolution.* New York: Random House, 1973.

McWilliams, Carey. *North from Mexico: The Spanish-Speaking People of the United States.* New York: Greenwood Press, 1968.

———. *Ill Fares the Land: Migrants and Migratory Labor in the United States.* Boston: Little, Brown, and Company, 1942.

Meier, Matt S., and Feliciano Rivera. *The Chicanos: A History of Mexican-Americans.* New York: Hill and Wang, 1972.

Mills, C. Wright. *The Marxists.* New York: Dell Publishing Co., 1975.

Moheno, Querido. *Sobre el Avia Sangrienta.* México, D.F.: Editorial Andrés Botas e Hijo, 1922.

Montejano, David. *Race Labor Repression, and Capitalist Agriculture: Notes from South Texas, 1920–1930.* Berkeley, Calif.: Institute for the Study of Social Change, 1977.

———. *Anglos and Mexicans in the Making of Texas, 1836–1986.* Austin: University of Texas Press, 1987.

Muñoz, Ignacio. *La Verdad sobre los Gringos.* México, D.F.: Ediciones Populares, 1961.

Navarrete, Alfredo. *Alto a la Contrarrevolución.* México, D.F.: Testimonios de Atlacomulco, 1971.

Paredes, Américo. *A Texas-Mexican Cancionero: Folksongs of the Lower Border.* Urbana: University of Illinois Press, 1976.

———. *With His Pistol in His Hand: A Border Ballad and Its Hero.* Austin: University of Texas Press, 1971.

Pelling, Henry. *American Labor.* Chicago: University of Chicago Press, 1960.

Perlman, Selig. *A History of Trade Unionism in the United States.* New York: Macmillan Company, 1922.

———. *A Theory of the Labor Movement.* New York: Macmillan Company, 1937.

Pitt, Leonard. *The Decline of the Californios: A Social History of the Spanish-Speaking Californians, 1846–1890.* Berkeley: University of California Press, 1966.

Poblete Troncoso, Moisés. *El Movimiento Obrero Latino Americano*. México, D.F.: Fondo de Cultura Económica, 1946.

Pope, Dorothy Lee. *Rainbow Era on the Rio Grande*. Brownsville: Springman-King Co., 1971.

Rayback, Joseph G. *A History of American Labor*. New York: Free Press, 1966.

Reisler, Mark. *By the Sweat of Their Brow: Mexican Immigrant Labor in the United States, 1900–1940*. Westport, Conn.: Greenwood Press, 1976.

Richardson, Rupert N. *Texas: The Lone Star State*. Englewood Cliffs, N.J.: Prentice-Hall, 1958.

Rodea, Marcelo. *Historia del Movimiento Obrero Ferrocarrilero, 1890–1943*. México, D.F., 1944.

Rodríguez Cabo, Mathilda. *La Mujer y La Revolución*. México, D.F.: Frente Socialista de Abogados, 1937.

Romo, Ricardo. *History of a Barrio: East Los Angeles*. Austin: University of Texas Press, 1983.

Rosenbaum, Robert J. *Mexican Resistance in the Southwest: "The Sacred Right of Self-Preservation."* Austin: University of Texas Press, 1981.

Rosenberg, Daniel. *New Orleans Dockworkers: Race, Labor, and Unionism, 1892–1923*. Albany: State University of New York Press, 1988.

Ross, Stanley R. *Fuentes de la Historia Contemporanea de México: Periódicos y Revistas*, Vol. 1. México, D.F.: Unión Gráficas, 1965.

Rubel, Arthur J. *Across the Tracks; Mexican Americans in a Texas City*. Austin: University of Texas Press, 1966.

Salazar, Rosendo, and José G. Escobedo. *Las Pugnas de la Gleba*. México, D.F.: Editorial Avante, 1923.

Saenz, José de la Luz. *Los México-Americanos en la Gran Guerra y Su Contingente en Pro de la Democracia, La Humanidad y La Justicia*. San Antonio, Tex.: Artes Gráficas, 1933.

San Miguel, Guadalupe, Jr. *"Let All of Them Take Heed": The Mexican American Quest for Educational Equality in Texas, 1918–1980*. Austin: University of Texas Press, 1987.

Snow, Sinclair. *Samuel Gompers and the Pan American Federation of Labor*. Durham: University of North Carolina, 1965.

Southwestern Bell Telephone Company. *Economic Survey of Texas*. St. Louis: General Commercial Engineering Department, 1928.

Stambaugh, J. Lee, and Lillian J. Stambaugh. *The Lower Rio Grande Valley of Texas*. San Antonio, Tex.: Naylor Company, 1954.

Steen, Ralph W. *Twentieth Century Texas: An Economic and Social History*. Austin, Tex.: Steck Company, 1942.

Stowell, Jay S. *The Near Side of the Mexican Question*. New York: George H. Doran Co., 1921.

Taylor, Paul S. *An American-Mexican Frontier: Nueces County, Texas*. Chapel Hill: University of North Carolina Press, 1934.

————. *Mexican Labor in the United States: Dimmit County, Winter Garden District, South Texas*. University of California Publications in Economics, Vol. 6. Berkeley: University of California Press, 1930.

Thompson, Edward P. *The Making of the English Working Class*. New York: Vintage Books, 1966.

Turner, John Kenneth. *Barbarous Mexico*. Chicago: Charles H. Kerr and Company, 1910.

Villarello Vélez, Ildefonso. *Historia de la Revolución Mexicana en Coahuila.* México: Talleres Gráficos de la Nación, 1970.
Weinstein, James. *The Corporate Ideal in the Liberal State, 1900–1918.* Boston: Beacon Press, 1969.
———. *The Decline of Socialism in America, 1912–1925.* New York: Vintage Books, 1969.
Wilkinson, Joseph B. *Laredo and the Rio Grande Frontier.* Austin: Jenkins Publishing Co., 1975.
Willard, Rex. *Status of Farming in the Lower Rio Grande Irrigated District of Texas.* U.S. Department of Agriculture Bulletin No. 665. Washington, D.C.: U.S. Government Printing Office, 1918.
Woodward, C. Vann. *Origins of the New South, 1877–1913.* Baton Rouge: Louisiana State University Press, 1951.
Zamora. Emilio. *El Movimiento Obrero Mexicano en el Sur de Texas, 1900–1920.* México, D.F.: Secretaría de Educación Pública, 1986.

Articles

Aguilar, Edingardo, and Salvador Hernández. "Notas Sobre Magonismo, 1900–1915." *Memoria del Segundo Coloquio Regional de Historia Obrera.* México, D.F.: Centro de Estudios Históricos del Movimiento Obrero Mexicano, 1979.
Almaguer, Tomás. "Interpreting Chicano History: The World System Approach to Nineteenth-Century California." *Review* 4 (Winter, 1981): 459–507.
———, and Albert Camarillo. "Urban Chicano Workers in Historical Perspective: A Review of the Literature." In *The State of Chicano Research on Family, Labor, and Migration: Proceedings of the First Stanford Symposium on Chicano Research and Public Policy,* edited by Armando Valdez, Albert Camarillo, and Tomás Almaguer. Stanford, Calif.: Stanford Center for Chicano Research, 1982.
Arroyo, Luis. "Chicano Participation in Organized Labor: The CIO in Los Angeles, 1938–1950: An Extended Research Note." *Aztlán* 6 (Summer, 1975): 227–303.
———. "Notes on Past, Present, and Future Directions of Chicano Labor Studies." *Aztlán* 6 (Summer, 1975): 137–49.
Bainford, E. F. "Industrialization and the Mexican Casual." *Proceedings of the Fifth Annual Convention of the Southwestern Political and Social Science Association.* Fort Worth: SP&SS Association, 1924.
Barragán, Leticia, Rina Ortiz, and Amanda Rosales. "El mutualismo en el siglo XIX." *Historia Moderna* 3 (October, 1977): 2–10.
Barton, Josef J. "Land, Labor, and Community in Nueces County: Czech Farmers and Mexican Laborers in South Texas, 1880–1930." In *Ethnicity on the Great Plains,* edited by Frederick C. Luebke. Lincoln: University of Nebraska Press, 1980.
Briggs, George W. *The Housing Problem in Texas: A Study of Physical Conditions under Which the Other Half Lives.* Pamphlet, privately reprinted from the *Galveston Daily News,* November 19–December 17, 1911.
Brody, David. "The Old Labor History and the New: In Search of an American Working Class." *Labor History* 20 (Winter, 1979): 111–26.

Bryan, Samuel. "Mexican Immigrants in the United States." *Survey,* September 7, 1912, 728–29.

Bustamente, Jorge. "The Historical Context of Undocumented Mexican Immigration to the United States." *Aztlán* 3 (Fall, 1972): 257–81.

Cadenhead, Ivie E., Jr. "The American Socialists and the Mexican Revolution of 1910." *Southwestern Social Science Quarterly* 43 (September, 1962): 103–17.

Cardoso, Lawrence. "Labor Emigration to the Southwest, 1916 to 1920: Mexican Attitudes and Policy." In *Mexican Workers in the United States: Historical and Political Perspectives,* edited by George C. Kiser and Martha Kiser. Albuquerque: University of New Mexico Press, 1979.

Carr, Barry. "Las Peculiaridades del Norte Mexicano, 1880–1927: Ensayo de Interpretación." *Historia Mexicana* 22 (January–March, 1973): 320–46.

Case, Robert. "La Frontera Texana y los Movimientos de Insurrección en México, 1850–1900." *Historia Mexicana* 14 (1965): 415–52.

Christian, Carole E. "Joining the American Mainstream: Texas's Mexican Americans during World War I." *Southwestern Historical Quarterly* 92 (April, 1989): 559–95.

Cline, C. L. "The Rio Grande Valley." *Southwest Review* 25 (April, 1940): 239–55.

Crowell, Chester T. "Strange News from Texas." *American Mercury* 4 (March, 1925): 323–30.

Cumberland, Charles C. "Mexican Revolutionary Movements from Texas, 1906–1912." *Southwestern Historical Quarterly* 52 (January, 1949): 301–24.

———. "Border Raids in the Lower Rio Grande Valley, 1915." *Southwestern Historical Quarterly* 57 (January, 1954): 285–311.

Esquivel, Servando I. "The Immigrant from Mexico." *Outlook* 125, May 19, 1920, 131.

Fuller, Roden. "Occupations of the Mexican Born Population of Texas, New Mexico, and Arizona, 1900–1920." *Journal of the American Statistical Association* 23 (March, 1928): 47–64.

Galarza, Ernesto. "Mexicans in the Southwest: A Culture in Process." In *Plural Society in the Southwest,* edited by Edward H. Spicer and Raymond H. Thompson. New York: Weatherhead Foundation, 1972.

García, Mario. "Racial Dualism in the El Paso Labor Market." *Aztlán* 6 (Summer, 1975): 197–221.

———. "The Chicana in American History: The Mexican Women of El Paso, 1880–1920: A Case Study." *Pacific Historical Review* 49 (May, 1980): 315–37.

———. "Americanization and the Mexican Immigrant, 1880–1930." In *From Different Shores: Perspectives on Race and Ethnicity in America,* edited by Ronald Takaki. New York: Oxford University Press, 1987.

Gerlach, Allen. "Conditions along the Border—1915: The Plan de San Diego." *New Mexico Historical Review* 63 (July, 1968): 195–212.

Glover, Robert W., and Allan G. King. "Organized Labor in Texas." In *Dynamics of Growth: An Economic Profile of Texas,* edited by Louis J. Rodríguez. Austin: Madrona Press, 1978.

Gómez-Quiñones, Juan. "Plan de San Diego Reviewed." *Aztlán* 1 (Spring, 1970): 124–32.

————. "Toward a Perspective on Chicano History." *Aztlán* 2 (Fall, 1972): 1–49.

————. "The First Steps: Chicano Labor Conflict and Organizing, 1900–1920." *Aztlán* 3 (Spring, 1972): 13–49.

————. "Piedras Contra La Luna, México en Aztlán y Aztlán en México: Chicano-Mexican Relations and the Mexican Consulates, 1900–1920." In *Contemporary Mexico: Papers of the IV International Congress of Mexican History,* edited by James W. Wilkie, Michael C. Meyer, and Edna Monzón de Wilkie. Berkeley: University of California Press, 1976.

————. "On Culture." *Revista Chicano-Riqueña* 5 (Spring, 1977): 29–47.

————. "Mexican Immigration to the United States and the Internationalization of Labor, 1848–1980: An Overview." In *Mexican Immigrant Workers in the U.S.,* Anthology no. 2, edited by Antonio Ríos-Bustamante. Los Angeles: UCLA Chicano Studies Research Center Publications, 1981.

————. "Notes on an Interpretation of the Relations between the Mexican Community in the United States and Mexico." In *Mexican–U.S. Relations: Conflict, and Convergence,* edited by Carlos Vásquez and Manuel García y Griego. Los Angeles: UCLA Chicano Studies Research Center Publications, 1983.

————, and Luis Leobardo Arroyo. "On the State of Chicano History: Observations on Its Development, Interpretations, and Theory, 1970–1974." *Western Historical Quarterly* 7 (April, 1976): 155–85.

————, and Antonio Ríos-Bustamante. "La Comunidad al Norte del Río Bravo." In *La Otra Cara de México: El Pueblo Chicano,* edited by David Maciel. México, D.F.: Ediciones "El Caballito," 1977.

————, Antonio Ríos-Bustamante, et al. "Preludio al Futuro: Pasado y Presente de los Trabajadores Mexicanos al Norte del Río Bravo, 1600–1975." In *La Otra Cara de México: El Pueblo Chicano,* edited by David Maciel. México, D.F.: Ediciones "El Caballito," 1977.

————. "The Origins and Development of the Mexican Working Class in the United States: Laborers and Artisans North of the Río Bravo, 1600–1900." In *El Trabajo y los Trabajadores en la Historia de México,* edited by Elsa C. Frost, Michael C. Meyer, and Josefina Z. Vázquez. México, D.F.: Colegio de México, 1979.

Gompers, Samuel. "Reasons for Immigration Restrictions." *American Federationist,* April, 1916, 253–56.

González, Jovita. "American Invades the Border Towns." *Southwest Review* 15 (Summer, 1930): 469–77.

Green, George. "The ILGWU in Texas, 1930–1970." *Journal of Mexican American History* 1 (Spring, 1971): 144–69.

Green, James R. "Tenant Farmer Discontent and Socialist Protest in Texas, 1901–1917." *Southwestern Historical Quarterly* 81 (October, 1977): 133–54.

Green, Jim. "Culture, Politics and Workers' Response to Industrialization in the U.S.," *Radical America* 6 (January, February 1982): 101–28.

————. "Struggling with Class Struggle: Marxism and the Search for a Synthesis of U.S. Labor History." *Labor History* 28 (Fall, 1987): 497–514.

Guerra, Francisco Xavier. "Territorio Mimado, Mas Allá de Zapata en la Revolución Mexicana. NEXOS 6 (May, 1983): 33–43.

Gwin, J. Blaine. "Immigration along Our Southwest Border." *Annals of the American Academy of Political and Social Science* 93 (January, 1921): 126–30.

Handman, Max S. "The Mexican Immigrant in Texas." *Political and Social Science Quarterly* 7 (June, 1926): 33–41.

Hager, William M. "The Plan of San Diego: Unrest on the Texas Border in 1915." *Arizona and the West* 5 (Winter, 1963): 327–36.

Hall, Covington. "With 'Pope' Hickey in Texas." *International Socialist Review* 16 (December, 1915): 378–80.

Harger, Charles M. "The New Era of the Ranch Lands." *American Review of Reviews* 44 (November, 1911): 580–90.

Hart, John Mason. "U.S. Economic Hegemony, Nationalism, and Violence in the Mexican Countryside, 1876–1920." In *Rural Revolt in Mexico and U.S. Intervention,* edited by Daniel Nugent. San Diego, Calif.: Center for U.S.-Mexican Studies, University of California, San Diego, 1988.

Henderson, Dwight F. "The Texas Coal Mining Industry." *Southwestern Historical Quarterly* 68 (October, 1964): 207–19.

Henderson, Peter V. N. "Mexican Rebels in the Borderlands, 1910–1912." *Red River Valley Historical Review* 2 (Summer, 1975): 207–19.

Hernández Álvarez, José. "A Demographic Profile of the Mexican Immigration to the United States, 1910–1950." *Journal of Inter-American Studies* 8 (July, 1966): 471–96.

Hickey, Thomas A. "The Land Renters Union in Texas." *International Socialist Review* 13 (September, 1912): 239–44.

Holman, Charles W. "The Tenant Farmer, Country Brother of the Casual Worker." *Survey,* April 17, 1915, 62–64.

Johnson, Alvin S. "Mexico in San Antonio." *New Republic,* June 24, 1916, 190–91.

Leonard, W. E. "The Population of Texas and Its Potentialities as a Labor Force." *Bulletin of the University of Texas,* January 10, 1915.

Limón, José. "El Primer Congreso Mexicanista de 1911: A Precursor to Contemporary Chicanismo." *Aztlán* 5 (Spring-Fall, 1974): 85–117.

Longoria, Mario D. "Revolution, Visionary Plan, and Marketplace: A San Antonio Incident." *Aztlán* 12 (Autumn, 1981): 218–20.

Maroney, James C. "Labor's Struggle for Acceptance: The Houston Worker in a Changing Society, 1900–1929.: In *Houston: A Twentieth Century Urban Frontier,* edited by Francisco A. Rosales and Barry J. Kaplan. Port Washington, N.Y.: National University Publications, 1983.

Márquez, Benjamín. "The Politics of Race and Class: The League of United Latin American Citizens in the Post-World War II Period." *Social Science Quarterly* 68 (March, 1987): 85–101.

Marshall, F. Ray. "Some Reflections on Labor History." *Southwestern Historical Quarterly* 75 (October, 1971): 139–57.

Meyers, William K. "La Comarca Lagunera: Work, Protests and Popular Mobilization in North Central Mexico." In *Other Mexicos: Essays on Regional Mexican History, 1876–1910,* edited by Thomas Benjamin and William McNellie. Albuquerque: University of New Mexico Press, 1984.

Miller, Richard U. "American Railroad Unions and the National Railways in Mexico: An Exercise in Nineteenth Century Proletarian Manifest Destiny." *Labor History* 15 (Spring, 1974): 239–60.

Montgomery, David. "To Study the People: The American Working Class," *Labor History* 21 (Fall, 1980): 485–512.

Montgomery, Robert H. "Keglar Hill." *Survey,* May 1, 1931, 171, 193–95.

Nelson-Cisneros, Victor. "La Clase Trabajadora en Tejas, 1920–1940." *Aztlán* 6 (Summer, 1975): 239–65.

———. "UCAPAWA Organizing Activities in Texas, 1935–1970." *Aztlán* 9 (Spring–Summer, 1978): 71–84.

Putnam, Frank. "Texas in Transition." *Collier's,* January 22, 1915, 15.

Reese, James V. "The Evolution of an Early Texas Union: The Screwmen's Benevolent Association of Galveston, 1866–1891." *Southwestern Historical Quarterly* 75 (October, 1971): 158–85.

Richmond, Douglas W. "La guerra de Texas se renova: Mexican Insurrection and Carrancista Ambitions, 1900–1920." *Aztlán* 11 (Spring, 1980): 1–32.

Rosales, Francisco, A., and Daniel T. Simon. "Chicano Steel Workers and Unionism in the Midwest." *Aztlán* 6 (Summer, 1975): 267–75.

Roy, Janet. "The Life of Minera, Texas." *Southwestern Historical Quarterly* 49 (April, 1946): 510–17.

Sandos, James A. "The Plan of San Diego: War and Diplomacy on the Texas Border, 1915–1916." *Arizona and the West* 14 (Spring, 1972): 5–24.

Shapiro, Harold. "The Labor Movement in San Antonio, Texas, 1865–1915." *Southwestern Social Science Quarterly* 36 (September, 1955): 160–75.

Shabot A., Esther. "La Unión de Mecánicos Mexicanos y la Huelga de 1906." *Memoria del Segundo Coloquio Regional de Historia Obrera.* México, D.F.: El Centro de Estudios Históricos del Movimiento Obrero Mexicano, 1979.

Slayden, James L. "The Mexican Immigrant: Some Observations on Mexican Immigration." *Annals of the American Academy of Political and Social Science* 93 (January, 1921): 121–26.

Wright, Chester M. "Mexico, The Hopeful: A Survey of Her Political and Industrial Situation as She Takes Her First Steps in Reconstruction." *American Federationist,* December, 1920, 1087–94.

Zamora, Emilio. "Chicano Socialist Labor Activity in Texas, 1900–1920." *Aztlán* 6 (Summer, 1975): 221–36.

———. "Las Escuelitas: A Texas-Mexican Search for Educational Excellence," In *Los Tejanos: Children of Two Cultures,* Published proceedings of the South Texas Head Start Bilingual-Bicultural Conference. Edinburg: South Texas Regional Training Office, 1978.

———. "Sara Estela Ramírez: Una Rosa Roja en el Movimiento." In *Mexican Women in the United States: Struggles, Past and Present,* edited by Magdalena Mora and Adelaida del Castillo. Los Angeles: UCLA Chicano Studies Research Center Publications, 1980.

Index

271